W9-CBR-377

Complete Handyman do-it-yourself Encyclopedia

do-it-

- Home Modernizing
- Home Repair and Improvement
- Auto Repair and Maintenance
- Appliance Repair
- Furniture Building
- Interior Home Projects
- Exterior Craft Projects
- Gardening
- Use of Hand and Power Tools
- Boat Building
- Boat Handling
- Fishing and Fishing Equipment
- Hunting and Hunting Equipment
- Camping and Camping Equipment
- Hobbies and Crafts
- Radio, TV and Electronics
- Electrical Installation

Complete Handyman yourself Encyclopedia

A COMPILATION OF SPECIAL INTEREST PROJECTS AND MANUALS FOR THE REPAIR AND CARE OF HOMES, AUTOS, APPLIANCES, HOBBY EQUIPMENT.

by the editors of

Science & Mechanics

1

ABRASIVES

AUTOMOBILE ENGINES

H. S. STUTTMAN CO., INC. *publishers* New York, N.Y. 10016

COPYRIGHT © 1975 BY
H. S. STUTTMAN CO., INC.

ISBN 0-87475
Library of Congress Catalog Card No. 74-21375

No part of the text or illustrations in this compilation may be reproduced without written permission. Manuscripts were produced by DAVIS PUBLICATIONS, INC.

All instructions and diagrams have been checked for accuracy. However, success and safety in working with tools depend on individual accuracy, care, caution and skill. For this reason, the authors and publishers cannot guarantee the result of any project, nor assume responsibility for damage to property or injury to persons. In using any tools, building any projects, or carrying out any procedures, persons do so entirely at their own risk.

PRINTED IN THE UNITED STATES OF AMERICA

3P-2578-70(150)

INTRODUCTION

MODERN SCIENCE AND TECHNOLOGY have surrounded us with a vast assortment of products whose proper function affect our daily lives. Our homes, our automobiles, all our appliances, as well as our hobby and recreational equipment are the end result of applied science and technology and we take it for granted that these products will always function properly. Therefore, we are invariably annoyed when a malfunction deprives us of their use and enjoyment.

This annoyance becomes more aggravated when even minor repairs and adjustments are difficult to obtain and result in constantly increasing costs. The words "do-it-yourself" have, therefore, become of utmost importance when applied to maintaining and increasing the value, comfort, beauty and performance of practically everything you own or hope to acquire.

THE COMPLETE HANDYMAN "DO-IT-YOURSELF" ENCYCLOPEDIA represents the combined efforts of the writers, editors and technical consultants of Science & Mechanics magazine. With this authoritative background, these volumes can provide the "how-to" answers to practically any question pertaining to mechanical techniques and crafts.

In this new work, the authors have demonstrated that a reader can be motivated with the desire and equipped with the knowledge to "do-it-yourself." With just a few basic tools (skilled craftsmen even show you how to use them), the reader acquires confidence to:

construct a cabinet . . . change a spark plug . . . catch a bass
fix an air conditioner . . . upholster a chair . . . navigate a boat
paint a car . . . grow a bonzai garden . . . waterproof a cellar
install a bathroom . . . repair a carburetor . . . reload a shot shell
make a storm window . . . tile a floor . . . install electric outlets
maintain a pool . . . tune an engine . . . expand a room

The wide range and diversity of projects and techniques is amply demonstrated in the accompanying Table of Contents. This skillful combination of practical projects with instructions in the craft techniques for completing these projects is what the COMPLETE HANDYMAN DO-IT-YOURSELF ENCYCLOPEDIA is about. The reader quickly discovers, or gradually develops, basic skills as he becomes familiar with the craft techniques that help execute each project. Simplified, yet authoritative and jargon-free, instructions are combined with informative step-by-step self-teaching illustrations that encourage the reader to acquire new skills and improve on those he already has. Because the reader is exposed to this wide diversity of *attainable* projects, he is motivated to refine and improve on his methods for creating, building and repairing. The fun and enjoyment in each project is heightened in the knowledge of the substantial savings that have been effected.

The reader's attention is called to legal and safety aspects to many of the licensed crafts which prompt the editors to include a warning note. Some community local laws and regulations prohibit anyone but licensed professionals from doing certain jobs. In such cases, a practical knowledge of the craft enables the reader to better evaluate both the cost and quality of work performed.

To make this set more useful to the reader, and to encourage browsing and using each volume as a source of ideas, four cross referenced aids are provided. The alphabetic headings at the top of each page cover broad classifications of projects and techniques. The caption underneath each heading is the title of a project, craft or technique that may logically fall within this alphabetic heading. At the end of most articles "See also" references direct the reader to other articles dealing with the same general subject under another alphabetic entry. Alphabetic cross references shown at the bottom of a page call attention to an article that appears under another alphabetic heading. A complete alphabetic Index by subjects and topics is contained in the back section of Volume 21 and will provide aid in quickly locating information within any topic.

In producing this work, the authors were fortunate in having the advice and guidance of Mr. Joel Davis, President and Publisher of SCIENCE & MECHANICS PUBLICATIONS, INC. The publishers wish to express their gratitude for his assistance and admiration for his dedication to the task of showing readers how to "do-it-yourself."

H. S. STUTTMAN CO., INC.
PUBLISHERS

EDITORIAL BOARD

Editor in Chief	Joseph Daffron
Executive Editor	Burt Murphy
Production Editor	Maureen Gardella
Associate Editors	Sandra Skea Frank Cogan
Editorial Assistants	Frances Barnes Constance Barbara Brenda Jackson Leslie S. Spector

TECHNICAL CONSULTANTS

Appliance Repair	George Meyerink
Automotive	Paul Weissler
Boat Building	Hal Kelly
Boating	Thomas Bottomley
Camping	Andrew Carra
Electronics	Len Buckwalter
Fishing	Jim Martenhoff
Furniture Construction	John Capotosto
Gardening	Lillian Borgeson
Home Remodeling	Jorma Hyypia
Hunting	Richard Dietz
Mobile Homes	Marley Cole
Painting	George Daniels
Photography	Burt Murphy
Recreational Vehicles	Robert Behme
TV, Hi-Fi and Stereo	Stephen B. Gray
Water Sports	Thomas Hardman
Workshop Projects	Steve Ellingson
Workshop Techniques	Ralph Treves

PUBLISHING STAFF

Executive Guidance	Joel Davis
Design	Donald D. Wolf and Margot L. Wolf
Art	Jeffrey M. Langkau Babcock Studios

CONTRIBUTORS

Initials at end of articles identify the author

M.C.A.	M. C. Anderson
S.B.	Sylvia Bashline
F.J.B.	F. J. Bauer
D.B.	Dave Beatie
B.B.	Bob Behme
R.L.B.	Robert Lee Behme
R.B.	Ron Benrey
F.B.	Fred Blakemore
G.B.	George Bodmer
L.M.B.	Lillian M. Borgeson
T.M.	Thomas Bottomley
R.A.B.	Raymond Bridge
J.B.	Jacklyn Buboltz
L.B.	Len Buckwalter
J.C.	John Capotosto
T.C.	Tim Christansen
F.C.C., JR.	Fred C. Clark, Jr.
F.C.	Frank Cogan
M.C.	Marley Cole
P.A.C.	Paul Corey
H.K.C.	H. K. Cox
N.C.	Norman Crawford
P.C.	Pete Czura
B.W.D.	Byron W. Dalrymple
G.D.	George Daniels
H.L.D.	Homer L. Davidson
R.J.D.	R. J. DeCristoforo
R.D.	Richard Dietz
W.R.D.	William R. Dodd, Jr.
M.E.D.	M. E. Dowd
J.D.	John Duffett
D.D.	Dave Duffey
M.E.	Milt Evans
T.F.	Tom Faulkner
M.E.F.	Mark E. Fineman
H.F.	Herbert Friedman
M.F.	Marv Frydenlund
M.G.	Maureen Gardella
I.G.	Imre Georgenvi
J.G.	Jerry Gibbs
H.R.G.	H. R. Gleyre
T.G.	Townsend Godsey
K.G.	Ken Grant
T.H.	Thomas Hardman
M.H.	Marvin Harper
B.H.	Bill Hartford
F.H.	Frank Hegemeyer
L.H.	Lou Heiner
M.A.H.	Margaret Herbst
R.H.	Robert Hertzberg
O.E.H.	O. E. Hopper
C.R.H.	Clinton R. Hull
J.H.	Jorma Hyypia
H.F.J.	Herman F. Johnson
S.J.	Sam Julty
H.K.	Hal Kelly
J.K.	John Krill
E.P.K.	Emil P. Kushner
E.P.K., SR.	Emil P. Kushner, Sr.
J.L.	John Lauderdale
G.L.	George Laycock
R.F.L.	Robert F. Lewis
R.L.	Ray Lorenz
E.M.L.	Edwin M. Love
T.M.C.	Ted McCawley
G.M.C.	Gary McClellan
T.M.	Ted Mann
J.M.	Jim Martenhoff
F.M.	Frank Martin
A.M.	Anthony Mastey
C.R.M.	Charles R. Meyer
G.M.	George Meyerink
E.M.	Ellison Michel
S.M.M.	Stephen M. Miller
W.G.M.	Willis G. Misch
E.A.M.	Edward A. Morris
G.E.M.	Gordon E. Morrison
L.M.	Les Morrow
B.M.	Burt Murphy
M.N.	Martin Nolsen
J.O.	Joseph Olivari
P.P.	Pat Perrett
F.P.	Franklynn Peterson
R.G.P.	R. G. Puckett
C.D.R.	Charles D. Rakes
N.R.	N. Raskhodoff
A.N.R.	Alexander N. Retsoff
J.L.R.	Judith L. Reynolds
C.R.	Chuck Richards
V.H.R.	Victor H. Ries
S.R.	Stanley Rosenfeld
J.R.	Jim Rutherfoord
R.S.	Robert Scharff
D.S.	Don Shiner
P.K.S.	Patrick K. Snook
J.S.	Jack Speirs
J.R.S.	James R. Squires
H.S.	Harry Stavert
B.S.	Bob Steindler
E.M.S.	Eleanor M. Stothart
H.P.S.	Harold P. Strand
A.S.	Andy Sugar
D.M.S.	David M. Swartwout
B.T.	Bill Thomas
J.B.T.	Jack B. Thornton
A.T.	Arthur Trauffer
R.T.	Ralph Treves
P.W.A.	Paul Wahl
C.F.W.	Charles F. Waterman
D.W.	David Weems
P.W.	Paul Weissler
R.W.	Robin White
G.L.W.	Glen L. Witt
A.Y.	Alan Young

CONTENTS

ABRASIVES
AUTOMOBILE ENGINES
1

ABRASIVES
What You Should Know about Abrasives 25

ADDITIONS, HOME
How to Plan Your Home Additions 32

ADHESIVES
All about Adhesives 39

AIR CLEANERS
Servicing Your Car's Thermostatic Air Cleaner 46

AIR CONDITIONERS
What You Should Know about Air Conditioners 51
Seasonal Maintenance for Your Air Conditioner 61
How to Repair Your Room Air Conditioner 64

ALARMS, BURGLAR
Install a Burglar Alarm 69
Install a Burglar Alarm in Your Car 75
Burglar-proof Your Car's Tape Player 78
Light Sensor Alarm 80

ALTERNATOR, AUTO
Maintaining Alternator Output 85

ALUMINUM
How to Make Screens and Storm Windows 90
Maintaining Your Aluminum Boat 102

ANTENNAS
How to Erect a Rooftop Antenna 104
Citizen's Band Radio Antenna 110

ANTI-POLLUTION
Pollution Control Systems 116

ANTIQUING
All about Antiquing 123

APPLIANCE REPAIR
Trouble-shooting Home Appliances 126

ATTIC
Finishing an Attic Room on a Small Budget 136

AUTOMOBILE
Make an Automobile Headlight Switch 148

AUTOMOBILE ENGINES, ADVANCES IN
How the Wankel Rotary Engine Works 151

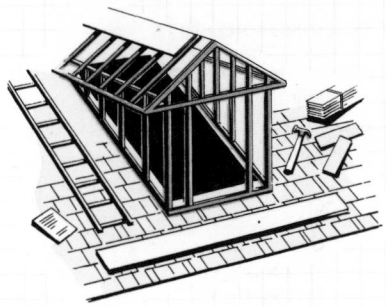

BALL JOINTS
BOAT ENGINE
2

BALL JOINTS
Repairing Worn Ball Joints 161

BARBECUE
Build a Backyard Barbecue 164

BARS
Inexpensive Bar Cabinet 166
Shaving Bars 171
Build This Rustic Bar 175

BASEMENTS
How to Take Care of Your Basement 180
A New Way to Insulate Your Basement 186

BASS FISHING
Tying Flies and Bass Bugs 189

BATHROOMS
Ceramic Tiling Your Bathroom 194
Plastic Bathroom Walls 204

BATTERIES
Guarding Your Car's Battery 211
Buying a Battery for Your Boat 217
Getting the Most Out of Small Batteries 219

BEARINGS
Servicing Your Car's Wheel Bearings 225
How to Change Engine Bearings 230

BEDS
Build These Bunk Beds 235
Race Car Bed 240
Three-in-one Wallbed Unit 244

BICYCLES
What You Should Know about Bicycles 250
How to Fix Bicycles 259

BINOCULARS
How to Buy Binoculars 264

BIRD FEEDERS
Bird Feeding Stations 270

BLENDERS
Repair Your Blender 276

BOAT BUILDING
Plywood and Lumber 281
How to Build Plywood Boats 287

BOAT BUILDING PROJECTS
Build a Buck Board 294
Deep-vee Sea Angler 299
Build an Islander 308

BOAT ENGINE
Spark of Life for Your Engine 311

BOAT HANDLING
CANOE
3

BOAT HANDLING
How to Handle a Bigger Boat 315

BOATING
How to Inspect a Boat 321
Launching Your Boat from a Trailer 323
How to Test Your Own Boat 329

BONSAI
Bonsai 334

BOOKCASE
Decorative Bookshelf-table 339
Lectern Bookcase 344
Build a TV Cabinet-bookcase 348

BOTTLE CUTTING
Make Your Own Glassware 351

BREEZEWAYS
Screen Your Patio or Breezeway 353

BRICKWORK
"Homescaping" with Bricks 360

CABINETS
Library Wall Cabinet 370
Console Cabinet and Mirror 376
Corner Display Cabinet 384
How to Buy Cabinetmaker's Supplies 390

CAMPERS
All about Campers 396
Tailgate Extension for Your Van 406

CAMPFIRES
Anatomy of a Campfire 408
How to Choose Campfire Wood 410

CAMPING
How to Get Started Camping 414
Camper's Check Lists 418
How to Camp in Foul Weather 423
How to Read Weather Signs 428
Take Your Camera Camping 432
Care for the Camping Camera 436

CAMPING EQUIPMENT
How to Lash Tent or Bedroll 440
Quick-light Camp Lantern 442
Preventive Maintenance for Your Gear 443
Make Your Own Sleeping Bag 447

CANDLE MAKING
How to Make Decorative Candles 452

CANOE
How to Travel by Canoe 457
Canoe Portage Rig 463

CARBURETORS
CLUTCH
4

CARBURETORS
Put New Life in Your Carburetor 469
How to Rebuild a Four-barrel Carburetor ..476

CAR TOP
Car Top Luggage Rack 484

CARTS
Build a Chef's Cart 487
Garden Cart Planter 491

CARVING
How to Carve Decorations in Wood 495
How to Make High Relief Carvings 501

CASSETTE TAPE PLAYER
Ten Steps to Cassette Player Repair 506
How to Repair Car Tape Players 510

CAULKING
How to Seal Your House against the Weather 513

CEILING TILE
Direct Ceiling Installation 517
A New Ceiling with Furring Strips 521
Install a Suspended Ceiling 527

CERAMICS
How to Throw Pottery without a Wheel 531

CHAISE
Build a Sun-sauna Chaise 537
Enjoy a Two-place Chaise 542

CHIMNEYS
How to Maintain Your Chimney 547

CHINA CABINET
Break-front China Cabinet 550

CHISELS
How to Use Chisels 558

CHOKE, AUTOMATIC
How to Service Your Automatic Choke 566

CIRCUITS, ELECTRICAL
Adding a Circuit 573

CITIZEN'S BAND RADIO
All about Citizen's Band Radio 578
How to Use CB Radio 589

CLOCKS
Build a Banjo Wall Clock 594
Two Grandfathers Clocks You Can Build 597

CLOSETS
Make Closet Space Do Double Duty 608
Four Cedar Closets You Can Build 609

CLUTCH
How to Maintain Your Car's Clutch 615

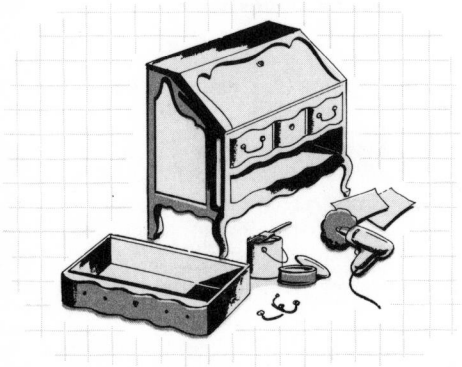

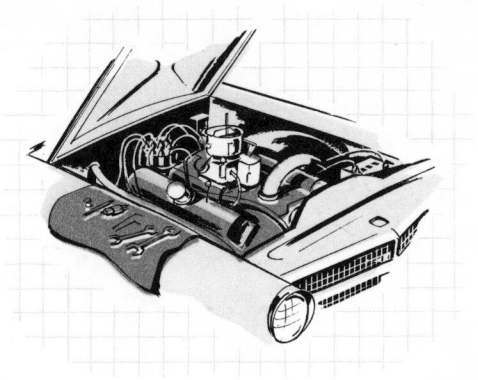

COFFEE MAKERS

DESKS

5

COFFEE MAKERS
How to Repair Coffee Makers 623

COLOR TELEVISION
How to Adjust Your Color TV 631
How to Change a Color TV Tube 641

COMMUNICATIONS
Communicating with Light Waves 647

COMPACT CARS
Turbocharge Your Compact Car 652

CONCRETE
How to Mix and Pour Concrete 657
How to Repair Masonry 662

CONCRETE BLOCKS
How to Create Decorative Block Screens and Partitions 667

CONCRETE, DECORATIVE
How to Cast Decorative Concrete Objects..675

COOLING
How to Cool Your Home without Air Conditioning 680

COOLING SYSTEMS, AUTO
Maintaining Your Car's Cooling System 684

CRAFT PROJECTS
How to Make Decorative Plaques 694
Make Toys and Jewelry Flash 699

CRAFTSMANSHIP
Wilderness Craftsmanship 702

CUPOLA
Dress Up Your House with a Cupola 707

DARKROOMS
Build This Inexpensive Darkroom 710
Make Your Own Safelight 716

DC GENERATOR, AUTO
Servicing Your Car's Generator 718

DEACON'S BENCH
How to Build a Deacon's Bench 725

DECKS
How to Build a Wooden Patio Deck 728
How to Build Wooden Decks 738

DECORATIONS
Pennsylvania Dutch-style Decorating 745

DECOUPAGE
How to Decorate with Decoupage 748

DECOYS
Make a Flying Decoy 754
Making Your Own Decoys 757

DESKS
Build an Antiqued Secretary Desk 762
Do-it-yourself Colonial Desk 768
Build a Corner Desk Set 771

DIMMER, LIGHT
ELECTRICITY
6

DIMMER, LIGHT
How to Install Light Dimmers 777

DIRECTION FINDERS
Wilderness Direction Finders 782

DISC BRAKES
Servicing Your Disc Brakes 786

DISHWASHER
How to Repair Your Dishwasher 791

DISPLAY CABINET
Safe Storage for Your Sporting Equipment..801

DOCKING, BOAT
The Techniques of Docking Your Boat 806

DOORBELL, CHIMES
Change the Sound of Your Front Door 815
Easy Installation of Doorbells 822

DOORS
How to Free Sticking Doors 827
How to Paint a Door 830

DORMER
Build a Dormer on a Weekend 831

DOWELS
Dowels and Their Uses 837

DRAINS
What to Do if the Drain Clogs 842

DRAWERS
Making Cabinet Drawers and Doors 849
Instant Drawers for Your Workshop 855

DRILL ATTACHMENTS, POWER
Making the Most of Portable Electric Drills..856

DRILL PRESS
Make Difficult Drilling Jobs Easy with a Machine 863
Routing with a Drill Press 869

DRIVEWAYS
How to Patch a Driveway 875

DRUM BRAKE SERVICE
Servicing Drum Brakes Yourself 876
Trouble-shooting Power Brakes 887

DUCK BOAT
How to Camouflage Your Duck Boat 891

EARLY AMERICAN
Traditional Dry Sink with a Modern Elegance 898
Building a Colonial Hutch 900
Dutch Colonial Seats for Your Front Porch..904
Build a Colonial Canopy Bed 906

EGG DECORATIONS
Egg Masterpieces are Easy to Make 909

ELECTRICAL, AUTO
Servicing Electrical Controls in Your Car ..911
Checking Dashboard Gauges in Your Car ..915
How to Make Electrical Connections 920

ELECTRICITY
How to Understand Electrical Terms 922
Analyzing Your Home Electrical System 924

ELECTRIC RANGE
FIREPLACE
7

ELECTRIC RANGE
How to Repair Electric Ranges 931

ELECTRONIC COOKING
All about Microwave Ovens 942

ELECTRONICS
The Practical Language of Electronics 948
The Gem of the Electronics World 951
Getting the Static Out of Your Boat Radio ..960
Electronic Equipment for Weekend Mechanics 966
Build a Battery-powered Mini-beacon 973

EMERGENCY BOAT REPAIRS
Making Emergency Repairs while Afloat 974

ENCLOSURE, BATHROOM
An Easy Way to Enclose Your Bathtub 979

ENGINE
Cut Down on Gasket Replacements 982
How to Revive a Faltering Starter 989
Servicing Your Engine's Tappets 994
Taking Care of Your Engine 1000

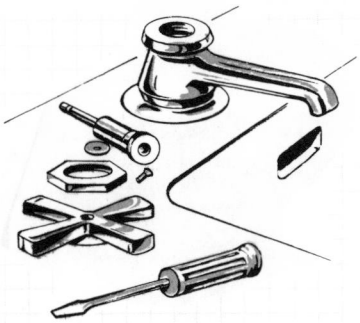

ENGINES, SMALL
How to Maintain and Repair Small Engines 1010

EXERCISE EQUIPMENT
Easy-to-build Jogging Machine 1014
Rowing Exercise in Your Home 1020

FAUCETS
How to Repair a Dripping Faucet 1027
Replacing Your Kitchen Faucets 1032

FENCES
Three Easy-to-build Fence Designs 1036

FENCE-STORAGE SHED
Build a Storage Area into Your Fence 1042

FERTILIZERS
Selecting the Right Fertilizer for Your Lawn and Plants 1048

FILTERS
How to Change Your Car's Filters 1051

FINISHING, WOOD
Stocking Your Refinisher's Cabinet 1057
How to Prepare Wood for Finishing 1062
How to Stain and Finish Fine Wood 1067

FIREPLACE
Repair and Maintenance of Your Fireplace 1073
Add a Fireplace to Your Home 1080

FIRST AID
GARAGE REMODELING

8

FIRST AID
First Aid and Medicine for Campers 1085

FISHING
Where to Learn Fly Casting 1090
Twelve Tricks to Take More Fish 1093
How to Identify the Fish You Catch 1097

FISH PREPARATION
How to Fillet a Fish 1103

FLOORS
Refinishing Your Wood Floors 1106
How to Paint Wood or Concrete Floors 1110
Using Wax to Polish Your Floors 1112

FLOORS, BRICK
How to Lay Plastic Brick Floors Yourself ..1114

FLOORS, TILING
Installing Pre-glued Floor Tiles 1116
How to Install a Parquet Floor in a Day 1119
How to Install Cove Base Molding 1122

FLOWER CARE
Increasing the Life of Cut Flowers 1124

FLOWERING BULBS
Choosing and Planting Spring-flowering Bulbs 1126

FLUORESCENT LIGHTING
Trouble-shooting Fluorescent Lights 1134
Indoor Gardening with Fluorescent Lights 1141

FOYER
Easy-to-install Stone Foyer 1144

FUEL PUMP
Repairing Your Fuel Pump 1147

FUELS
How to Choose a Heating System 1151

FURNITURE, CHILDREN'S
How to Build a Cradle 1160
Build a Child's Footlocker 1163

FURNITURE, INDOOR
Contemporary Coffee Table 1168
Modular Entertainment Center 1170
Cabinet for All Your Sewing Needs 1174
Build a Space-saving Wardrobe 1178
Build This Modern Desk 1183

FURNITURE, OUTDOOR
Build a Rocker for Your Patio 1187
Put a Swing on Your Lawn 1191
Patio Table 1195

FURNITURE, USED
How to Buy and Restore Used Furniture ..1199
How to Rebuild an Old Rocker 1204

GAME BOARDS
Make This Plastic Game Board 1208
Build a Chessboard-topped Game Table ..1211

GARAGE DOOR, OVERHEAD
How to Maintain Garage Doors 1218
Install an Automatic Garage Door Operator 1223

GARAGE REMODELING
Convert Your Garage to Living Space 1229

GARDENING
HOME IMPROVEMENT
9

GARDENING
Green Thumb Tips 1239
How to Root Cuttings 1243
How to Prepare Your Garden for Winter ..1245
How to Water Gardens, Lawns and Trees..1248

GARDEN PLANNING
Choosing Garden Favorites 1255
How to Make a Home Landscaping Plan ..1263
Plants That Solve Gardening Problems 1273

GARDEN TOOL SHED
Build a Little Red Barn 1280

GLASS
How to Cut and Install Window Glass 1289

GRAFTING
How to Graft Trees and Shrubs 1292

HANDICRAFTS
Making Mosaics with Beans and Seeds 1296
Making Animal Toys from Shells 1297

HAND TOOLS
How to Select Tools 1298
How to Tighten Bolts Precisely 1324

HEATING SYSTEMS, HOME
Reducing Your Cooling and Heating Bills..1328
How to Maintain and Repair Hot Air Gas Furnaces 1334
Bringing Your Electric Water Heater Back to Life 1340
Balancing Hot Water Heating Systems 1342

HEAT RISER, AUTO
Servicing Your Car's Heat Riser 1347

HERBS
Raising Your Own Herb Garden 1349

HIGH FIDELITY SYSTEMS
Servicing Hi-fi's, Radios and Television Sets 1355

HIKING
Making the All-purpose Back Pack 1363
Making Your Own Pack Frame 1366
Packing Your Back Pack 1370

HOME IMPROVEMENT
A New Face for Your Old Home Front 1372
How to Add a Room to Your House 1377

HOME OWNERSHIP
LASER
10

HOME OWNERSHIP
Costs Versus Livability in Building a Home 1393
Cutting Initial Construction Costs 1396
Financial Advantages of Owning a Home..1405

HOME SECURITY SENSORS
Installing Home Security Sensors 1407

HOPPERS
Constructing Multi-sided Columns and Hoppers 1411

HULLS
Which Hull Type is Right for You 1417

HUNTING
You May Not Have Missed That Bird 1419
Duck Hunters, Don't Ignore Those Ponds..1423
Tips on Dove Hunting 1426

HYDRAULICS
How Hydraulic Brakes Work 1430

IGNITION SYSTEM, AUTO
How the Ignition System Works 1433
How to Service Electronic Ignition Systems 1434

ILLUMINATION
How to Plan Kitchen Illumination 1438

INLAY WOODWORKING
How to Make Inlaid Veneer Pictures 1446
Make Decorative Inlaid Turnings 1452
Make Decorative Inlays 1458

INTERCOMS
Choosing a Home Intercom System 1464

IRONS
How to Repair Steam or Dry Irons 1471

JIGS
Four Table Saw Jigs to Meet All Your Needs 1476

KITCHENS
Planning an Ecological Kitchen 1481
How to Arrange Kitchen Appliances 1489
Improving Your Household with Plastic Laminates 1496
How to Replace a Kitchen Sink 1500

KNIVES AND AXES
Choosing and Maintaining Knives and Axes 1502

KNOTS
Good Knots Mean More Fish 1511
Tying Useful Knots 1516

LADDERS
Ladders In and Around Your Home 1519

LAND SAILER
A Sailboat for Land Lovers 1526

LANDSCAPING
Enhancing the Beauty of Your Home with Landscaping 1533

LASER
Using Laser Beams for Voice Transmission 1542

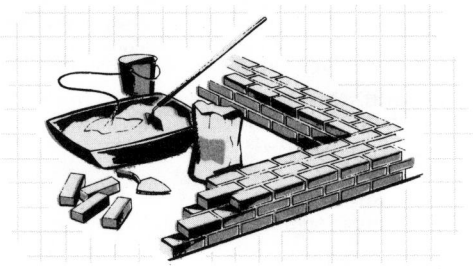

LATHE
MODEL CAR LAYOUT
11

LATHE
The Wood-turning Lathe 1547
Duplicating Odd Shapes with a Lathe Jig..1559

LAUNDRY ROOMS
Laundry Planning in Your Home 1563
Build This Modular Laundry Center 1567

LAWNS
Choosing and Maintaining a Lawn for Your Yard 1573
Buying the Right Grass Seed for Your Lawn 1579

LIGHTING
Increasing the Beauty of Your Garden with Lighting 1582

LOCKS
Repairing Door Locks 1586

LOOM
Constructing a Table Top Loom 1590

LUMBER
Buying the Right Lumber Grade for Your Needs 1595
Make Your Own "Antiques" from Scrap Lumber 1602
Making Furniture from Crates 1605
Convenient Storage for Extra Lumber 1611

LURES
Overhauling Your Fishing Lures....1615

MACROPHOTOGRAPHY
Join the Small World of Macrophotography 1620

MAINTENANCE, BOAT
Giving Your Boat a Spring Painting 1627
Spring Check List for Your Boat 1631

MAINTENANCE, CHAIN SAW
Repairing and Maintaining Your Chain Saw 1636

MASONRY
Concrete Improvements Around Your Home 1643
Stopping Leaks in Masonry Walls 1654

MICROPHONES
Building a Directional Microphone for Experiment or Fun 1658
Building a Highly Sensitive Parabolic Microphone 1665

MINIBIKES
Choosing the Right Minibike 1668

MIXER
How to Repair Electric Mixers 1671

MOBILE HOMES
Shopping for Mobile Homes 1677
Choosing a Site for Your Mobile Home 1682
Self-defense for the Mobile Home Buyer..1685
Finishing the "Finished" Mobile Home 1690

MODEL CAR LAYOUT
Building a Hideaway Track for Your Model Cars 1694

MOLDINGS
PAINT SPRAYERS
12

MOLDINGS
What You Can Do with Moldings 1701

NAILS
All about Nails and Nailing 1707

NAVIGATION
Boating's "Rules of the Road" 1711
The Simple Way to Steer by Compass 1722
All about Folk Navigation 1730

NOISE
Noise and Your Homesite 1734

OIL, ENGINE
How to Stop Engine Oil Loss 1743

ORGANIC GARDENING
All about Organic Gardening 1748

ORNAMENTS, LAWN
Decorate Your Lawn with a Wishing Well..1759
Casting Your Own Lawn Birdbath 1763
Add a Restful Air to Your Yard 1764
Build a Lamppost for Your Front Yard 1765

OUTBOARD MOTORS
Choosing an Outboard Motor 1770
Maintaining Your Outboard Motor 1772
Motorize Your Canoe 1777

OUTDOOR COOKING
Cooking Convenience at the Campsite 1789
Portable Flameless Cooker 1782
Improvising Cooking Rigs
at the Campsite 1784

OUTDOOR LIFE
Living Off the Land 1787
Campsite Cooking with Foil 1792

OVENS
A Lightweight Back Pack Oven
You Can Make 1798

PADDLE WHEELER
Build a Pogo Stern Wheeler 1800

PAINT
How to Estimate Paint Requirements 1806
Paint with Brushes, Pads or Rollers 1807

PAINTING
How to Prepare Surfaces for Painting 1813
Paint Wood or Fabric with Dyes 1815
Make a Marble Table Top Out of Plywood..1816

PAINTING, AUTO
Paint Your Car Like a Pro 1819

PAINTING, HOUSE
Painting Problems and
How to Solve Them 1827
All about Exterior House Painting 1832
All about Painting Your Home's Interior 1845

PAINT SPRAYERS
Spray Painting with an Aerosol Can 1854

PANELS
PICTURE FRAMING
13

PANELS
How to Install Wall Paneling 1855
How to Build with Translucent Panels 1881

PAPER DISPENSER, KITCHEN
Build a Kitchen Paper Dispenser 1891

PARSONS TABLE
How to Make and Cover a Parsons Table..1894

PARTITIONS
How to Make Spring Pole Partitions 1900

PARTS REPLACEMENT, ENGINE
How to Change Engine Parts 1903

PATCHING
How to Patch Plaster Walls 1914
How to Repair Holes in Wallboard 1918

PATIOS
The Basics of Patio Design 1919
How to Build a Patio Screen 1923

PATTERNING, SHOTGUN
Checking Your Shotgun's Pattern 1926

PEST CONTROL
Coping with the Insect World 1931

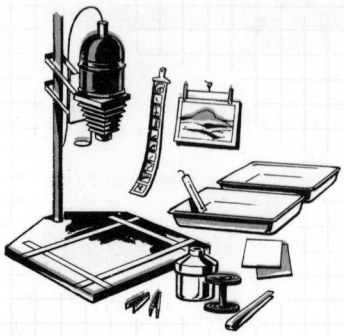

PHOTOGRAPHY
Photography for Beginners 1937
Photography on the Camp Trail 1949
Photographing Your Favorite TV Scenes ..1955
How to Photograph People 1959
How to Photograph Infants Successfully ..1964

PHOTOMICROGRAPHY
3-D Photographs through a Microscope..1972
Take Electronic Flash Photos
through a Microscope 1983

PICNIC TABLE
Build This Picnic Table 1997

PICTURE FRAMING
How to Make Your Own Picture Frames ..1999

PLASTICS, FABRICATING
REPAIRS, AUTOMOBILE
14

PLASTICS, FABRICATING
How to Make a Wine Rack
of Acrylic Sheet 2009
Build This Plastic Etagère 2013

PLAYHOUSE
Build an A-frame Playhouse 2016

PLUMBING
Householder's Guide to Plumbing 2018
Plumbing Tips 2024

POOL TABLE
Build Your Own Pool Table 2026
How to Build a Bumper Pool Table 2042

POWER STEERING, AUTO
Understanding Your Car's
Power Steering 2048

POWER TOOLS
All about Power Tools 2052
Power Tool Safety Check Lists 2064

PRINT MAKING
How to Make Linoleum Prints 2066

PROJECTOR, OVERHEAD
How to Build an Overhead Projector 2070

PUBLIC ADDRESS SYSTEMS
How to Operate a Public Address System..2079

QUICKSAND
What to Do about Quicksand 2084

RACING BOAT
How to Build a Mini-hydrofoil 2086

RADIAL ARM SAW
How to Use a Radial Arm Saw 2092
Boring and Routing with a Radial Arm Saw 2099

RADIO
How to Restore a Vintage Radio 2104
Restoring a Clock Radio 2110

RAFT
Build a Raft for Youngsters 2113

RAILINGS, IRON
Improve Your Home with Wrought Iron Railings 2118

REFRIGERATOR
Maintaining and Repairing Your Refrigerator 2121

RELOADING
Reloading Ammunition for Your Weapon ..2128
How to Hand Load Ammunition 2132

REMOTE CONTROL SWITCHES
Low-voltage Remote Control Switching 2138

REPAIRS, AUTOMOBILE
How to Spot That Noise and Quiet It 2142
How to Repair Dents and Rust-outs 2151
All about Paint Sprayers 2156

ROOFS / SCIENCE PROJECTS 15

ROOFS
Enlarge Your Home by Raising the Roof....2163
All about Roofing 2175
Repairing Roofs and Gutters 2183
Resurfacing a Flat Roof 2188

ROOM DIVIDERS
Use Louvered Panels to Divide a Room 2192

ROTARY ENGINE, MINI
Mini Wankel for Model Airplanes 2196

ROUTER
What You Can Do with a Portable Router....2198

RUNABOUTS
Build a Motorized Surfboard 2210
Build a Sailing Dinghy 2218
This Lightweight Pram Is Easy to Build 2221

SABER SAW
How to Use a Saber Saw 2227
Tricks You Can Do with a Saber Saw 2234

SAFETY, BOAT
What to Do about Boating Accidents 2238
How to Trailer a Boat Safely 2242

SAFETY, WATER
Keep Yourself and Your Family Safe from Drowning 2248

SAILING
Sailing for Beginners 2254

SANDERS
How to Use a Pad Sander 2259

SAUNA
Install a Sauna Bath in Your Home 2265

SAW
Handsaws and How to Use Them 2277

SCIENCE PROJECTS
All about Air Cannons 2280
Experimenting with Loudspeakers 2286
Schlieren Bench Makes Sound Wave, Heat Visible 2292
See How Lenses Work with a Smoke Box Optical Bench 2302
How to Mold Plastic Prints 2311

SCREENS / SPARK PLUG 16

SCREENS
How to Make Your Own Window Screens 2317

SCUBA DIVING
How to Get Started Snorkeling or Scuba Diving 2319

SECURITY, HOME
Attention-getting Alarm Generator 2327

SERVERS
Movable Drop Leaf Server 2330
Build a Roll-about Server 2337

SHARPENING
Sharp Edges Make Short Work 2341
All about Sharpening Stones 2346
How to Keep Tools Sharp 2352
How to Sharpen an Electric Razor 2358

SHELLS
How to Collect Sea Shells 2360

SHELVES
Mirror-back Georgian Wall Shelf 2365
Four Ways You Can Stretch Your Garage 2368
How to Build Simple Utility Shelves 2374

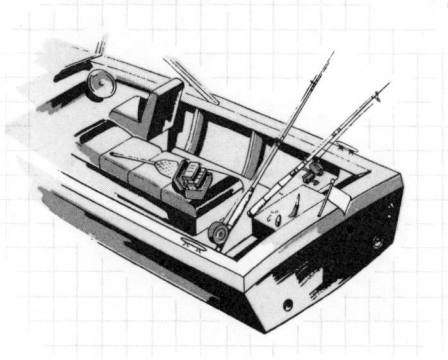

SHOCK ABSORBERS, AUTO
Testing and Replacing Your Car's Shock Absorbers 2375

SHOOTING
How to Get Your Weapon in Shape 2378
How to Make Your Own Ammunition 2381
Improve Your Marksmanship with a Small Shooting Range 2386
All about Trapshooting 2389
All about Skeet Shooting 2397

SHOOTING TECHNIQUES
How to Deal with Recoil 2406

SHOTGUN
Learn Shotgunning at Home 2409
The Basics of Shotgun Chokes 2411

SHOT SHELLS
Selecting the Best Shot Size 2414

SHOWER
Portable Shower for Your Camper or Trailer 2416

SHOWER DOOR
Install a Break-resistant Acrylic Shower Door 2419

SHUTTERS
How to Build Your Own Shutters 2422

SIDING
How to Select Siding for Your Home....2425
Stopping Leaks in Wood Siding 2435

SITE SELECTION
How to Evaluate a Vacation Homesite 2437

SKIFF, HUNTING AND FISHING
Build a Lightweight Hunting and Fishing Skiff 2442

SLED
Jump the Bumps with a Single-runner Sled 2449

SNAKES
Playing It Safe with Snakes 2452
What to Do about Snakebite 2454

SOLVENTS AND STRIPPERS
How to Remove Paints and Varnishes 2458

SPARK PLUG
Trouble-shooting Your Engine's Spark Plugs 2461

SPEAKERS
Build a Nine-unit Stereo Speaker 2471

SPICE RACKS
Two Spice Racks for Your Kitchen 2478

SPLICING
How to Splice Wire Like a Pro 2482

SPOT REMOVAL
How to Remove Spots from Rugs and Carpets 2484
How to Remove Stains from Floors 2485

STAINING
All about Wood Staining 2488

STAPLE GUN
How to Use a Staple Gun 2494

STEREO
How to Choose Stereo Equipment for Your Home 2497
How to Place Speakers for Four-channel Sound 2501
Build a Pair of Bookshelf Speakers 2505
Put Your Stereo Speakers in End Tables 2511
Bring Your Hi-fi Sound Outdoors with an Extension Speaker 2518

STONEWORK
Four Ways to Build with Stone 2521
How to Install Curbs, Edging and Ground Cover 2525
What You Should Know about Retaining Walls 2527

STORAGE
Storage Unit for a Folding Bed 2531
Food Storage Unit 2534
Store Your Small Appliances in a Hutch 2537
Divider Unit Combines Desk and Storage Space 2541

STORAGE, BOAT
Build a Storage Port for Your Boat 2553
Getting Your Boat Ready for Storage 2559

STORAGE, SPORTING GOODS
Cabinet Holds Sports Gear 2564

STORAGE WALL
Decorative Storage Wall 2572
How to Make a Free-standing Storage Wall 2578

STORM DOORS AND WINDOWS
How to Install Acrylic Safety Glazing 2583

STROBE
Record Action with Inexpensive Strobe 2587

STUCCO
How to Repair Stucco Surfaces 2597

SURFBOARD
Keep Your Surfboard in Top Condition 2601

SURVIVAL
Make Yourself Freeze-proof 2604
Protect Your Feet from Frostbite 2607
Emergency Shelters for Hikers 2609

SWIMMING
Make Yourself Drown-proof 2610
Basic Swimming Strokes 2614
Swimming Underwater 2621

SWIMMING POOL TOOLS 18

SWIMMING POOL
How to Select Your Swimming Pool 2625
The Care and Maintenance of Your Swimming Pool 2628

TABLES
Drop Leaf Coffee Table 2634
How to Assemble an Elegant Coffee Table 2638
Book and Magazine Table 2641
How to Make a Fold-away Table 2643

TABLE SAW
How to Use a Table Saw Like a Professional 2647

TAPE RECORDERS
Solving Minor Tape Recorder Problems 2656
All about Recorded Tape 2661

TELEPHONE
Guard Your Telephone Privacy with a Scrambler 2665

TELEVISION REPAIR
Television Repair Tips 2671
Getting the Most from Your TV 2676
How to Service Portable TV Sets 2689

TENTS
How to Pitch a Tent 2701
Wind-proof Your Tent 2706
For a Superior Tent, Make it Yourself 2707
How to Repair and Maintain Your Tent 2709

TILE, CARPET
Installing Carpet Tile 2715

TILE, CERAMIC
Decorate Your Fireplace with Ceramic Tile 2719

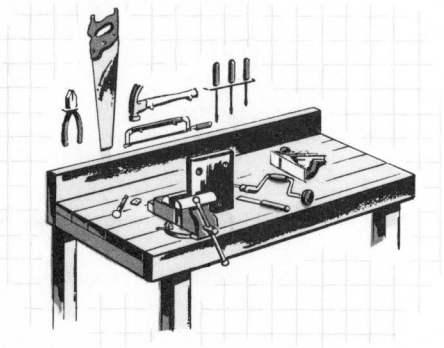

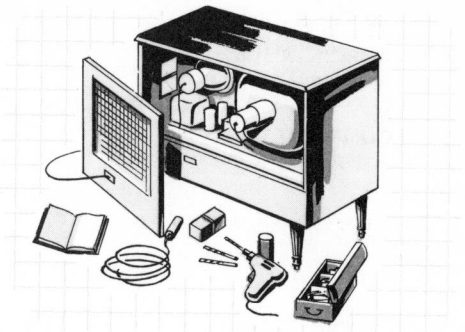

TIRES
How to Buy and Maintain Automobile Tires 2725

TOASTER
How to Repair Your Toaster 2733

TOILET
How to Repair a Faulty Flush Tank 2738
How to Stop Toilet Sweating 2743

TONE AND CHORD GENERATOR
Build a Tone and Chord Generator 2745

TOOL CADDIES
Keep Your Tools Ready with This Handy Carrier 2750
Build a Sawhorse Mini-workshop 2753

TOOL CHEST
Two Tool Chests You Can Build 2760

TOOLS
Maintaining Hand Tools 2764
Get the Most from Your Portable Circular Saw 2768
Get the Most from Your Chain Saw 2773

TOOLS, GARDEN UPHOLSTERY 19

TOOLS, GARDEN
How to Choose Garden Tools 2779

TOOL TECHNIQUES
How to Choose the Right Saw Blade 2782
Twin-blade Cutting with a Table Saw 2788
Decorative Cuts with Common Shop Tools 2792
Jointing with Wood Shapers 2797
Shaping and Cutting Large Workpieces 2804

TRAILERING
How to Select a Trailer Hitch 2807
Tips for Trailer Towing 2810

TRAILERS, BOAT
Buying a Trailer for Your Boat 2814
Maintaining Your Boat Trailer 2821
Lights for Your Boat Trailer 2827
Bring along Your Boat and Your Trailer 2829

TRAILERS, TENT
Equip Your Tent Trailer with a Trunk 2832

TRAINING BOAT
Learn to Sail in a Pram 2837

TRANSMISSION, AUTO
Servicing Your Car's Automatic Transmission 2847

TRASH COMPACTORS
How to Repair a Trash Compactor 2853

TRAYS
How to Make Wood Trays and Lazy Susans 2860
Build a Butler's Tray Table 2865

TREES
What Homeowners Need to Know about Trees 2872

TROLLING TECHNIQUES
How to Troll for Fish 2885
Fish with Outriggers 2891

TROUT
Professional Secrets for Taking Trout 2893

TUNE-UP, ENGINE
Tuning Your Car's Engine 2902
How to Tune a Wankel Engine 2918

UNFINISHED FURNITURE
How to Enamel Unfinished Furniture 2925

UPHOLSTERY
Keep Your Car's Upholstery in Good Condition 2928

VACUUM CLEANER — WILDLIFE

20

VACUUM CLEANER
How to Repair Your Vacuum Cleaner 2933

VACUUM GAUGE
Pinpointing Engine Ailments with a Vacuum Gauge 2937

VALVES
How to Do an Engine Valve and Ring Job 2943
Adjusting Valves for Maximum Engine Performance 2953

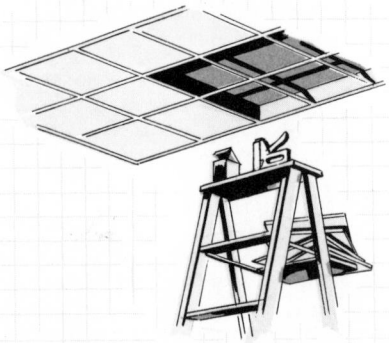

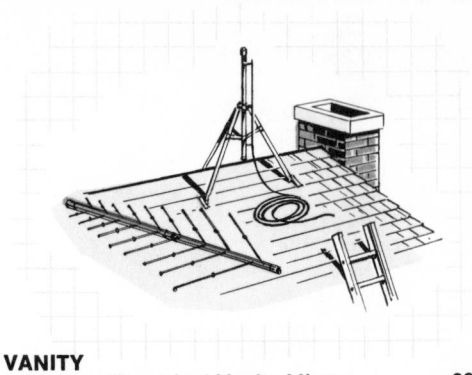

VANITY
Make a Theatrical Vanity Mirror 2957
Combination Vanity Table and Writing Desk 2960

VENTILATION
How to Ventilate with Kitchen and Bathroom Fans 2965

WAFFLE IRON/GRILL
How to Repair Waffle Irons and Grills 2974

WAGON
Build a Patio Flower Wagon 2979

WALKIE-TALKIE
Walkie-Talkie Repair 2980

WALLBOARD
How to Install Gypsum Panel Walls 2984

WALL COVERINGS
How to Prepare Walls for Papering 2993
How to Hang Wall Coverings 2996
Using Imitation Stone Wall Coverings 3002

WALL DECORATIONS
Wall and Counter Decorating Ideas 3004

WALL SWITCHES
How to Select Combination Electrical Switches 3010
How to Use Surface-mounted Electrical Wiring 3015

WASHER AND DRYER
How to Repair Your Automatic Washing Machine 3018
How to Repair Your Clothes Dryer 3028

WATER SKIING
How to Practice Water Skiing on Dry Land 3035
Rate Your Ability on Water Skis 3038
Tricks You Can Do on Water Skis 3043
How to Slalom on a Water Ski 3048
How to Water Ski on Your Bare Feet 3053

WEATHER
Be Your Own Weatherman 3057

WEATHER-STRIPPING
Keep Your House Warm with Weather-stripping 3069

WILD FLOWERS
How to Identify Wild Flowers 3073

WILDLIFE
The Camper's Guide to Animal Intruders 3077
Recognizing Animal Tracks 3082
How to Make Casts of Animal Tracks 3085

WIND GAUGE

INDEX

21

WIND GAUGE
Measure Wind Speed with an Anemometer 3087

WINDOW REPAIR
How to Rebuild Windows the Easy Way 3100

WINDOWS
Solving Problems in Windows and Doors 3102
How to Install Double-pane Insulating Windows 3106
Brighten a Dull Window with a Shadow Box 3110

WINE CELLAR
Combination Buffet and Wine Cellar 3114

WIRING, ELECTRICAL
How to Work Safely with Electricity 3118
Safe Wiring Indicator 3123
How to Rewire Old Lamps 3126
Wiring an Extra Room 3129

WOOD BENDING
How the Experts Bend Wood 3139

WOODWORKING
How to Finish Edges and End Grains 3145
The Basics of Dadoing and Rabbeting 3152
All about Joints and Joinery 3157
Machine Molding of Flat Stock 3167

WORKBENCH
Build Your Own Workbench 3174
Make a Modern Multi-purpose Workbench 3182
Hobbyist's Low-voltage Power Supply 3196

WORKSHOP
How to Lay Out Your Workshop 3198
Wall-mounted Workshop Desk 3202

YARN
How to Decorate with Felt and Yarn 3205

ANATOMY OF A HOUSE
Structural Transparencies....facing page 3208

INDEX 3209

CREDITS

In striving to make this publication as complete, accurate and up to date as possible a great deal of assistance and technical information was obtained from manufacturers trade association and governmental agencies. The editors are deeply grateful to all of them for their help and wish to thank the following organizations for the illustrations they have made available:

AMF Swimaster
Airstream, Inc.
Allied International Films Ltd.
American Plywood Association
Amspec, Inc.
Apeco Recreational Vehicles
Armstrong Cork Company
Aromatic Red Cedar Closet Lining Manufacturers Association
Arrow Fastener Co., Inc.
Baths International, Inc.
Behr-Manning
Bertram Yacht
Black and Decker Manufacturing Company
Borden Chemical Division, Borden Inc.
Boy Scouts of America
The Brewster Corporation
W. Atlee Burpee Co.
Champion Spark Plug Company
Dayton Products, Inc.
The Decro-Wall Corporation
Department of Commerce
Disston, Inc.
Dupont Building Products
Dupont Paint Company
Duro-Test Corporation
Eastman Kodak Company
Environmental Science Service Administration
Filon Division of Vistron Corporation
Florida News Bureau
Fluidmaster
Formica Corporation
Frigid, Inc.
Frigidaire Division, General Motors Corp.
GTE Sylvania, Inc.
General Electric Company
Georgia-Pacific Corporation
Glen L. Marine
Hartline Products Co., Inc.
Homelite A Textron Division
The Hoover Company
Hotpoint
Hunt Manufacturing Company
In-Sink-Erator Division, Emerson Electric Company
Interlux
International Paint Company
JFD Electronics Corporation
Jackson & Perkins
Johnson Motors Division of Outboard Marine Corp.
Lecomar, Inc.
Luger Industries
MRL Inc.
The Magnavox Company
Malak Photographs, Ltd.
Masonite Corporation
The Maytag Company
Mazda Motors of America, Inc.
Mercury Marine
Meridian Yachts
Michigan Tourist Council
Benjamin Moore and Company
National Paint, Varnish, and Lacquer Association
National Swimming Pool Institute
Nebraska Game Commission
New York State College of Agriculture and Life Sciences
New York State College of Human Ecology
Northern Stone Supply, Inc.
NuTone Division, Scovill Housing Products Group
Oakridge Industries
Old Town Co.
Ozite Corporation
Pittsburgh Paint Company
Plastronics, Inc.
Plexiglas
Portland Cement Association
Power Tool Institute, Inc.
Quaker Manufacturing Company
RCBS Incorporated
Red Devil, Inc.
Reynolds Aluminum
Rockwell Manufacturing Company Power Tool Division
Rohm and Haas Company
Morris Rosenfeld & Sons
School Products Co., Inc.
Schwinn Bicycle Company
Set Products
Sharon Communications, Inc.
Sherwin-Williams Paint Company
Simpson Timber Company
The Sony Corporation
Stanley Door Systems
Stanley Power Tools Division of The Stanley Works
The Stanley Works
Sunbeam Appliance Company
The Swan Corporation
Swim Gard, Inc.
Swingline, Inc.
Switchpack Systems, Inc.
Texas Parks and Wildlife Department
3M Company
Tibbals Flooring Company
Tile Council of America
True Temper Corporation
U. S. Coast Guard
U. S. Department of Agriculture
U. S. Department of the Interior, Fish and Wildlife Service
U. S. Forest Service
United States Gypsum
U. S. Plywood Division of Champion International
Wallcovering Industry Bureau, Inc.
Watco-Dennis Corp.
Western Wood Products Association
Wheeler, Knight & Gainey, Inc.
Wilson Imperial
Winnebago Industries, Inc.
J. Wiss & Sons Co.
York Division, Borg-Warner Corp.
Zenith Radio Corporation

Steve Ellingson construction projects appear through the courtesy of UB Newspaper Syndicate, 15125 Saticoy St., Van Nuys, Cal. 91409.

VOLUME 1

ABRASIVES

WHAT YOU SHOULD KNOW ABOUT ABRASIVES: How to choose and use old standbys like sandpaper, plus new buffing and polishing materials 25

ADDITIONS, HOME

HOW TO PLAN YOUR HOME ADDITIONS: Refinish your basement, attic, garage or breezeway to add space, increase equity 32

ADHESIVES

ALL ABOUT ADHESIVES: For decorating a window shade, repairing a camera or building a model boat, there's an adhesive that will do the job 39

AIR CLEANERS

SERVICING YOUR CAR'S THERMOSTATIC AIR CLEANER: Neglect of these vacuum and temperature controlled devices can lead to engine stalling and poor gas mileage 46

AIR CONDITIONERS

WHAT YOU SHOULD KNOW ABOUT AIR CONDITIONERS: Here's how to narrow down a field of more than 3,000 types, models and sizes to the unit that meets your requirements 51

SEASONAL MAINTENANCE FOR YOUR AIR CONDITIONER: Get this job done in the spring for dependable summer-long operation 61

HOW TO REPAIR YOUR ROOM AIR CONDITIONER: You can keep your machine working and save on repair bills by replacing some broken parts yourself 64

ALARMS, BURGLAR

INSTALL A BURGLAR ALARM: Here's how to select an alarm, and instructions for a complete alarm system 69

INSTALL A BURGLAR ALARM IN YOUR CAR: Shrill alarm sounds whenever trunk, hood or doors are tampered with 75

BURGLAR-PROOF YOUR CAR'S TAPE PLAYER: This alarm requires only four components, and you can install it quickly 78

LIGHT SENSOR ALARM: This system's photocell "eyes" can detect an intruder's shadow as he passes an ordinary light bulb 80

ALTERNATOR, AUTO

MAINTAINING ALTERNATOR OUTPUT: This job is advanced for a novice, but an experienced mechanic can handle it 85

ALUMINUM

HOW TO MAKE SCREENS AND STORM WINDOWS: Do the job yourself with inexpensive aluminum components and a few simple tools 90

MAINTAINING YOUR ALUMINUM BOAT: That hull is tough and corrosion-resistant, but choose an antifouling paint with care 102

ANTENNAS

HOW TO ERECT A ROOFTOP ANTENNA: Putting an antenna on your roof is easier than it looks, and it can give your TV set and FM radio a sharp boost in performance **104**

CITIZEN'S BAND RADIO ANTENNA: Your CB radio gear will only work as well as your antenna. Here's how to pick one out and how to choose a location for it **110**

ANTI-POLLUTION

POLLUTION CONTROL SYSTEMS: Neglect of these devices can lead to poor performance, increased engine wear **116**

ANTIQUING

ALL ABOUT ANTIQUING: Follow these steps to achieve a professional-looking result on a piece of furniture—whether it's an old relic or brand new **123**

APPLIANCE REPAIR

TROUBLE-SHOOTING HOME APPLIANCES: Here's how to do everything you can, depending on your tools and experience, to head off those costly visits by the repairman **126**

ATTIC

FINISHING AN ATTIC ROOM ON A SMALL BUDGET: Unused attic space in your home can be converted economically into an attractive living area **136**

AUTOMOBILE

MAKE AN AUTOMOBILE HEADLIGHT SWITCH: This device will keep your car lights on while you walk to your door, then turn them off automatically **148**

AUTOMOBILE ENGINES, ADVANCES IN

HOW THE WANKEL ROTARY ENGINE WORKS: Few moving parts and relatively small size keynote the revolutionary Wankel **151**

What You Should Know about Abrasives

How to choose and use old standbys like sandpaper, plus new buffing and polishing materials

Non-woven synthetic fiber pads impregnated with abrasive particles for finish sanding, scouring, etc. Colors indicate the coarseness grade.

WHETHER YOU CALL IT SANDPAPER or coated abrasive, it's the same thing and it does the same jobs. The readily available abrasive types are five in number. The one you use depends on the job to be done and the material involved.

There's a technique in using any of these abrasives to get the best result. To see the overall picture let's look at the abrasives first, then the methods of using them.

Flint, a natural abrasive, is the oldest of the common woodworking types still widely used. It has a short working life and relatively poor cutting power. But, being the lowest in price, it's a very popular type for work that clogs the abrasive quickly and requires frequent replacement, as in heavy paint removal. It is grayish white, but acquires a yellowish tinge from the adhesive that holds it to the paper backing. And, as it looks like sand, it can probably be credited with keeping alive the term "sandpaper." It is a good choice for small sanding jobs and any work that requires a cheap, throw-away abrasive.

Garnet is another natural abrasive. It has much sharper cutting edges (when crushed) than flint, and is much harder. So it cuts faster, lasts longer, and is a good low cost woodworking abrasive. It is easy to recognize by its red color—the same red color that makes large pieces attractive when faceted and polished for jewelry use.

Emery, also a natural abrasive, was once the major metal-finishing type. It is black, slow-cutting and short-lived. But, its rounded, slow-cutting crystals have very good polishing qualities that give it a lasting place in the workshop. It is also used by tradition-minded craftsman and by those unfamiliar with the more efficient artificial abrasives now available for cutting rather than polishing action.

Aluminum oxide, a reddish brown artificial abrasive, is perhaps the most versatile and widely used of the synthesized types. Being extremely tough and sharp, it is excellent for wood, metal, and the majority of other materials usually handled in the home workshop. It far outlasts any of the natural abrasives, and cuts much faster, though it costs somewhat more.

Silicon carbide, a blue-black artificial abrasive, is almost as hard as the diamond, and the sharpest of all five common abrasive types. But its crystals are too brittle

accident prevention: see safety
acrylic glazing material: see glass
acrylic resin adhesive: see adhesive
acrylic safety glazing: see storm doors and windows
acrylic sheet: see plastics, fabricating

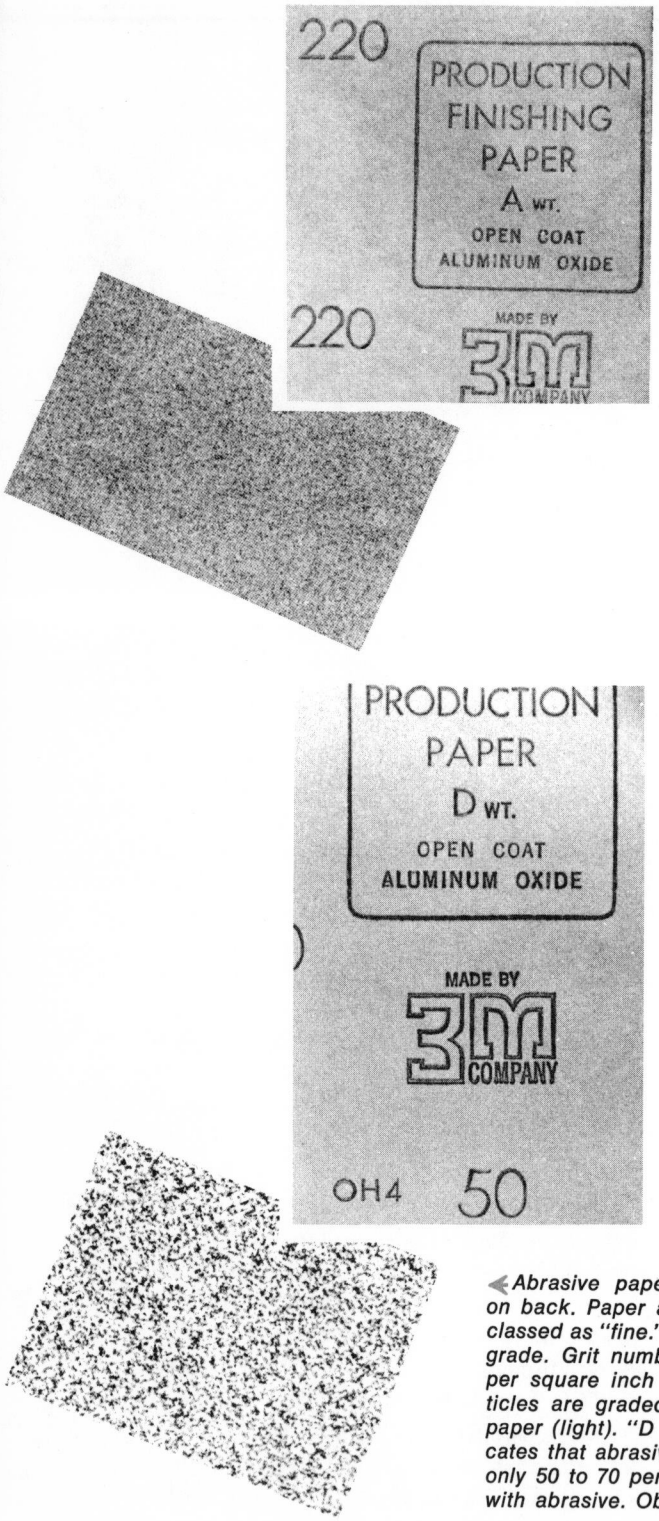

for general use on metals like iron and steel. It is a good choice, however, for softer metals like aluminum and bronze, because it cuts very fast without excessive speed or pressure. It also has ample strength for use on glass, and is widely used in glass work. It is the ideal abrasive, too, for many soft materials like leather. It is, in fact one of the leading abrasives in shoemaking and shoe repair.

All of these abrasives are readily available at hardware stores, though silicon carbide may not be stocked by some because of its more specialized applications. If you can't obtain it through local sources, contact an abrasive manufacturer for your nearest source of supply.

Pumice and rottenstone are natural abrasives not commonly available retail in coated abrasive form. They are obtainable, however, in fine powdered form through paint stores, and are widely used in producing the desired sheen in fine furniture work. The powder is mixed with No. 10 motor oil, or similar light oil, to make a creamy paste. (Water mixtures and others are sometimes used.) The technique of application is described later.

The coarseness of coated abrasives is measured in several ways, according to the type of the abrasive, its application, and to some extent, the market to which it is sold.

Industrial users, for example, prefer to specify coarseness by grit size—the minimum size sieve openings through which the

Abrasive paper carries specification labels on back. Paper at top is 220 (finishing) grade, classed as "fine." Paper at bottom is 50 (coarse) grade. Grit numbers indicate number of holes per square inch in sieves through which particles are graded. "A wt." indicates weight of paper (light). "D wt." is heavy. Open coat indicates that abrasive particles are spaced out so only 50 to 70 percent of paper area is covered with abrasive. Objective: reduce clogging.

abrasive grains will pass. (The extra fine and super fine sizes are graded by air flotation and water sedimentation processes.) An extra coarse abrasive might have a grit size of 16, extra fine might be as high 600 (each representing the number of sieve openings in a given area.)

Some users, on the other hand, still think in terms of the old symbol system, using 0, 2/0, 3/0, etc. And many home shop workers like the simplified terminology of extra fine, fine, medium, etc.

A coarseness grading term from at least one of these systems will be found printed on the back of your sandpaper (coated abrasive). The grit size is also printed on screen-backed abrasive. The non-woven pad types, however, usually have to be identified as to coarseness by color. Check on this where you buy unless you find the coarseness grade printed on the package.

The backing of coated abrasives is usually paper or cloth, though combinations are also used for special purposes. For most workshop applications a paper backing is the choice, with cloth backing reserved for heavy duty jobs, as in some forms of metal work. In general, lighter weight backings of either type are used with fine grit sizes for flexibility. Heavier backings go with coarser grits that are likely to be used under conditions of greater stress.

Open coat abrasive paper is made with abrasive grains separated by pre-set distances so that the abrasive covers only about 50 to 70 per cent of the surface. The gap between abrasive particles greatly reduces clogging with sanded material. This type can be used for most sanding work with a saving in time and expense, and is available from the usual sandpaper sources.

Wet-or-dry coated abrasive can be used with water or other liquids to wash away abraded material. Use it on car body work and other jobs requiring very fine abrasive that would be subject to frequent clogging.

Sanding methods depend on the job, and whether the work is done by hand or power. The number of different grades of coarseness the job requires depends on the initial roughness of the surface to be smoothed. If you are starting with rough wood, for example, as it might be after cutting to size on a workshop table saw, you would start sanding with a 50 or 60 grit size, sand with the grain, and continue until the entire surface has the same sanded texture. Then switch to a grit size of about 100. Work in stages to a finishing grit size around 220 or 240, never skipping more than one grit size when switching from one stage to the next. If the wood is smooth surfaced (as dressed lumber from the lumberyard) you can start with a grit size around 120. All this, assuming you want an extremely fine finish. After sanding, it is extremely important that all dust be removed from the work. Otherwise, dust specks will appear in whatever finish is applied.

As the finishing grit size used varies somewhat with the species and condition of the wood (seasoning, etc.) it helps to try the steps on a scrap if one is available. The final bare finish on some hardwoods can be improved by ending with a finer grade than would be required on the common soft woods. The finish applied to the wood must also be sanded between coats, preferably with very fine grit finishing paper in the 320 to 400 range. If your hardware store doesn't stock paper this fine you can get it from auto supply dealers, as it is used in auto body work. The final coat is not sanded.

In metal work the best abrasive in most instances is aluminum oxide. Use it to remove rust, starting with a coarseness suited to the roughness of the corrosion. Then work up to the final smoothing in stages, as with wood. To avoid frequent clogging of the abrasive, use an open coat type. On badly corroded surfaces a flexible disk sander on a power drill speeds the work greatly. Sanding disks are readily available in hardware stores in all the grit sizes likely to be needed. Do not expect to bring the metal to a mirror finish. An attractive satin type finish is usually obtainable, however. This makes a good base for painting.

Shaping with sandpaper is also easy with the aid of the flexible disk sander. The procedure is suited to many woodworking jobs, and is best carried out with aluminum oxide abrasive. As an example, if you have cut a toy boat hull to rough shape with a saber saw or compass saw, you can use the disk sander to provide the rounded contours.

The technique calls for keeping the disk moving over the areas to be shaped. The outer half of the disk radius does most of the work. Apply enough pressure to flex the disk slightly against the work. But do not apply enough pressure to slow the disk appreciably. High r.p.m. is best for fast cutting.

Practice on a scrap before tackling an actual project. Wear glasses or goggles during the work; abrasive grains that occasionally fly off the disk could injure the eyes.

Work up from coarse to fine, as in ordinary wood finishing, and the end product will be as smooth as conventional woodwork. On many jobs, the disk-shaping procedure does the job faster and better than any other tool.

Using a powdered abrasive, like pumice, is a simple matter. The purpose is the reduction of a high gloss to a softer sheen—desirable on many furniture projects. Mix the pumice (available from paint stores) with inexpensive No. 10 motor oil to form a creamy paste. Rub this paste over the work with a soft cloth and light pressure. Wipe off the paste frequently to examine the effect. The pumice works fairly fast, and can cut through the finish if you go too far without stopping to check the results. Be careful along corners and on sharply rounded areas, because it is easy to apply too much pressure at such points and cut through the surface coating you are working on. With moderate care, however, the pumice and oil method produces very attractive results and is surprisingly easy. Wipe the finished job throroughly to remove all traces of the paste and oil residue.

Abrasive pads can do much the same job without the need for cleanup. Your best bet is to try the grades on a concealed area of the piece to be rubbed, starting with the finest. A minute of rubbing will usually tell the grade best suited to the job. Steel wool can be used for this purpose, too, but usually requires more work to produce equivalent results.

Power sanders are made in various basic types that should be matched, where possible, to the type of work. Some of the more versatile types can be used for a wide variety of jobs.

Reciprocal sanders operate with a back-and-forth motion, much like with-the-grain

➤ *Rubbing down ribbon top table to give satin finish, using abrasive pad.*

Steel abrasive sheet has thousands of punched holes that produce surface like fine grater. These can be shaped to form tools, work like combination rasp and abrasive. Made in sandpaper sizes, they can be cut with shears.

Use steel wool for dulling with minimum finish removal, also for cleaning, preparing for wax over finish. Twisted into cord form, it works in carvings, lathe turnings and similar forms.

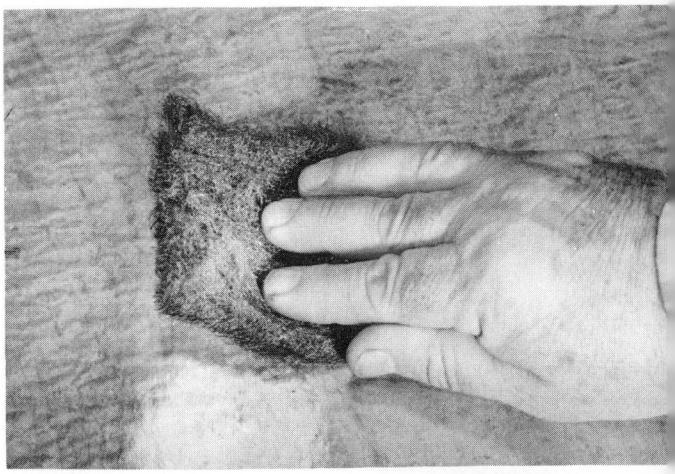

Abrasive on plastic screen has high degree of flexibility, comes in different coarseness grades (see text), and can be cut to size required. Use on contoured surfaces where paper backing can't conform.

To sand to square cornered edge by hand, pull abrasive paper tightly around wood sanding block, sand with grain.

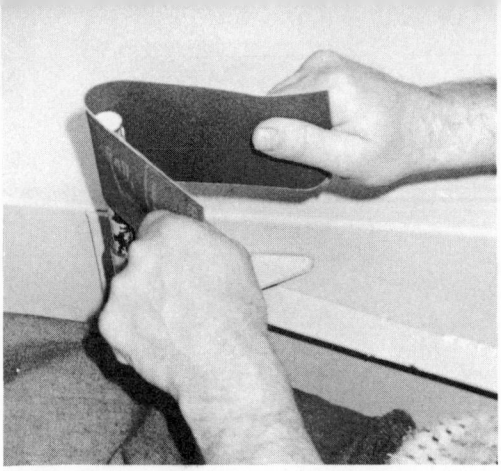

Use "shoe shine" method to smooth round objects like shaft ends. Here, 80 grit aluminum oxide cloth is being used to strip protective paint from new axle ends so wheel bearings will slide on easily.

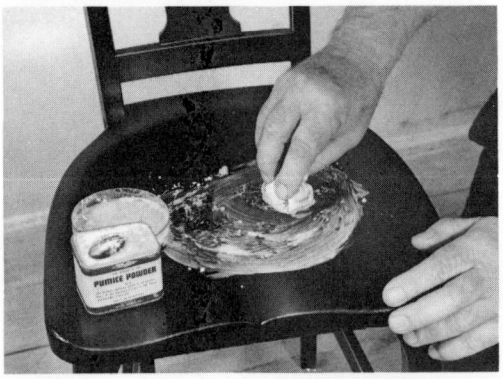

hand sanding. They do the same job as hand sanding, but do it faster. And they should be used with the same grit size stages as in hand sanding.

Orbital sanders (sometimes combined in dual types for selective reciprocal or orbital motion) move the sandpaper in a small rotary orbit. Instead of moving back and forth, the sandpaper combines a side motion, producing an "orbit" about ⅜" diameter. The orbital motion is very useful where the wood grain meets from several directions, as at a miter. Instead of sanding with the grain on one piece and crosswise on the other, as a reciprocal sander would, the orbital type sands with the same rotary motion on both pieces. Both this and the reciprocal type are good finishing sanders for most work.

To soften high gloss on newly finished furniture, rub (after finish is hard) with pumice and oil paste of creamy consistency, using pad of soft cloth. No. 10 motor oil is suitable for mix. Wipe off paste at frequent intervals to check finish and make sure you don't rub through.

Power sanders. Upper left is belt sander, fast cutting, good for large jobs on flat surfaces. Upper right is orbital sander, good finishing. Lower right, power drill with flexible disk sander. It is good for rough work and rounding and shaping of wood. At lower left is a ball joint disk sander, which can be used in a power drill for finish sanding. It has almost no tendency to dig in, as ball joint lets power drill tilt without tilting disk.

The belt sander provides a uni-directional motion by means of an abrasive-coated belt that operates much as the treads of a bulldozer. Hence, it is essential to keep a good grip on the sander to keep it from "running away" across the work. The motors in these sanders are usually much more powerful than those in other types, and they are fast cutting when used with coarse grit belts. For the fastest cutting they are often used at a 45 degree angle across the wood grain, first in one direction, then the other. Final smoothing is with the grain.

Disk sanders are made in three basic types. The flexible disk sander, probably the most common and inexpensive, is simply a rubber disk with a center shaft for mounting in a power drill chuck, and a centered screw flange gripping the abrasive disk. This type cuts fast and is suited to rough work like paint removal and wood shaping, as mentioned earlier. For finer work it must be used with great skill and care.

The rigid disk sander is often mounted in place of the blade of a table saw. The sandpaper is stuck to the disk with a special "peelable" adhesive that permits abrasive removal and replacement quickly and easily. This type can be used for smoothing and for wood trimming, much as a planing machine might be used.

The ball joint disk is also a rigid form. But the sandpaper disk is attached in the same manner as on the flexible disk, by a screw-flange at the center. The ball joint permits this disk to be used flat on the surface of the work, driven by a power drill. The centered screw flange is recessed so it does not contact the work surface, and the ball joint prevents the disk from digging in if the power drill is tilted during the operation. This is also a good finishing type of sander in the low price range.

All power sanders should be used with progressively finer grit sizes in finishing work, and must be kept moving over the work. If allowed to stand still while running they will cut a recess in the work surface. The technique of use, however, is quickly acquired. The best bet, practice on scrap material before tackling your first project. G.D.

See also: POWER TOOLS; ANTIQUING; PAINTING.

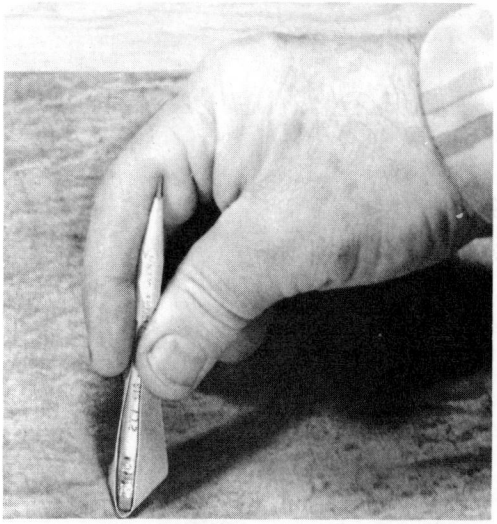

▲ *To sand small blemish areas, wrap strip of abrasive paper around rubber eraser of pencil.*

◄ *To sand flat surfaces that may be slightly irregular (as a cupped board) use flannel or felt pad between abrasive paper and wood sanding block. This lets abrasive surface conform to that of wood being sanded.*

How to Plan Your Home Additions

Refinish your basement, attic, garage or breezeway to add space, increase equity

One place to look for additional space in your home is at the top. Here, an attic has been refinished inexpensively into a cheerful bedroom for two children.

YOUR HOME may be your castle, but are there also times when it does not live up to your expectations? Then perhaps it is time to provide the extra room you need for recreation, sleeping, craftwork, or to house a live-in relative.

The cost of converting an unfinished basement or attic, or even a breezeway or garage into extra living space need not be prohibitive. You can cut the total conversion cost to a third or even a quarter of a contracted job by doing much or all of the work yourself because, in most instances, labor costs far exceed the cost of materials.

Do-it-yourself home improvement is now easier than ever thanks to the availability of materials that eliminate much of the hard work that you would have had to do for a similar conversion only a decade ago. Examples of easy-to-use construction materials include self-stick floor tile, beautifully prefinished wall paneling of several varieties and almost endless designs, colors and textures, and attractive ceiling coverings that can be installed in a professional manner by anyone. So, it doesn't make much sense for the average homeowner to spend, say, from fifteen hundred to two thousand dollars on a home improvement job that he can do in his spare time for perhaps five hundred dollars.

The secret of success really comes down to one thing: careful planning. Plan all major design features of the new room in detail before buying materials or starting work; shop thoroughly for the best construction materials for your purpose (should walls be of plywood, hardboard or gypsum board, for example); compare prices of competitive materials, but do not sacrifice quality for cheapness; buy lumber in standard sizes and in lengths that minimize waste; seek reliable information concerning proper installation of construction materials that are unfamiliar to you.

Evaluate the relative merits of finishing an attic or basement, or perhaps adding an extension onto your home. Each home, and

additive, oil: see oil, engine
additive, transmission: see transmission, auto

the space requirements of the family that lives in it are to some degree unique; the type of space expansion that was ideal for your neighbor may be a poor choice for you. So study in detail the pros and cons of converting all possible areas in your home. You might be surprised to conclude that the area that initially seems least attractive is in fact the best place in the home for improvement.

Basement. To this day you can find people—including some architects—who turn thumbs down on basement improvements on the grounds that below-grade rooms are damp, dingy and especially depressing if there are no windows. This may have been true in the past, but a basement room that is properly finished, properly illuminated, and equipped with dehumidifying equipment if necessary can be as pleasant as any other room in the home. Also, it is one of the best places for relatively noisy activities —within reasonable limits of course. For example, you wouldn't want to work in a woodworking shop under a bedroom when someone is sleeping. On the other hand, if you are trying to sleep, would you prefer that your teenagers dance above or below you?

A typical basement does not exhibit the cold and hot seasonal temperature extremes that are normal for attic areas. Thus cooling and heating is easier and less expensive, and there is no need to buy insulating materals for a roof.

The very first dollars spent on basement improvement can make the area more usable. For example, just by laying an inexpensive vinyl asbestos floor on the concrete sub-base you have an area that is much better for use as a play area. If money is on the short side, just paint concrete or block walls to add visual appeal at lowest possible cost.

Before starting more extensive improvements, take a critical look at your basement stairs. If they are too steep or flimsy, or if there is inadequate headroom (perhaps because of heating ducts), rebuild the stairway first. By adding a landing, and making the stairs turn a right angle, you may be able to provide extra headroom. Is there now a basement door leading to the yard? If not, consider adding one for convenience and safety. This outside entrance is especially important if you intend to put a woodworking shop in the basement. How else would you get large pieces of lumber into the shop? In fact, it may be impossible to get the 4-by-8 foot wall paneling for your recreation room into the basement until you add that outside entrance.

Wall paneling can be supported by a framework made of 2-by-3 or 2-by-4 studding, or you can save on lumber costs by using 1-by-2 or preferably 1-by-3 furring attached to the masonry wall. But what about electrical outlets? Clearly, these could not be set into walls where the space between the foundation and paneling is only one inch. This is a good example of the kind of oversight in initial planning that could lead to grief and be costly later on.

Basic electrical wiring is not difficult for any reasonably adept do-it-yourselfer who takes the trouble to consult readily available reference material. Just be sure that you understand local wiring regulations and that you have your work inspected by a town official before you bury it under paneling. By following the sensible rules established for your protection, you will have a safe place in which to live and play, and you can avoid unnecessary alterations. For example, if you install the ungrounded kind of outlet you have in your living room, in the basement, the electrical inspector will surely insist that you replace them with grounding type receptacles.

Analyze your basement area carefully during the initial planning stage to make sure that every cubic foot of usable space will be utilized to best advantage. For example, you probably have large sewer pipes running a couple of feet above the basement floor, along one or more walls. These should be hidden behind the new paneling, of course, but why run the paneling straight to the ceiling and thereby waste some excellent storage space? Instead, plan for cupboards or built-in bookcases above the pipes. Also, remember to use removable panel sections wherever there are clean-out plugs in the sewer piping.

Are you hard-pressed to find a good place to add that sauna you would like to have? Take a tip from one imaginative Finn who put his steam bath under a porch just off the kitchen by excavating and building a small room under the porch and adding a connecting door through the basement wall. A curtained-off corner of the basement recreation room served as a dressing room. Another advantage of placing the steam bath *outside* of the main house area is that it can be aired out easily to keep excessive moisture out of the house.

No basement improvements should be attempted if there is any problem whatever with excessive moisture or actual water leakage into the basement. Correct such faults before the remodeling begins and, to make sure all is well, wait until after a prolonged rainy spell before starting on major basement improvements. It can be heartbreaking to see water seeping under the new paneling you have so carefully installed. If complete waterproofing of the basement just isn't feasible at reasonable cost, you might be wiser to look for extra room in some other part of the house.

Attic. Finishing an attic is no more difficult than improving the basement unless dormers must be added to obtain more light, ventilation and/or headroom. But even the construction of a new dormer can be handled by a reasonably competent do-it-yourselfer. Small gable ("doghouse") dormers are useful mainly to provide light and ventilation; a larger shed dormer is

➤ *Not a window in sight, but refinished basement is still attractive. Note space-saving spiral staircase at right. One caution: don't decide to finish your basement until you are sure it is not incurably damp.*

Building an actual extension is the most costly way of increasing usable space. Improving existing space—attic, basement, garage or breezeway—is cheaper.

used where extra headroom is required. You will also probably find that it is cheaper to build a shed dormer than to construct two or three doghouse dormers. Often, the original roof can be kept in place until the dormer is largely completed. Another possibility is raising a portion of the original roof to form the roof of a shed dormer; this is not as difficult or costly as one might think, but it is not the kind of job a do-it-yourselfer should attempt single handed.

It is especially important to provide sufficient headroom at the top of the attic stairs. If headroom cannot be achieved by adding a dormer, it may be possible to relocate the stairway, or to install a stairway that emerges where there is more headroom. For example, a prefabricated metal spiral stairway may be the ideal solution. And don't overlook the possibility of building a new stairway *outside* of the existing house structure. This could be especially convenient if the lower end of the stairway can lead to an outside door as well as to the lower floor of the house.

If the attic area is to be used for relatively noisy activities during evening hours, consider adding sound insulation to the floor. At least plan on using a thick carpet with a resilient pad underneath. If such wall-to-wall carpeting is to be used, do not waste money installing a fine hardwood floor that will never be seen.

A bathroom in the attic area is desirable, especially if the area is to be used for sleeping or for accommodating overnight guests. Try to locate the bathroom over an existing bathroom on the lower level to keep plumbing costs down.

Do not stint on insulation in the attic ceiling and walls. Use the best and heaviest insulation you can. You will then be more comfortable, and spend less on heating and air-conditioning expenses.

If the attic ceiling slants, try to make the knee walls at least four feet high to permit easy furniture placement. Don't overlook the possibility of adding storage drawers that slide through the walls into the unused portions of the attic, near the eaves. But, box in the drawer areas and insulate thoroughly. Other left-over areas of the attic, even if only high enough to be crawl spaces, should be made accessible for storage of items that are not used frequently.

Provide plenty of electrical outlets to power TV sets, radios, electric toys, and perhaps even space heaters in lieu of conventional hot water or hot air systems.

Garage conversion. If you don't mind leaving the car out in the open, or if you can provide a carport or other shelter elsewhere on your property, the existing garage can probably be converted into a very useful living area. The conversion may be quite easy, and cost less than you might think, because you already have a roof and three walls (the garage doors must be replaced by a fourth wall). The garage floor probably slopes toward the front, or toward a central water drain, and this will have to be leveled before you can add a tile floor. If headroom in the garage permits, it may be preferable to install a wooden floor at a somewhat higher level to bring the floor of the converted garage to the same level as the floors in the rest of the house. But be sure to scrub out all grease and oil from the original garage floor before covering it with a new floor, to eliminate all possibility of unwanted odors seeping into the room.

You may want to keep the garage ceiling where it is, or raise it higher, perhaps even form a cathedral ceiling. But do not start pulling out existing joists indiscriminately until you have found some other way to hold the garage structure together. If there is good storage space above the garage ceiling, make it available by adding a spiral staircase, or perhaps a fold-down

BASEMENT FINISHING COSTS

Item	Unit Cost	Quantity Needed	Cost
Vinyl asbestos floor tile	33¢/sq. ft.	320 sq. ft.	$106
Prefinished plywood panels	$8 each	18	144
2-by-4 for wall framing	18¢/foot	576 ft.	104
Acoustic ceiling tile	30¢/sq. ft.	320 sq. ft.	96
1-by-2 furring for ceiling	5¢/ft.	340 ft.	17
			$467 +tax

The basic cost of finishing a 16 by 20 foot basement area was around $500 in terms of early 1973 prices for medium quality floor tile, wall paneling and ceiling tile. To the estimated $467 add the cost of such incidentals as nails, adhesive to apply wall paneling, staples for ceiling tile, and purchase of rental of stapler. Also add expenditures for electrical wiring, fixtures, possibly professional service to connect the new wiring to the main circuit breaker system. If you hire professional contractors to do the whole job, expect a total cost that is three to four times as much as the materials cost.

An attached garage is often a good prospect for refinishing to add living space to a house. Here, refinishing is under way, with new subflooring in place over the old garage floor.

Use of prefinished wood paneling is one way to cut costs of home improvement. Here paneling is being installed in a new addition to a house.

staircase. The attic, even if small, is an ideal place in which to store sporting equipment, games, or lumber if you make the garage into a shop.

If the garage door leading into the interior of the house now connects with the kitchen, it might be preferable to relocate it so that traffic can flow into and through a family room, living room or hallway. But before you start tearing out walls to create doorways, make certain that the walls do not contain water or heating system pipes that would be hard to relocate.

Plan new electrical wiring to suit the power requirements of the kind of room you are planning. Conventional wiring is adequate for a recreation room or den. But you should install heavier wiring, and several separate branch circuits, if the area is to be used for a shop containing such power tools as circular or radial arm saws, sanding machines, drill press.

The kind of paneling you use on the walls depends on how the room is to be

used. A rumpus room where the kids will bang around should have plastic coated walls that are resistant to impact and easy to clean. Less rugged paneling can be used in a sitting room, or where no violent play is anticipated. For a shop or studio, consider using perforated hardboard which will make the hanging of tools or paintings a joy.

If the garage wall is of conventional wood construction, new paneling can be installed on the existing studding quickly and easily. If you have concrete walls, you will first have to add furring. Remember that thin, 1-by-3 furring can save you money but you would have to run new electrical wiring on top of the new paneling.

Porches and breezeways. If the garage you are converting to new uses is connected to the house by means of a breezeway, you should close in the breezeway as well so that getting to the new room will not entail dashing across a cold, windswept no-man's land.

Even if you leave the garage untouched, conversion of the breezeway into an all-seasons living area may be desirable. How useful this area would be for your needs depends on the size of the breezeway as is, or after expansion. Small or large, be sure that it is made just as weatherproof as the remainder of the house. Do not stint on insulation, and use double-glazed windows and sliding glass doors. Don't overlook the probable need of a radiator or two. If extending the conventional house heating system to this area is too complicated or costly, consider installing electrical heating units into the breezeway walls.

An open porch can also be converted into a closed-in room for year-around use provided it is at least nine feet in its shorter dimension, and if it has—or can be made to have—direct access to the kitchen, dining room, family room or hallway. If your main reason for doubting the wisdom of closing in the porch is that you would miss the cooling breezes during the summertime, just plan your renovation to include large screenable windows.

New wing. Suppose your basement is too wet for finishing or you have no basement, the attic has insufficient headroom, there is no porch or breezeway, and you can't bear the thought of evicting the family bus—then what? Your only recourse is to add a new extension to the house. This is bound to be the most costly way to solve your space problem because you must pay for new exterior as well as interior walls, insulation, and a supporting foundation. But if you do all or most of the work yourself, the cost may not be at all prohibitive.

You face at least two new planning problems if you decide to add an extension to your home. First, you must be sure that you have enough space on your lot, so that the addition does not violate set-back-requirements, and you must obtain approval of your building plan from the local building department. Secondly, unlike home improvements made inside your existing building, the new addition will be visible to neighbors. Be sure that the addition blends well with the existing structure and that it does not convert your home into an eye-sore that your neighbors will resent. If you have doubts about the visual aspects of the planned addition, consult an architect, or at least an experienced builder. And it wouldn't hurt to show your plans to your nearest neighbors to get their reaction, provided you can take honest criticism without feeling offended. Remember, you won't enjoy your new living space to the fullest extent if you see neighbors scowling across the backyard fence. J.H.

See also: ATTIC; BASEMENTS; BATHROOMS; BREEZEWAYS; DORMERS; ELECTRICITY; GARAGE; HOME IMPROVEMENT; PAINTING, HOUSE; PANELS; ROOFS; WALL COVERINGS; WALLBOARD.

All about Adhesives

For decorating a window shade, repairing a camera or building a model boat, there's an adhesive that will do the job

MATCH a modern adhesive to the job and you can bond almost any material. Often the joint will be solid and waterproof in five minutes or less with a strength running to tons per square inch.

One versatile acrylic adhesive, for example, has been applied with a toothpick to mend a broken camera control and smeared on with a brush to bond an aluminum patch to the cracked iron hub of an earth moving machine.

There are epoxy glues that harden almost as fast on almost as many materials. One kind of epoxy holds heart pacers together. And, there are resocinol resin glues that bond boats together without nails, screws, or other metal fastening, so ruggedly that even after 20 years they have no leaks and require no caulking. And, there are completely flexible multi-resin adhesives that turn to rubber in minutes with such strength you can patch your work pants, your sail or your convertible top with greater strength than stitching. And there are less spectacular glues for everyday jobs. Some are so simple to use you just squeeze them on to a joint, stick the parts together and forget it. No clamps, no fuss.

Large hardware stores stock most of the modern glues. The remainder are available through marine suppliers or directly from the manufacturer. To pick the right one for the job at hand you need only the basic facts. For these, let the following data serve as your guide.

Acrylic resin adhesive. The fastest setting adhesive generally available. Based on the same formula used in high strength white dental fillings (you'll recognize the aroma) it sets in as little as five minutes to a strength of three tons per square inch. It is a two-part type (liquid and powder) with setting time varying from 5 to 20 minutes, according to the mixing proportions of the two components. A stiff mix gives short setting time, as wet mix longer setting time. It bonds to most materials including wood, metal, and ceramics. It is completely waterproof and widely used in marine repair work. It is also well suited to many types of delicate repair work, as on cameras, record players, etc. Clamping is no problem because parts can be hand-held while the adhesive sets. Sold in two-container packages consisting of two cans, or can and plastic jar combination.

Aliphatic resin glue. A leading furniture glue, this is a one-part beige liquid type that dries clear. It can also be colored with water soluble dyes to match the wood finish to be used. It is unaffected by most common finishes. Tackiness is similar to old style hot animal glues, making it pos-

aerial: see antennas
aerosol painting: see paint sprayers
a-frame playhouse: see playhouse
air cannon: see science projects

sible to stick gluing blocks in furniture frame corners without clamping. Where clamps are required, glue is usually firm enough for clamp removal in about an hour. Allow overnight for complete set. It is moisture-resistant, but not waterproof. It is sold in squeeze bottles.

Buna-N adhesive. Originally developed for aircraft use, this is a one-part, thick beige liquid that will bond almost any material with a completely flexible and waterproof bond. It can bond fabric to metal or wood, metal to glass, even to bond patches to work clothes with greater strength than stitching.

Joints are usually pressed together while the applied adhesive is still wet.

In fabric-to-fabric bonding the dried adhesive-coated surfaces may be placed together and bonded by heating from the outside of one fabric piece, as with a flatiron. Sold in tubes and cans.

Broken nib of camera exposure guide (at pencil tip) was permanently reattached with acrylic adhesive. The job took about 10 minutes. The same adhesive was used to bond an aluminum patch over the cracked cast iron hub of an earth moving machine.

Casein glue. A strong, inexpensive adhesive with good moisture resistance (not waterproof) and gap-filling qualities that are useful in woodworking. It is a cream colored powder that must be mixed with water for use. It stiffens shortly after mixing, then becomes creamy on re-stirring. Follow the manufacturer's instructions carefully, and *do not* add water at the pre-stiffened stage. No longer widely available, it is stocked by cabinetmakers' supply houses and large hardware suppliers under various brand names.

Cellulose nitrate cement. Often called household cement or model airplane cement, this is a one-part water resistant adhesive, usually clear. (Some forms are tinted to make coated areas visible during work.) Dries firm enough for gentle assembly handling in unstressed work after an hour or two, for regular handling, overnight. It is sold largely in tubes.

Contact cement. Developed for bonding plastic laminates to plywood counters, and similar applications. Available in very quick-drying (flammable) types and in non-flammable form. It is applied to both meeting surfaces to be bonded, and

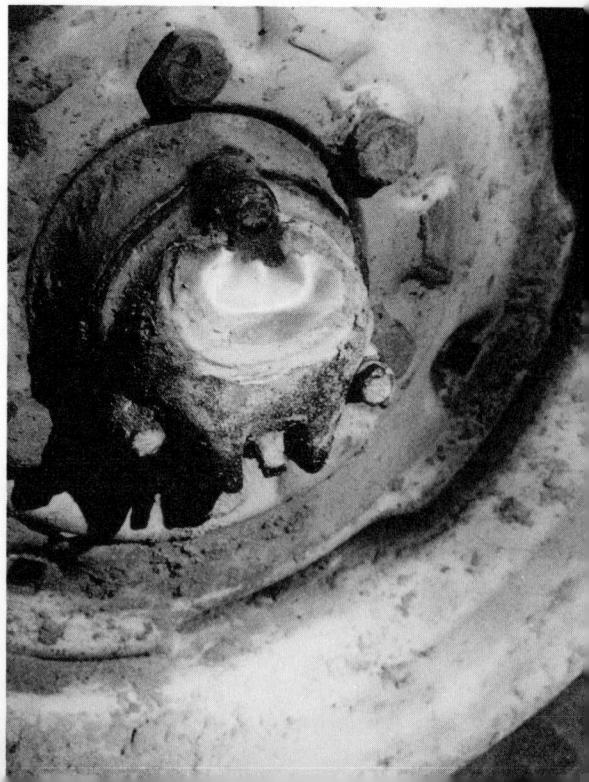

allowed to dry completely. A wrapping paper "slip sheet" is then placed between the coated surfaces so they can be aligned without touching each other. The sheet is slipped out while the parts are held in alignment, permitting the cement-coated surfaces to come into contact. Permanent bond is made instantly on contact. A rubber roller is used to assure firm, full-area contact and work any trapped air bubbles outward to escape at edges. Contact cement is widely available through hardware stores under many brand names, mainly in cans, but occasionally in tubes.

Epoxy glue. A two-part adhesive comprising a liquid resin and liquid hardener. Available in both clear and opaque types, this is a completely waterproof adhesive that bonds most materials. The usual types set firm overnight and continue to increase in strength for a week or more. They are often used in marine fiberglassing and hull repairs. Quick-setting types are available with hardening times as short as 10 minutes. As formulas vary widely, follow the manufacturer's instructions in mixing and using any epoxy. In buying, specify the characteristics you require, clear, etc. Sold by hardware and marine suppliers under many brand names.

Epoxy, water-phase type. Relatively new to the retail market, this type may be used either as a coating or as an adhesive, and, prior to setting, can be washed from brushes and tools with water. Once hard, it is completely waterproof. It is a two-part type. Two liquid components are mixed in equal proportions for use. Complete setting time is around eight hours. Unmixed left-

For two-part glues like resorcinol resin twin measuring cups and twin measuring spoons are a must, so no trace of hardener can accidentally get into the resin remaining in the original can. Paint one spoon handle white, the other black, and use dark one for dark glue component, light one for light component.

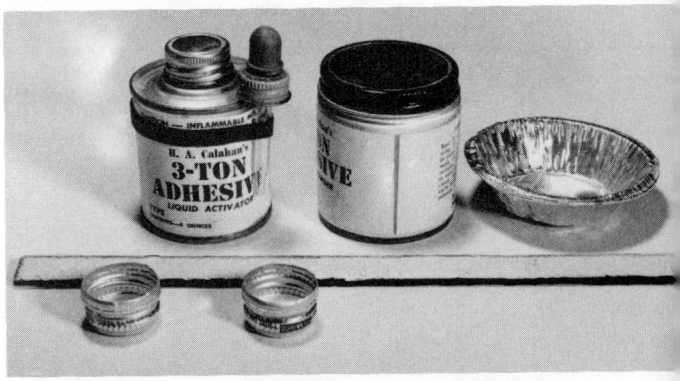

For small job gluing, as with acrylics, keep medicine dropper rubber-banded to can of liquid component. Use flat stick to portion out powder, and break off fresh section of stick for each use. For small-quantity mixing use screw-off pop bottle caps, after removing plastic gasket. For slightly larger batches, use aluminum cookie cups.

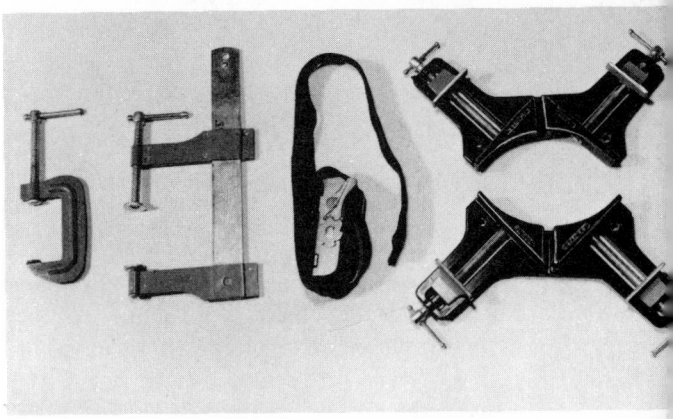

Clamps for most jobs. C-clamp at left is made in many sizes. Bar clamp next to it serves same purpose, but extends quickly to bridge wide gap, locks automatically for screw tightening. Band clamp to right of it can be wrapped like a belt around irregular work and drawn tight by turning built-in ratchet with wrench or screwdriver. Miter clamp at right locks mitered work like picture frames.

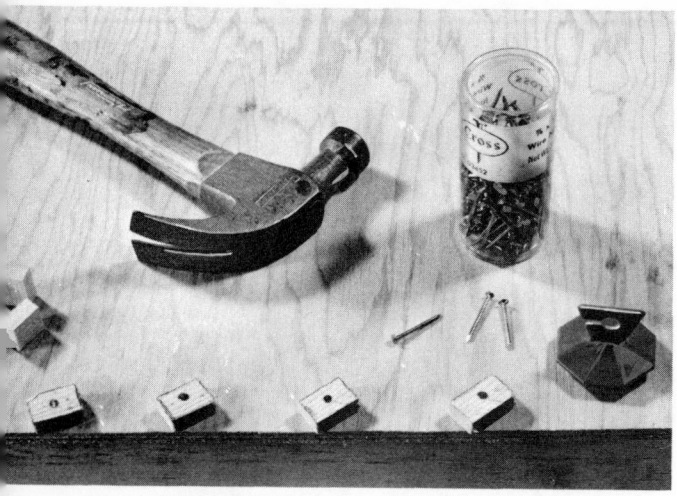

Nailing blocks can take the place of clamps where too many clamps would be required. Brads are driven through small wood blocks, tight, holding long glue line firmly.

Nailing blocks are easily removed (with nails or brads) after glue has set. Here, nail puller has lifted one block and brad from the work.

overs last indefinitely if containers are tightly closed. It is made in clear, white, and colored forms, and can be tinted with the same dry colors used in cement work.

It can also be mixed with portland cement (follow instructions on the adhesive containers) to make a high strength bonding filler for masonry repairs and similar jobs. The adhesive cement mix has a much shorter setting time than the adhesive alone, so plan to work accordingly. Ideal for fiberglassing seams on plywood porches and decks, it also is used with mineral granules for non-skid surface around swimming pools. It is sold in twin cans.

Hide Glue. This is available mainly in liquid form through hardware stores, though some cabinetmakers' supply houses still stock the traditional flake and sheet form. The latter forms must be water-soaked, then heated for use. Known as "hot glue," this type must be applied to joints and clamped before cooling. In the common liquid form it is used like any other one-part liquid glue. Usually it will harden overnight into a bond that is stronger than wood, but it is not very moisture resistant.

Hot-melt resin glues. Polyethylene-base types are used in electric glue gun cartridges. They bond to most materials, and are waterproof and moderately flexible. Because they harden by cooling, they are in the fast-setting class and require quick assembly of the parts to be glued. They are sold in cartridge form to fit specific glue guns.

Multi-resin hot melt glue is also available for special uses without a glue gun. These usually are sold in foil trays, and are melted on a heating device, such as a hot plate. Types like "Hot Grip" are used for bonding to plastics that will not accept other adhesives, such as polyethylene and polypropylene.

Neoprene-base adhesives. These are the types widely used in caulking guns to mount wall paneling. Now, combination resin forms are also used in house frame construction to bond sheathing to framing.

Characteristics vary with the brand, and the manufacturer's instructions should be followed carefully.

Polyester resin glue. Best known as a boat fiberglassing adhesive, this type is also a strong, quick-setting, waterproof wood glue that can be used clear or colored with pigments sold for the purpose. It is a two-part type. A liquid resin and a liquid catalyst are mixed just before use. Typically, a specified number of drops of catalyst from a small squeeze bottle are stirred into a quart or pint can of the resin. A portion of the resin may be poured off and mixed with a corresponding portion of catalyst. The amount of catalyst is important; an excess will harden the resin before it can be applied.

Temperature of the working area is also a factor because hardening time shortens as the working area temperature rises. Temperature-hardening time charts are available from suppliers for many resin brands. Do not apply a chart for one brand to another brand of resin; formulas vary widely.

Polyester resin glue is sold in cans, usually with plastic tube of catalyst in a plastic overcap, by boatyards, marine suppliers and large hardware outlets. Shelf life of unused resin varies with brand and storage conditions, so buy it fresh, as needed.

Polysulphide. Also known as Thiokol, this type is widely used as a marine caulking compound, though it is also a strong, completely waterproof adhesive with great flexibility and unusual vibration-damping qualities. The two-part form requires the mixing of two thick pastes. The one-part form sets by reaction with moisture in the air. When set, polysulphide is actually synthetic rubber, so mixed leftovers may be formed into gaskets, tires for toy wheels, etc. Molds with oiled surfaces may be used.

Polyvinyl acetate glue. This is the familiar one-part "white glue." It is easy to use and stronger than wood, but its strength is affected by high humidity and high temperature. It is a handy woodworking glue for joints that do not require the glue, alone, to sustain a prolonged load. (Most furniture joints are designed so the wood takes the load, the glue holds the joint together.) This glue should not be used on bare metal because of possible corrosive effect. Sold in squeeze bottles under various brand names.

Squeeze-out of glue along glue line tells you if you have even clamp pressure along glue line. Note that more glue has squeezed out at clamp locations. Use more clamps or clamp work between two heavy pieces of scrap wood to distribute clamping pressure evenly.

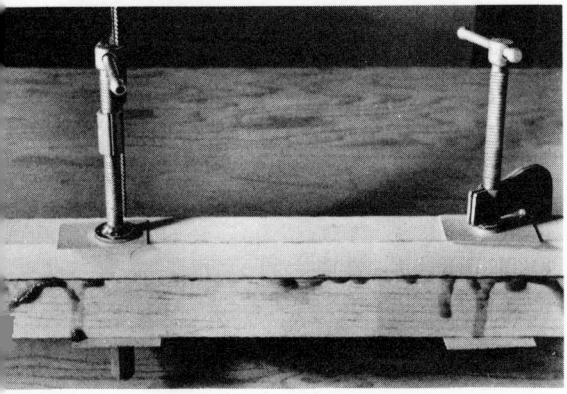

How tight should clamps be? Make test joint with scrap wood. Tighten clamps. Then, unclamp, and open joint. If meeting surfaces show coating of glue, pressure was not excessive. If clamped too tight almost all glue will be squeezed out of joint, making weak bond.

Resorcinol resin glue. This two-part (liquid and powder) glue is generally accepted as the best completely waterproof glue for wood. Originally developed for torpedo boat construction, it is stronger than wood, completely waterproof, (even in prolonged boiling) and unaffected by gasoline, oil, mild alkalis, mild acids, or common solvents. A working advantage: before hardening, it can be washed from brushes and tools with water.

Hardening time depends on temperature. Once components are thoroughly mixed according to manufacturer's instructions, the glue will cure in about 10 hours at 70 degrees, or in as little as 3½ hours at 90 degrees.

Mix proportions by volume are usually four measures of the liquid component to three measures of the powder. Very important: protect your eyes from both parts when mixing. And, before mixing, shake the closed can of powder thoroughly to "fluff" it. It tends to pack during storage, so volume measure is thrown off unless it is shaken up. Resorcinol resin glue is sold in twin cans by hardware stores and marine suppliers.

Rubber base adhesive. A one-part waterproof type that bonds to most materials, rubber base adhesive can be applied as a sealer even under water for emergency repairs. It should not be used where exposed to gasoline or oil, however, as both act on it as solvents. It is sold in tubes and cans by hardware stores.

Urea formaldehyde glue. Now usually called plastic resin glue, this is a one-part powder type that is mixed with water for use. It is stronger than wood, and highly water resistant but not quite waterproof. It is not a gap-filler type, however, and requires well fitted joints. Use this glue for general woodworking, especially where high humidity or high temperatures are likely, as it remains strong under both conditions. It is sold in cans under various trade names.

In woodworking, match the nature of the glue to the job. Thermoplastic adhesives can be softened by heat. Thermosetting ones can't. Thermoplastic glues (like white glue) shouldn't be used on joints where the glue alone must sustain a constant load, as in a simple lap joint. They are fine, however, in joints where the glue holds the joint together and the form of the joint takes the load, as where one part is notched into another.

For joints where the glue alone must take the load use a thermosetting type like plastic resin glue or resorcinol resin glue.

For plastics pick a glue that suits the particular material to be glued. Unless you're an expert, you can't tell the type of a plastic by looking at it. So select a glue (usually in a tube) that is labeled for use with plastics, often with a list printed on it. Try a small dab on a concealed part of the object to be bonded. After half a minute, wipe off the dab. If it leaves a shallow recess in the plastic, it has taken a "bite" and will usually do a good bonding job on it. This test works on thermoplastic

Use flexible spray adhesive to bond fabric to window shades. Spray adhesive on shade, apply fabric while adhesive is wet, spread smooth with hands, as shown.

Temporary adhesive that permits pull-off when necessary bonds abrasive paper to power sanding disk for table saw. Spray it on sanding disk, also on cut-to-fit abrasive paper (back), then press paper in place, aligned with disk. Paper can be peeled off when worn. New paper mounted in same way.

Hot-melt resin glue applied by glue gun bonds most materials, sets in seconds on cooling. Have parts ready for quick assembly before glue cools.

materials (a wide variety of plastics) but not on thermosetting types like Bakelite. For these, you need an adhesive that actually bonds to the material, as it can't bite into it by dissolving the surface. Try such adhesives as the epoxies, acrylics, and multi-resin-bond-anything types. Casein, if readily available, also bonds a wide range of materials.

Spray adhesives are made in many forms, and are usually flexible when set. Read the label on the container before you buy, to make certain the adhesive will bond the material you have in mind. Many are made for art work, as in bonding paper to backing board. They can be used for many other purposes, however. For example, a non-flammable type, was used to bond cotton fabric to a paper window shade. The shade was sprayed, and the fabric smoothed onto it while the adhesive was still wet. Always follow the manufacturer's instructions. G.D.

See also: BOAT BUILDING; FURNITURE; BASEMENTS; BATHROOMS; PATCHING.

TYPE OF ADHESIVE	BRAND NAME
Acrylic resin adhesive	3-Ton Adhesive; P.A.C. (plastic adhesive cement)
Aliphatic resin glue	Titebond
Buna-N adhesive	Pliobond
Epoxy glue	Ten-set Epoxy
Epoxy, water phase type	Dur-A-Poxy
Hide Glue	Franklin Liquid Hide Glue
Hot-melt resin glues	Thermogrip; Swingline
Polyester resin glue	Fibre-Glass-Evercoat
Polysulphide	Sav-Cote
Resorcinol resin glue	U.S. Plywood Resorcinol Waterproof Glue
Rubber base adhesive	Miracle Adhesive

Servicing Your Car's Thermostatic Air Cleaner

Neglect of these vacuum and temperature controlled devices can lead to engine stalling and poor gas mileage

THE THERMOSTATICALLY-CONTROLLED air cleaner was originally conceived to improve cold engine operation, and is now part of the anti-air-pollution package, on Ford, GM and Chrysler products. (Chrysler uses the GM device.)

The Ford and GM units do the same thing (although in somewhat different ways). They duct intake air over the exhaust manifold to preheat it for better combustion when the engine is cold. They keep the intake air at a temperature of about 100 degrees F. until the engine warms up. Each has a vacuum override system that bypasses the duct and opens the regular air cleaner neck or snorkel on hard acceleration. When the engine warms up, all the air comes from the air cleaner neck or snorkel.

The Ford system has a thermostatic assembly that holds a valve in the air cleaner intake neck so that exhaust-manifold-heated air flows into and through the air filter. As the engine warms, heating the air in the engine compartment, the thermostatic assembly lengthens, and through linkage, pivots the valve to restrict (and finally close) the opening to the duct over the exhaust manifold. The valve also can be pivoted by a vacuum diaphragm device that is spring-loaded. When the throttle is floored, the manifold vacuum drops, and the spring-loaded device pushes on another link to pivot the valve. But the basic action is the same in both situations: the valve closes against the exhaust manifold duct and opens the air cleaner intake neck or snorkel.

Except for this vacuum override, the pivoting of the valve is gradual, and in the middle of engine warmup, the air that goes into the carburetor is a mixture of preheated air from the exhaust manifold cut and colder air entering through the air cleaner intake neck or snorkel.

To check the system, start with the engine cold and off, and an air temperature of no more than 85-95 degrees F. The air cleaner intake neck or snorkel should be closed off by the valve. If it isn't closed, the linkage is binding or the thermostatic unit is defective.

As the engine warms up, the valve should move, closing off the duct for the exhaust manifold preheated air. If it doesn't, the thermostat is defective, the linkage is binding or the vacuum override is defective. The simplest procedure is to check the linkage first, then the vacuum device, and if they are good replace the thermostatic assembly.

Before the engine fully warms up, open the throttle. This will cause manifold vacuum to drop, and the spring in the vacuum device should force the valve to move and

Servicing Your Car's Thermostatic Air Cleaner 47

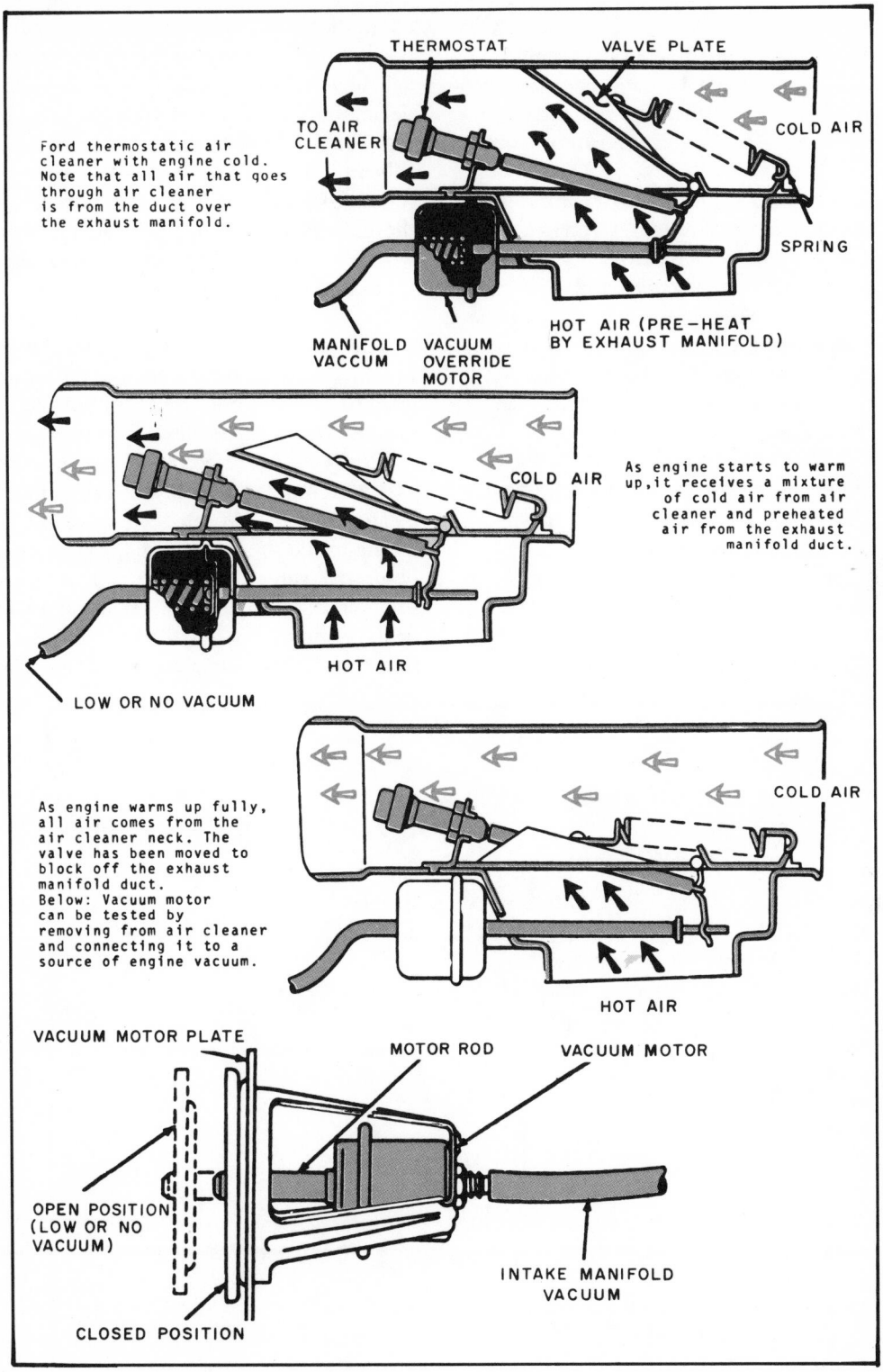

Ford thermostatic air cleaner with engine cold. Note that all air that goes through air cleaner is from the duct over the exhaust manifold.

As engine starts to warm up, it receives a mixture of cold air from air cleaner and preheated air from the exhaust manifold duct.

As engine warms up fully, all air comes from the air cleaner neck. The valve has been moved to block off the exhaust manifold duct.
Below: Vacuum motor can be tested by removing from air cleaner and connecting it to a source of engine vacuum.

open the air cleaner intake neck. If it doesn't, check for 15 inches of vacuum at the hose connection to the vacuum device (using an inexpensive vacuum-fuel pressure gauge, available at auto supply stores).

Low or no vacuum indicates a bad hose or connection. If vacuum is good, check the vacuum device. Remove the vacuum device from the air cleaner and connect it to a source of vacuum on the engine. (There should be one at the carburetor base, such as the PCV hose neck.) With vacuum applied, the device's link should be held against the entire assembly. Disconnect the hose and it should spring outward about a half inch. The vacuum device (called a "motor" by Ford) is not normally rebuildable. Replace it if it is defective.

When the engine is fully warm, the valve should close off the exhaust manifold duct and open the air cleaner intake neck. Just look into the air cleaner neck and see if it is open. Note: if the vacuum device operates the linkage and moves the plate, the linkage obviously is good. If a good vacuum device fails to move the linkage, it is binding. Free up linkage by working in a good solvent. (The aerosol type used for carburetor linkage is ideal for this purpose.) If the linkage is free and the vacuum device works outside the air cleaner, any defect in the system can be traced to the thermostatic unit.

The GM system, like the Ford, uses a pivoting valve in the air cleaner intake neck and the valve is connected by linkage to a vacuum diaphragm device. But here the similarity ends. The GM system incorporates a temperature sensor inside the air cleaner housing. When the engine is off, a spring inside the vacuum diaphragm device holds the valve against the exhaust manifold air duct. When the engine is started cold, vacuum passes through the sensor into the vacuum diaphragm device, open-

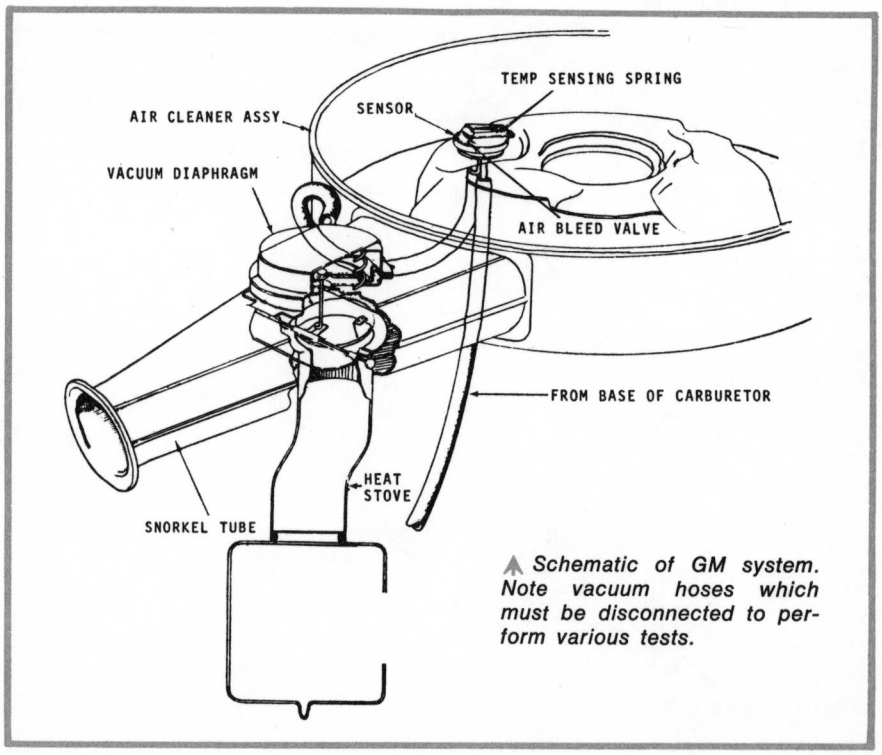

▲ *Schematic of GM system. Note vacuum hoses which must be disconnected to perform various tests.*

ing the exhaust manifold air duct and closing off the air cleaner intake neck. As the sensor heats up, it bleeds off vacuum to the atmosphere, and the pressure of the spring against the diaphragm inside the vacuum device moves the valve to close the exhaust manifold air duct.

On GM cars with double-snorkel air cleaners and four-barrel carburetor, only one snorkel has the temperature-sensitive arrangement and one duct over the exhaust manifold. The other has a vacuum diaphragm controlled valve and it closes off the snorkel. When the throttle is opened, manifold vacuum drops and a diaphragm spring forces open the valve to admit additional air for higher performance. The second snorkel works this way whether the engine is hot, cold or in-between.

To check the GM system, proceed as follows: With the engine cold and not running, the air cleaner intake neck should be open. Start the engine and one valve should close. As the engine warms up, that valve should move and cover the exhaust manifold air duct (which you will not be able to see), opening the air cleaner intake neck (which you will be able to see).

Before the engine fully warms, open the throttle, which will cause manifold vacuum to drop. The thermostatically-controlled valve should open (so should the other snorkel's valve on double-snorkel setups).

If the valve is in the wrong position with the engine off, the cause is binding linkage or a defective spring in the vacuum device. If the valve fails to close the air cleaner intake neck when the cold engine is started, check for at least eight inches of vacuum at the end of the hose that connects the carburetor base or intake manifold to the sensor in the air cleaner. Less than this amount indicates a defective hose or connection.

If vacuum is good at the sensor, check it at the vacuum device hose connection. If it is low, check the hose, and if this is good, replace the sensor. Adequate vacuum at this hose, combined with failure of the valve to move when the engine is started, indicates a leaking vacuum diaphragm device. Reconnect the hose and pinch it firmly (or kink it) to trap vacuum. The valve in the air cleaner neck should close off with the vacuum applied. If the valve doesn't do this, or if the valve starts to open with the hose firmly pinched or kinked, a leaking diaphragm is likely. This test is excellent as a general check of the vacuum device, as it will spot a minor leak before it becomes major.

Top: Pivoting valve of GM system. Valve should be open (as shown) when engine is warm and running. When engine is cold, valve should close air cleaner snorkel. Above: Air cleaner element removed. Vacuum sensor is at upper left, near center depression in air cleaner base.

Removing vacuum sensor from GM system (on Chrysler products).

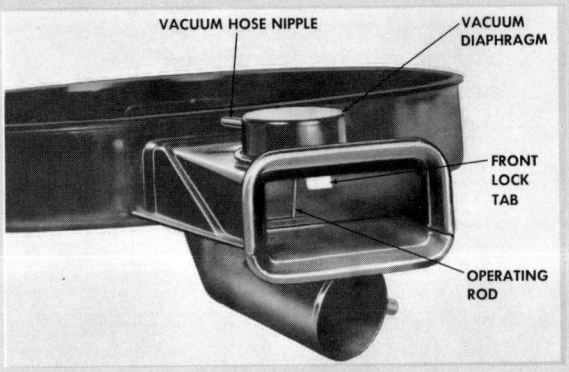

Closeup of vacuum diaphragm assembly from Chrysler products.

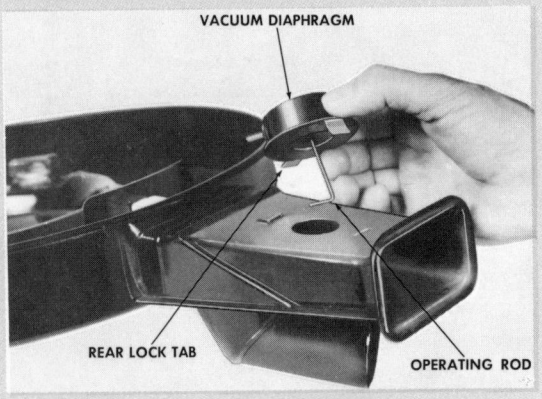

Removing vacuum diaphragm from Chrysler products.

Checking the snorkel valve that responds only to vacuum changes is simple. With the engine idling, the snokel should be closed off by the valve. Open the throttle (causing manifold vacuum to drop) and the valve should swing open. If you have an engine with a two-barrel carburetor and a double-snorkel air cleaner, one snorkel is strictly jazz. It's blocked off by a plate and that plate won't move.

There are all sorts of special thermometers and time-consuming techniques for checking thermostatic air cleaners to see if they are right within specifications. But the specifications are reasonably wide, and if the unit is out of specifications, the condition will probably show up with the engine dying immediately after starting, carburetor icing or poor gas mileage that can't be traced to something else. P.W.

See also: AUTOMOBILE ENGINES, ADVANCES IN; ANTI-POLLUTION; FILTERS.

What You Should Know about Air Conditioners

Here's how to narrow down a field of more than 3,000 types, models and sizes to the unit that meets your requirements

IF YOU ARE IN THE MARKET for an air conditioner, make your purchase as an informed consumer. Resist any impulse to dash out on a Saturday morning and "pick up" any air conditioner that an eager salesman assures you will be just right for your medium-sized bedroom. It might be just right—but only through sheer chance. But, why depend on luck when choosing wisely is easy, and you stand to save a considerable amount of money on both the initial investment and on year-by-year operating expenses.

About 55 different companies now manufacture a total of almost 3,000 models of room air conditioners in the U.S. The appliances include window, through-the-wall and combination cooler-heater models. The cooling capacities range all the way from about 4,000 BTU/hour to about 34,000 BTUs. There's nothing mysterious about the term BTU which is just an abbreviation for British thermal unit, a standard unit used to measure heat quantities. In this case the BTU/hour is the amount of heat that a given air conditioner can remove from the surrounding air in one hour. Thus a 10,000 BTU unit can remove twice as much heat from the air, in any given time, than a 5,000 BTU model. But as we shall see, there is a little more to picking the right air conditioner than deciding how many BTUs your unit should be able to handle. Not all 10,000 BTU units, even if superficially identical, are necessarily equally good.

Since the appliance uses electricity, your first job is to decide what type and size of air conditioner your existing power line can handle. House convenience outlets are usually rated at 115 volts and 15 amperes. If you want to avoid adding new wiring to your home, see if a 5,000 to 10,000 BTU/hr. unit drawing a maximum of 7.5 amperes will do the job (we will discuss later how to make such judgements). If it will, you can just plug it into the handiest wall outlet and be done with it. If you decide to buy a unit that draws as much as 12 amperes (typical 8,000 to 14,000 units), use a 115-

air filters: see filters
airplane, model: see rotary engine, mini
airport noises: see noise
air waves: see science projects
alarm generator: see security, home

volt, 15-ampere circuit, but make sure that no other electrical appliance is used on the same branch circuit at the same time. If you need still more cooling power (anywhere from 8,000 to 34,000 BTU), you will have to install a 230/208 volt circuit wired and fused for 15, 20, 30 or perhaps even 50 amperes depending on the current draw of the appliance you select. This circuit, independently fused, should supply power only to the air conditioner.

Types of systems. There are several types of air conditioning equipment, and each has special characteristics that make it suitable for specific applications. Refer to the *Air Conditioning Decision Guide* to determine what types probably would suit your needs, but remember that these are generalizations.

Central (whole house) air conditioning system. This type of system consists of an evaporator (cooling) coil, condenser coil (usually located outside the building), compressor, circulating refrigerant, two fans or blowers, and usually a humidity control and one or more air filters.

Warm, moist air, from inside the house is drawn by a fan blower through a filter and passes over cooling coils which absorb the heat. The heat is carried away by a refrigerant in tubes running to the outdoor condensing unit where the heat is transferred to the atmosphere by a fan in the condensing unit. The cooling coil also re-

AIR CONDITIONING DECISION GUIDE

The type of building you (1) already own or rent or (2) plan to build or rent in the future should be considered when you attempt to choose the basic type of air conditioning system that would probably be most economical and otherwise best suited for your needs. This two-choice decision guide will help you steer toward a good decision:

Type of Residence	First Consideration	Second Consideration
Planned New Construction:		
Single family home	Central A/C system	
Duplex	Two Central A/C systems	Zone systems
Mobile home	Self-contained or split system Central A/C	Mobile home room A/C
Add-on rooms for existing home	Air zone heating/cooling system	Room A/C unit
Vacation home	Heat pump units	Room A/C units
Existing Construction:		
Own single family home with warm air heating (ducts)	Central A/C system	
Own single family home with hot water heating (no ducts)	Room A/C units	
Own duplex apartment house with warm air heating (ducts)	Central A/C system	
Own duplex apartment house with hot water or individual heating systems	Air zonal cooling units	Room A/C units
Rent single family home	Room A/C units	Air zone system
Rent apartment	Room A/C units	
Own mobile home	Self-contained mobile home unit	

▲ *Central air conditioning for single family dwellings often is designed so that much of the mechanism is outside the house, as in this unit. Cooling coils are inside, where air blown over them is carried to various rooms by ducts.*

moves excessive moisture from the room air to effect dehumidification. The cooled and dehumidified air is circulated throughout the house through ductwork.

If your home has a heating system with ducts running to all parts of the house, the central air conditioning system can make use of the existing ducts *unless* (1) the furnace is in very cramped quarters and there is not enough room for the new equipment, (2) the ductwork goes only to a few central locations, or (3) the house is only partially heated or inadequately heated by a central heating system.

You can save money, use space more efficiently, and have a single control if you install a combination air conditioning and central heating system using common ductwork in a new house before construction is completed. But there are conditions wherein central air conditioning is not feasible: (1) the home is in a warm climate where central heating is unnecessary, (2) the building is used only occasionally in cold weather (vacation retreat, for example), (3) the building is occupied by more than one family and separate heating-cooling systems for each are desirable, (4) the building will frequently have unoccupied areas or rooms

▼ *Central air conditioning can be installed in various ways. At top left, cooling coils are in existing hot-air ducts. Where there is no hot-air heating system, ducts can be installed in attic (top right) or beneath floor (bottom).*

and (5) special heating or structural considerations call for use of ductless hot water heating.

Central combination systems. In a new structure, any one of four different types of central air conditioning can be installed, separately or in conjunction with the heating system: (1) basement installation having the evaporator coil and air distributor fan inside and the condenser outside of the building, (2) ground level installation in which the system is located in a closet or utility room (condenser outside), (3) attic installation with ductwork running to all parts of the building and (4) roof mount installation where all of the cooling equipment is on the roof (not suitable for combination heating-cooling systems).

Zonal combination heating-cooling systems. Zone heating and cooling units are efficient, uncomplicated, relatively low in cost and eliminate the need of ductwork and heavy conduit wiring. The units consist of single packages containing complete air conditioning equipment plus an electric heating coil grid. A common fan disperses the warm or cool air. These are especially suitable in such places as add-on rooms where individual control of temperature and humidity are desirable. They can be left off when the room is unoccupied. Installation is in an opening cut into an outside wall near where a 220-volt outlet is available.

Room window units. These units are very popular because they can be added to existing homes very quickly and easily, just by mounting into a window opening. If you are shopping for this type of air conditioner, be especially careful to buy good equipment that meets your needs best. One manufacturer of air conditioning equipment has determined that Americans are using 26 billion kilowatt hours of electricity unnecessarily and spending $543 million a year more than necessary on electricity for room air conditioners. The waste in electricity and dollars is attributed to purchase and use of air conditioners that are inefficient or have *too much* capacity for the area to be cooled. A room air conditioner should have an energy efficiency rating (EER) of eight or more to assure minimum electricity costs and maximum efficiency. If you buy the wrong size unit, or one that operates inefficiently, you may double or even quadruple the basic cost within five years.

Room air conditioners are made to operate off 115-volt or 208/230-volt power lines. If you have an outlet providing the higher voltage near the window where the air conditioner is to be installed, you can use a unit having greater cooling capacity than is provided by most 115-volt jobs (top limit about 14,000 BTU/hr. capacity). Moreover, the higher capacity units are said to work more efficiently (not necessarily in terms of amount of cooling per dollar of electrical cost), and they are likely to have more comfort features than do the lower-capacity 115-volt units. Just bear in mind that a *room* air conditioner is just that —a room conditioner—so don't expect it to cool your entire house or apartment. Even if it were large enough in terms of BTU capacity, you would have big problems keeping air circulating from room to room to maintain an even coolness throughout your habitat.

The operating cost (cost of electricity) of a room air conditioner can range from about $24 to more than $123 per year, assuming an operating period of 1,440 hours and an average kilowatt hour cost of two cents for electrical power. You will keep the operating cost on the low side if you buy a unit having the highest efficiency rating (EER), consistent with other factors that must influence your purchase decision.

Insist that the dealer demonstrate your tentative choice of air conditioner so that you can evaluate the noise level, at both high and low speeds. Remember that the unit may sound noisier in your home in the quiet of the night than it does in a store having a much higher background noise level. If you find heavy insulation in the air chamber behind the air discharge grille, you have evidence that the manufacturer has paid at least some attention to sound control.

The features found on different models and brands of air conditioners are not all the same. Look for and consider the desirability of the following: exhaust control for removal of smoky or stale air from the room; vent setting to bring outside fresh air into the room quickly; thermostat control plus automatic fan shut-off control so that the fan stops when the room air is as cool as you want it; air directors that help control air flow into the room so as to avoid annoying drafts. Also be sure that the selected unit has both the UL (Underwriters Laboratories) seal of approval and the AHAM (Association of Home Appliance Manufacturers) certified seal. Also examine the name plate which shows the model number and rated capacity, the BTU rating and wattage. Using the model number, use the AHAM chart provided by the dealer to verify the efficiency rating for that particular unit.

Heat pumps. These are window air conditioning units that provide both heating and cooling. They are especially popular for use in vacation homes, and in permanent homes in warm climes where winters are very mild. In northern areas they can be used for supplemental heating in the winter and for efficient cooling in the summer.

Heat pumps can reverse operation and take warmth from the outside air and bring it into the room to be heated. Surprisingly, the heat pump will extract warmth from the atmosphere even when the temperature is quite low. Heat pumps look much like regular window air conditioners, and they are installed just as easily.

Through-the-wall air conditioners. These are merely variations of window-type heat pumps in that they are installed in openings cut into the walls, rather than in windows. The main advantage is that use of the window for ventilation, illumination and visibility is not impaired.

Mobile home air conditioners. The heating ductwork is too small and the furnace blower capacity too weak in a typical mobile home to permit efficient integration of an air-conditioning unit. However, you can obtain a self-contained unit that fits neatly under the floor of the mobile home and connects to existing ductwork by means of flexible ducts. These units are especially good for small mobile homes having about 750 square feet of living space.

Another type of mobile home air conditioner, called a split system, consists of an evaporator unit which fits snugly under the floor, and a condensing unit outside, adjacent to the mobile home. This system is good for larger mobile homes. Whatever type you buy, be very sure that it operates very quietly so that you won't annoy neighbors and/or violate mobile park regulations.

Help your dealer help you. To shop intelligently for air conditioning equipment, you need to prepare yourself with facts and figures that either you or your appliance dealer can use to calculate the capacity unit you need. If you just ask a dealer to recommend a good unit for a "small bedroom," or whatever, he may try to do so. But don't be surprised if the cooler turns out to be too weak or too powerful.

If you reason that you can't go wrong by purchasing a unit that is a little bigger than that suggested by the dealer, you may be buying *poorer* performance at higher cost. The reason: an oversize unit can be worse than one that is undersized because it will cool the air too quickly; it won't have time enough to *dehumidify* the air properly. Thus the room may feel cool, but uncomfortably "clammy." If the calculated optimum cooling capacity should figure out to, say, 10,000 BTU, and you have a choice of a 9,000 or 11,000 BTU unit because the exact capacity model is out of stock, take the lower-capacity job. The only exception: if you live in a very dry section of the country where excess humidity is never a problem.

Before you go shopping, prepare a list showing the following information about the room where you plan to install the unit: floor area, room height, type of wall and ceiling insulation, whether there is another room above the one to be cooled, total glass area in windows and doors in the room, the type of glass used in the doors and windows (thickness, and whether they are of double-glazed insulating type), the number of people who normally use the room (to account for added body heat), the compass direction the room faces, whether the room receives direct sunlight or is shaded, and a list showing the wattage ratings of all heat-producing electrical devices and appliances in the room (light bulbs, TV sets, stereo sound equipment and the like).

Using such pertinent information, your dealer should be able to make a reasonably accurate estimate of your cooling needs. If your appliance dealer obviously does not attempt to calculate the cooling load, taking into consideration a reasonable number of the factors listed above, seek a more conscientious salesman in another store.

Of course you should also have some advance idea of whether you want a room air conditioner that mounts in a window, in a hole cut in the wall, or one that also doubles as a room heater. If the appliance is to be set into a wall, determine whether the selected wall area is clear of such obstructions as heating ducts, plumbing or hard-to-move electrical wiring.

Just where you locate the air conditioner in a room can make a very big difference

COOLING CAPACITY REQUIRED PER SQUARE FOOT OF FLOOR SPACE

APPROX. BTU CAPACITY REQUIRED	SPACE ABOVE ROOM BEING COOLED								
	OCCUPIED ROOM			ATTIC			INSULATED FLATROOF		
	AREA BEING COOLED HAS EXPOSED WALLS FACING								
	North or East	South	West	North or East	South	West	North or East	South	West
4,000	160	90	45	120	60	30	120	60	30
6,000	325	205	150	270	175	120	240	160	115
8,000	490	330	255	420	285	220	355	250	195
10,000	670	450	360	580	400	325	475	345	280
12,000	885	580	465	735	520	420	600	445	360
14,000	1200	720	580	900	640	525	730	540	445
16,000	—	880	690	1095	760	630	865	645	535
18,000	—	1090	820	—	885	745	1005	745	625
20,000	—	—	970	—	1030	855	1185	855	720
22,000	—	—	1185	—	1195	975	—	985	820
24,000	—	—	—	—	—	1120	—	1125	930
26,000	—	—	—	—	—	—	—	—	1060

NOTE: Based on an eight-foot ceiling height.

in how well it will perform. It should not be placed too close to the floor, too near an adjacent wall, or where an easy chair or sofa might obstruct air flow. If the air conditioner is placed where air circulation is hampered, the cooler thermostat may be fooled into "thinking" that the entire room is as cool as the stagnant air near the air conditioner, and it may cut off sooner than it should. This operating fault is called "short cycling."

New Efficiency Ratings. Since January 1, 1973 the Association of Home Appliance Manufacturers (AHAM) is providing specific, comparable information concerning the efficiencies of nearly 3,000 room air conditioner models sold under 55 different brand names.

The efficiency rating, or more accurately the *energy efficiency ratio* (EER) is calculated by dividing the BTU per hour of cooling by the watts of power used. Obviously, a unit of the same "size" that gives the most cooling per watt will cost less to operate than one that uses more power for the same amount of cooling. These EER ratings are published in a special directory that you should be able to see at any reputable air conditioner dealership. When comparing the ratings of different models and brands, just bear in mind that the higher the EER number, the more efficient is the unit in question.

Of course, your final choice should not be dependent solely on picking the highest available efficiency rating. It is possible that another model or brand of equipment may have a slightly lower efficiency ratio and still represent a better buy because it is quieter, has features not found on the competing model, or because it obviously is made more carefully or of more durable materials.

On the other hand, it would be most unwise to ignore the efficiency ratings, even if you have an unshakeable loyalty to one particular brand of appliance. For exam-

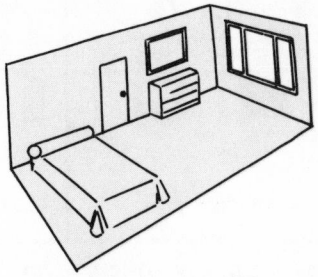

Height, width, and length of the area to be cooled

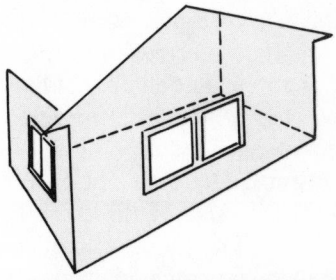

Number, sizes, and directions faced by windows

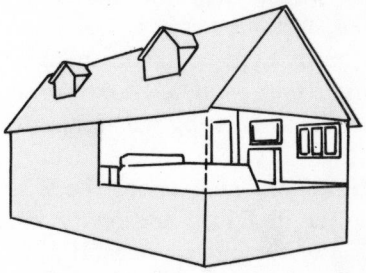

Location of space to be cooled within the building

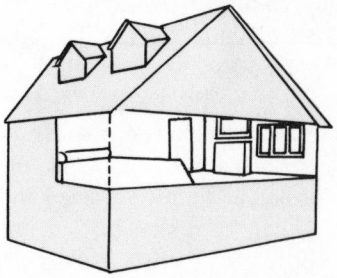

Direction of the longest side of the space to be cooled

Factors to consider when determining required air conditioner capacity include dimensions of the area to be cooled, the amount of window area and the compass direction it faces, the location of the space within the building and the compass direction faced by the longest outside wall.

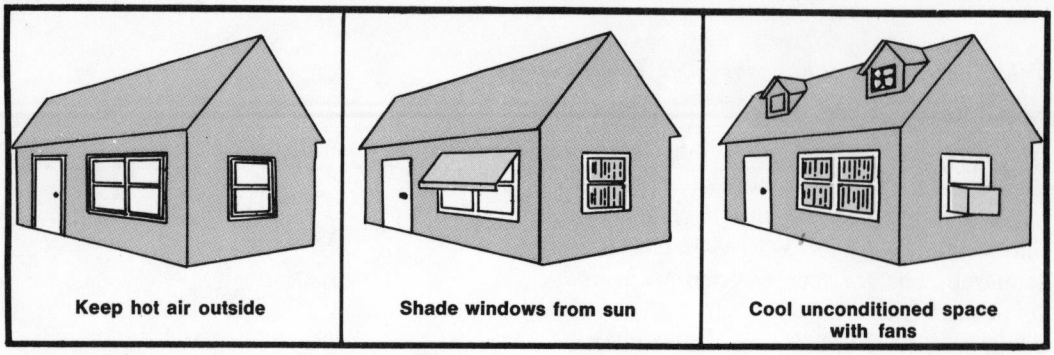

Use these tips to reduce your air conditioner's work load. Keep hot air outside by keeping storm windows on and making sure drafty cracks are caulked. Shade windows from the sun with awnings on the outside and shades, drapes or blinds on the inside. Cool unconditioned space with fans.

ple, one company offers two window model air conditioners rated at 14,000 BTU/hr. The 115-volt model has an EER rating of 10.2 whereas the 230/208-volt model is rated at only 6.0. Obviously, it will cost you a great deal more to operate the high-voltage model.

Even if a dealer does not have available a copy of the AHAM directory listing the EER ratings for all air conditioners, you can easily make such efficiency comparisons by calculating the efficiency ratios yourself. It is very easy to do. Each appliance must have a label indicating the cooling power in BTUs and the wattage. Just divide the first by the second to determine the EER. Above all, do *not* assume that air conditioners having the same cooling power in BTUs are pretty much the same. For example, one 10,000 BTU appliance listed in the AHAM directory draws 1,375 watts of power, so its efficiency ratio is 7.3; another 10,000 BTU appliance made by another manufacturer draws 1,850 watts to do the same amount of cooling work, so its efficiency ratio is a substantially lower 5.4. If you choose the second appliance, your electric bills will be larger than they need to be.

You can go a step further and calculate the approximate cost of electricity used to operate various models. You need to know the cost per kilowatt of electricity in your area, and you need to make a rough estimate of the number of hours you would probably operate the appliance throughout the year. For example, assume that electricity costs 2½ cents per kilowatt, and that you will operate your air conditioner 1400 hours each year, on the average. First calculate the *base annual cost per watt* by multiplying the cost of electricity by the hours of use, and then divide the product by 1,000 to convert the cost per kilowatt to the cost per watt:

$$\frac{\$0.025 \times 1400}{1000} = \$0.035$$

Armed with this basic figure, you can easily figure the approximate probable annual cost of operating any air conditioner, just by multiplying the base annual cost per watt (in this example, 0.035) by the wattage rating of the appliance in question. For example, consider the two 10,000 BTU units mentioned above. One draws 1,375 watts of power, so its operating cost per year would be about $48.12; the other unit draws 1,850 watts, so its operating cost would come to $64.75. The less efficient unit would, under these assumed circumstances, cost $16.63 more to operate each year.

When you stop to consider that you could easily throw away that kind of money—not just once but every year your air conditioner is in use—just through impulse buying, it's obvious that spending a little time figuring your real air conditioning needs is well worth the small effort involved. J.H.

COOLING-LOAD ESTIMATE FORM

Heat Gain From	Quantity	Factors				Quantity X Factor
1. WINDOWS: Heat gain from sun.		No shades*	Inside shades*	Outside awnings*	(Area x Factor)	
Facing northeast	_____ sq. ft.	60	25	20	_____	_____
Facing east	_____ sq. ft.	80	40	25	_____	_____
Facing southeast	_____ sq. ft.	75	30	20	_____	_____
Facing south	_____ sq. ft.	75	35	20	_____	_____
Facing southwest	_____ sq. ft.	110	45	30	_____	_____
Facing west	_____ sq. ft.	150	65	45	_____	_____
Facing northwest	_____ sq. ft.	120	50	35	_____	_____
Facing north	_____ sq. ft.	0	0	0	_____	_____
These factors are for single glass only. For glass block, multiply the above factors by 0.5; for double glass or storm windows, multiply above factor by 0.8.						
2. WINDOWS: Heat gain by conduction (total of all windows).						
Single glass	_____ sq. ft.			14		_____
Double glass or glass block	_____ sq. ft.			7		_____
3. WALLS: (Based on linear feet.)		Light construction		Heavy construction		
a. Outside walls						
North exposure	_____ ft.	30		20		_____
Other than north exposure	_____ ft.	60		30		_____
b. Inside walls (between conditioned and unconditioned spaces only)	_____ ft.		30			_____
4. CEILING: (Use one only.)						Enter one figure only
a. Uninsulated with no space above	_____ sq. ft.			19		_____
b. Insulation 1 inch or more, no space above	_____ sq. ft.			8		_____
c. Uninsulated with attic space above	_____ sq. ft.			12		_____
d. Insulated with attic space above	_____ sq. ft.			5		_____
e. Occupied space above	_____ sq. ft.			3		_____
5. FLOOR: (Disregard if floor is on ground or over basement.)	_____ sq. ft.			3		_____
6. NUMBER OF PEOPLE:	_____			600		_____
7. ELECTRICAL EQUIPMENT:	_____ watts			3		_____
8. DOORS AND ARCHES OPEN TO UNCOOLED SPACE:	_____ ft.			300		_____
9. SUBTOTAL:	xxxxxxx			xxxxxxx		_____
10. TOTAL COOLING LOAD: Btu per hour to be used for selection of room air-conditioner(s)	____ (Item 9) X _____ (Factor from map) =					_____

INSTRUCTIONS

The numbers of the following paragraphs refer to the correspondingly numbered item on the form:

1. Multiply the square feet of window area for each exposure by the applicable factor. The window area is the area of the wall opening in which the window is installed. For windows shaded by inside shades or Venetian blinds, use the factor for "Inside Shades." For windows shaded by outside awnings or by both outside awnings and inside shades (or Venetian blinds), use the factor for "Outside Awnings." "Single Glass" includes all types of single-thickness windows, and "Double Glass" includes sealed air-space types, storm windows, and glass block. Only one number should be entered in the right-hand column for item 1, and this number should represent *only the exposure with the largest load.*

2. Multiply the total square feet of *all* windows in the room by the applicable factor.

3a. Multiply the total length (linear feet) of all walls exposed to the outside by the applicable factor. Doors should be considered as being part of the wall. Outside walls facing due north should be calculated separately from outside walls facing other directions. Walls which are permanently shaded by adjacent structures should be considered as being "North Exposure." Do not consider trees and shrubbery as providing permanent shading. An uninsulated frame wall or a masonry wall 8 inches or less in thickness is considered "Light Construction." An insulated frame wall or a masonry wall over 8 inches in thickness is considered "Heavy Construction."

3b. Multiply the total length (linear feet) of all inside walls between the space to be conditioned and any unconditioned spaces by the given factor. Do not include inside walls which separate other air-conditioned rooms.

4. Multiply the total square feet of roof or ceiling area by the factor given for the type of construction most nearly describing the particular application. (Use one line only.)

5. Multiply the total square feet of floor area by the factor given. Disregard this item if the floor is directly on the ground or over a basement.

6. Multiply the number of people who normally occupy the space to be air-conditioned by the factor given. Use a minimum of 2 people.

7. Determine the total number of watts for lights and electrical equipment, except the air conditioner itself, that will be *in use* when the room air-conditioning is operating. Multiply the total wattage by the factor given.

8. Multiply the total width (linear feet) of any doors or arches which are continually open to an unconditioned space by the applicable factor. Where the width of the doors or arches is more than 5 feet, the actual load may exceed the calculated value. In such cases, both adjoining rooms should be considered as a single large room, and the room air-conditioner unit or units should be selected according to a calculation made on this new basis.

9. Total the loads estimated for the foregoing 8 items.

10. Multiply the sub-total obtained in Item 9 by the proper correction factor, selected from the map, for particular locality. The result is the total estimated design cooling load in Btu per hour. For best results a room air-conditioner unit or units having a cooling capacity rating as close as possible to the estimated load should be selected. In general, a greatly oversized unit which would operate intermittently will be much less satisfactory than one which is slightly undersized and which would operate more nearly continuously.

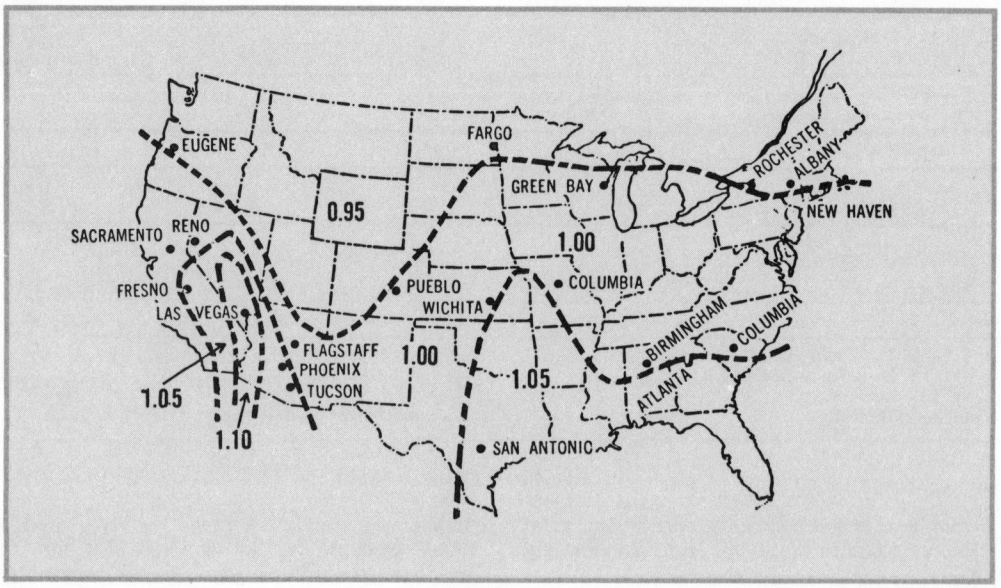

Seasonal Maintenance for Your Air Conditioner

Get this job done in the spring for dependable summer-long operation

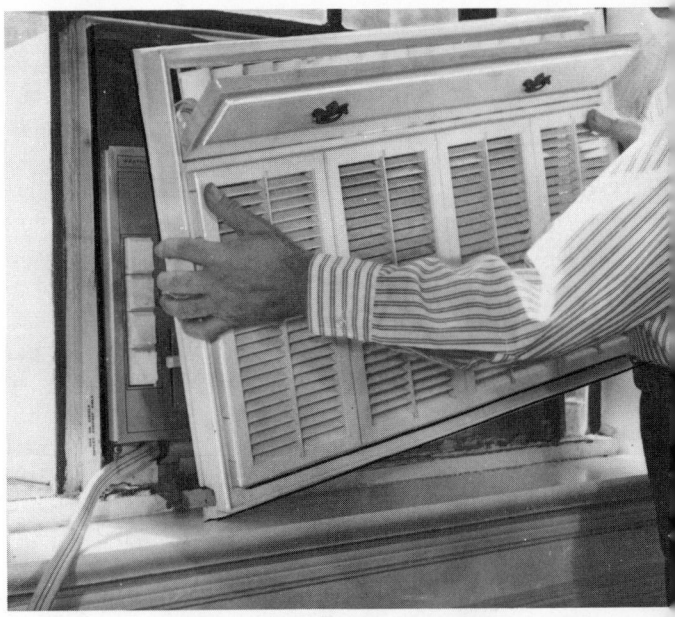

▲ *Room air conditioners need seasonal check-up to keep them trouble-free. A little attention beforehand will avoid costly breakdowns. First step is to lift off the front cover, held by spring clips.*

TAKE A LOOK at your air conditioner before the hot weather strikes. Just a few maintenance details may be all it needs to get it into shape for dependable performance all season.

Two routine chores, often overlooked, are quickly gotten out of the way. One is washing or replacing the filter, depending on the type. The other is cleaning the evaporator and condenser coils.

To get at the mechanism, remove the front cover panel. Every make of air conditioner has a panel that is held with clips and can be lifted off, though some have catches or retainer screws that must be loosened first.

With the front cover off, clean the deflecting louvers with a dry cloth or brush. To reach the condenser coils and fins, pull the machine forward from the housing in which it rests on small wheels or runners.

If the conditioner is installed in the window so that most of the housing extends on the outside, and the metal case is securely fastened, it is all right to pull the machine forward as it will remain balanced. However, if the machine is only partly mounted into the wall and most of the case projects into the room take the precaution of placing a wooden box or other support under the case before drawing out the chassis, which is quite heavy.

Use a vacuum cleaner with the brush attachment to remove accumulated lint and dust, making sure the ventilator fins are clear for air passage.

If necessary, reverse the vacuum hose to blow dust out of the fins. Wipe the coils and meter housing with a clean damp cloth. Check the fan meter to see if it has any lubricating cups and if so, add oil. Even the "permanent" type of motor bearings should be given a few drops of #20 motor oil.

The filter is located directly behind the front louvers, extending all the way across so it can be lifted out from the top. The woven plastic or metal type is renewed by flushing under a faucet. Wash in detergent if the filter is greasy. The fiberglass type should be replaced with a new one at the start of each season, and again each month to insure maximum cooling benefits.

Check the wiring to see that the terminals are tight and the cord insulation undamaged. Then slide the mechanism back and replace the cover.

Now think back to last summer to recall any breakdowns or annoyances with that particular unit. Did the fuses blow every so often? Was there a tinny rattle or excessive vibration? Some of these conditions can be corrected or at least alleviated.

Best cure for an overloaded circuit is to bring in a separate line for the air conditioner. This is not necessarily an extensive job, as a separate circuit line can be carried directly to the room concealed inside the walls, or through a conduit attached outside along the house wall. But if your house has inadequate wiring, installation of a larger electrical service may be required, and is worthwhile for efficient use of modern appliances.

Noise problems may be inherent in the operation of the machine, but sometimes they result from a loose hinge or missing gasket on the exhaust door. The source can be tracked down by operating the machine with the cover off.

Vibration in the walls results when an installation is not adequately braced. If the matter is sufficiently bothersome, fit a brace under the machine and insulate with rubber or felt padding. In any event, the opening should be tightly caulked both inside and on the outside.

Conditioners installed in double-hung windows should be thoroughly checked to make sure that the supports are adequate and that the sash is tight so that it doesn't rattle when the machine is running.

A frequent cause of service calls is a worn electric receptacle which results in the uncertain contact with the plug prongs. Replace the receptacle with a new one, or get the locking type of plug that twists into the receptacle and can't be dislodged by vibration. R.T.

▲ *Lift out filter located behind the condenser coils. Woven plastic type is cleaned under faucet. Other types should be replaced with new ones.*

◄ *Clean the air deflectors and casing with a brush or vacuum cleaner. Check the wire insulation and connections.*

▲ *With machine cover off, clean compressor coils, housing, etc., thoroughly with vacuum hose and damp cloth.*

▼ *Check electric cord and wall receptacle, which are common causes of conditioner failure.*

▲ *Where necessary, reverse vacuum hose to blow out lint from evaporator fins, and inside the case. Wipe fan meter with cloth, apply a few drops of oil to bearings.*

▼ *Check outside supports of large machines that extend out quite far from the window. If they are loose or rusted, replace them.*

How to Repair Your Room Air Conditioner

You can keep your machine working and save on repair bills by replacing some broken parts yourself

THE ROOM AIR CONDITIONER is a refrigeration unit plus some fans and filters. The filters remove the major dust particles from the air. The fans, usually mounted on each end of a single motor, move the air. One *recirculates* the room air over the evaporator (cooling coil) and the other blows the outside air over the condenser to cool it. Each is separated from the other by a wall to keep the room air and the outside air from mixing. A special door in this partition can be opened to allow some fresh air to mix with the room air.

Before condemning the air conditioner for not doing its job you must be certain that you are not expecting to cool a larger room than it was designed to do. And don't compare the operation of your machine with that of a friend, since the conditions of location and use will be different.

Air conditioners should be connected to a separate electrical circuit having large enough wire and fusing to handle its load. An approximate relation between B.T.U. capacity, wattage and wire size is shown in the accompanying chart.

B.T.U. Capacity	Volts	Watts	Wire Size	Fuse Size
10,000	115	1400	14	15
16,000	220	2650	14	15
20,000	220	3350	12	20

In many machines, removing the grill and inner enclosure will expose the controls and associated wiring. More extensive service to get at the fan and compressor will require removal of the outer enclosure assembly. Usually these parts are fastened with #6 or #8 hex-head slotted screws. Decorative trim is usually fastened with Phillips-head screws.

Basically, a medium sized standard screw driver, a Phillips-head screw driver, a set of nut drivers and a pair of channel-lock pliers should be all you need to remove the serviceable parts and clean the unit.

When cleaning the unit, remove the excess rust and paint over the rusty spots with a rust-inhibiting primer. This will do much to extend the unit's life.

Though you can see most of the parts when you remove the cover of your air conditioner (see drawing) it's best to disconnect any part from its wiring before checking it for electrical continuity. When you do, make a pencil sketch to remind you where the wires are connected. Wiring connections for this unit are shown in the accompanying wiring diagram.

To check the switch with your continuity tester, there should be no contin-

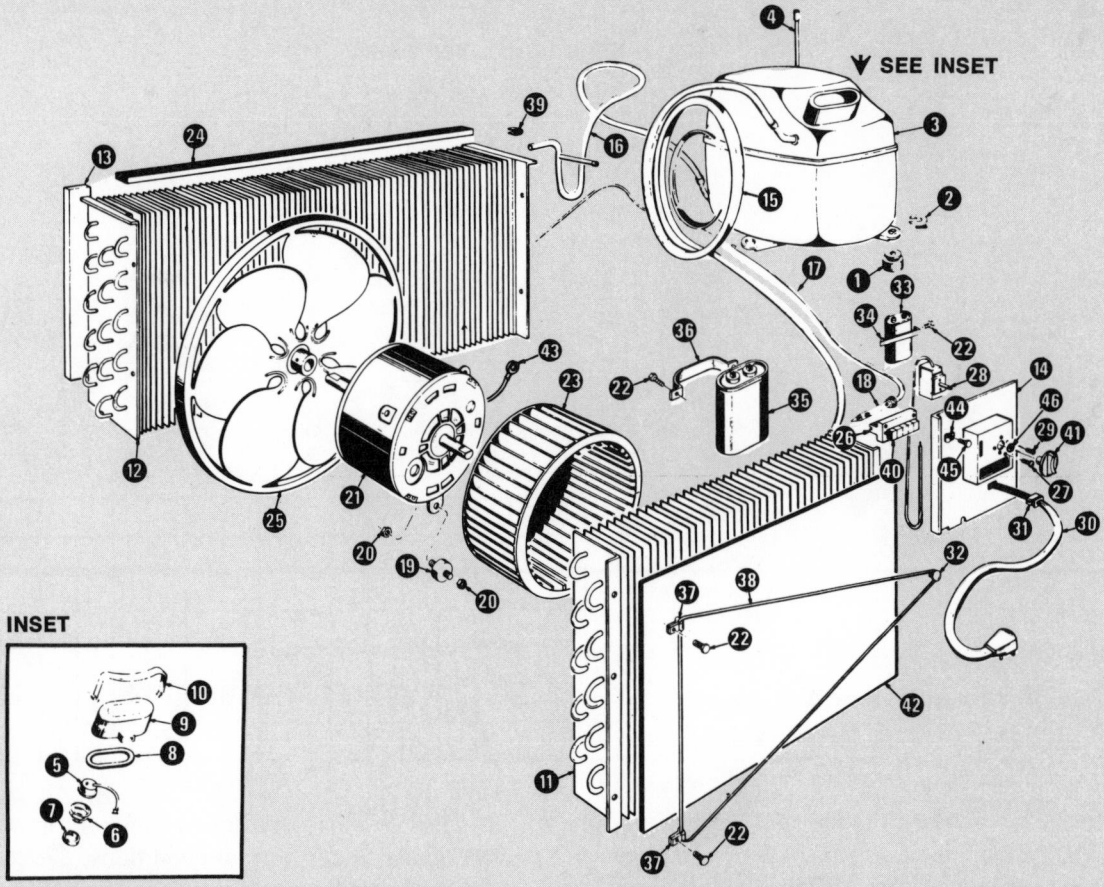

REF. NO.	PART NAME	QTY.
1	Compressor Isolator	3
2	Retainer Spring	3
3	Compressor	1
4	Compressor Charging Tube	1
5	Motor Protector	1
6	Protector Spring	1
7	Adaptor Protector	1
8	Cover Seal	1
9	Terminal Cover	1
10	Cover Strap	1
11	Evaporator Coil	1
12	Condenser Coil	1
13	Condenser Side Seal	1
14	Panel Assembly	1
15	Suction Tube	1
16	Discharge Tube Assembly	1
17	Restrictor Tube Assembly	1
18	Strainer .250 I.D.	1
19	Motor Isolator	3
20	1/4—20 Hex Nut Keps	6
21	Fan Motor—115 V.	1
22	No. 8—15x3/8″ Hex Washer Head Tapping Screw	As Required
23	Evaporator Blower Wheel	1
24	Condenser Top Seal	1
25	Condenser Fan	1
26	Pushbutton Switch	1
27	No. 8—32x3/8″ Round Head Phillips Machine Screw	2
28	Thermostat	1
29	No. 6—32x3/16″ Round Head Phillips Machine Screw	2
30	Power Cord	1
31	Strain Relief	1
32	Ratchet Rivet	2
33	Capacitor	1
34	Capacitor Strap	1
35	Fan Capacitor	1
36	Capacitor Strap	1
37	Clamp	3
38	Filter Retainer	1
39	"U" Type Clip	2
40	Pushbutton	5
41	Thermostat Knob	1
42	Unit Filter	1
43	Motor Ground Wire	1
44	Thermostat Bulb Clamp	1
45	No. 8x1/2″ Hex Head Sheet Metal Screw	2
46	Thermostat Knob Seal	1

WINDOW AIR CONDITIONER CHECKLIST

PROBLEM / POSSIBLE CAUSE	LOW LINE VOLTAGE	IMPROPERLY FUSED	WIRE OR PART SHORTED	DEFECTIVE STARTING RELAY	DEFECTIVE MOTOR—COMPRESSOR	THERMOSTAT SET TOO WARM	THERMOSTAT SET TOO COLD	FAN SPEED SET TOO SLOW	DEFECTIVE DEFROST THERMOSTAT	CLOGGED AIR FILTER	LOW OUTSIDE TEMPERATURE	LOOSE PARTS	FAN HITTING	SHIPPING BOLTS STILL TIGHT	NOT ENOUGH SLOPE TO OUTSIDE	DRAIN PLUGGED	ABNORMALLY HIGH HUMIDITY	INADEQUATE SEAL
BLOWS FUSES	√	√	√	√	√													
COMPRESSOR SHORT CYCLES	√			√	√			√	√	√								
NOISY OPERATION					√							√	√	√				
EVAPORATOR FROSTS UP							√	√			√							
UNIT RUNS TOO MUCH						√				√							√	
MOISTURE DRIPS INTO ROOM															√	√	√	√
WON'T START	√		√	√	√													

uity between the line and any other contact when switch is *off*. When turned to each other position, switch should show continuity.

The motor starting relay must show continuity when it is disconnected from the circuit. Contacts will open when motor reaches normal speed, as indicated by your test light. Motor relay must be mounted in correct position or it will not operate properly.

To test the motor starting capacitor, use an ohmmeter. But first disconnect capacitor leads and short its terminals to discharge it; otherwise you can get a strong shock.

With ohmmeter at its highest scale and connected to capacitor terminals, a low resistance reading will indicate a leak or short. On a good capacitor, the needle will swing to zero, then within a few seconds slowly change to a resistance reading of over 100,000 ohms. Check running capacitor the same way.

The overload protector should show continuity under normal conditions. Check the fan motor for continuity and for lubrication. The fan should spin freely when the blades are turned by hand.

The defrost thermostat normally opens at 30° F. to stop the compressor. Below this, for test, it must show no continuity. Above 60°, continuity should be shown. Between 30° and 60°, the stat will not show continuity when warming up, but will when cooling down.

The control thermostat will show continuity as the knob is turned, depending on room temperature. Failure to get a continuity change at some point near room temperature is cause to suspect this unit. Make sure that thermostat feeler bulb temperature is within the thermostat's operating range. Anything between 65° and 75° will do.

Unless you have special tools and some experience, don't get involved with the

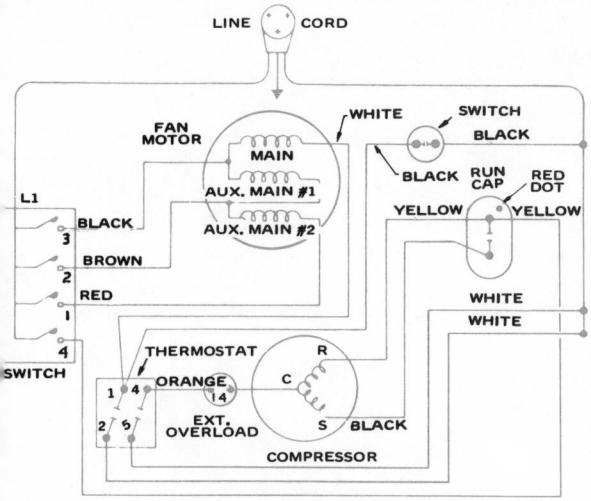

SCHEMATIC

REFRIGERATION SYSTEM

Simple Refrigerant Circuit

A. Dual capillary used with 4-row evaporators
B. Expansion valve used on 2¼ h.p. models only
C. All other models have single capillary

Fan switch is master switch; supplies current through thermostat to compressor on "Hi Fan" and "Lo-Fan" settings only. Thermostat controls compressor

Thermostat sensing bulb is located in room-air intake

Electrical wiring for an air conditioner diagramed schematically and pictorially.

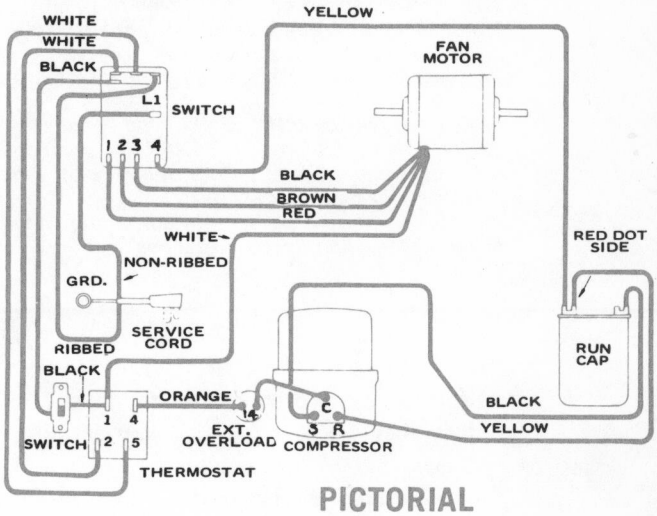

PICTORIAL

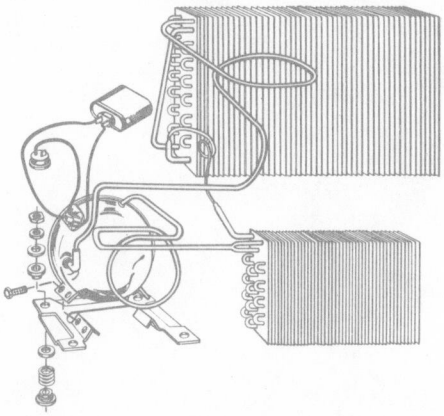

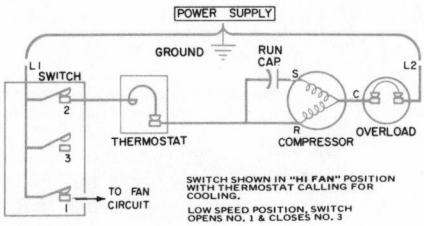

CONDENSATE FLOW SYSTEM

Evaporator condensate drains into insulated plastic pan beneath evaporator coil

Evaporator pan drains through tubes to plastic pan beneath condenser coil

Condenser fan blade slinger ring sprays water (from plastic pan beneath condenser) onto condenser coil

Overflow from condenser pan goes into unit base (unusual condition, caused by very high indoor humidity)

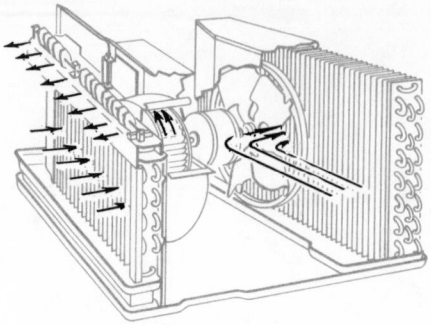

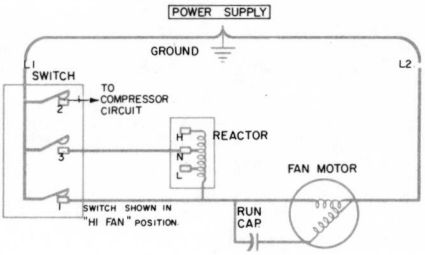

➤Filtered room air is pulled through evaporator coil
Cooled air discharged into room at high velocity by squirrel-cage blower wheel
Adjustable wafer-discs direct cooled air to left side, straight ahead or to right side of room
Condenser fan blade pushes air through full-width, full-height condenser coil
Condenser air pulled in through vents in sides of cabinet
Fan switch provides "Hi" or "Lo" fan speeds
Setting thermostat on "OFF THERM" (or "Fan only" on some models) allows operation of fan only at either high or low speed
Adjustable-tap reactor allows correcting high or low voltage fan speed variations

compressor, evaporator or condenser. Together, they form the sealed refrigerating system.

Should any of the parts prove to be defective, they will have to be removed and replaced. The best source of replacement parts for your air conditioner is from the manufacturer of the machine or the dealer who sold it. Usually the Yellow Pages listing under air conditioning equipment will include local dealers and suppliers of parts. G.M.

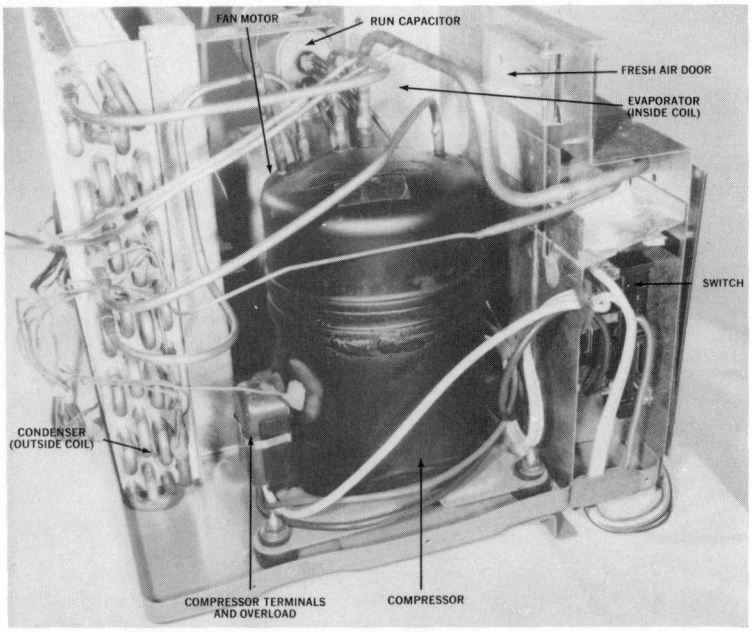

◄Shown are principal components of a typical air conditioning unit.

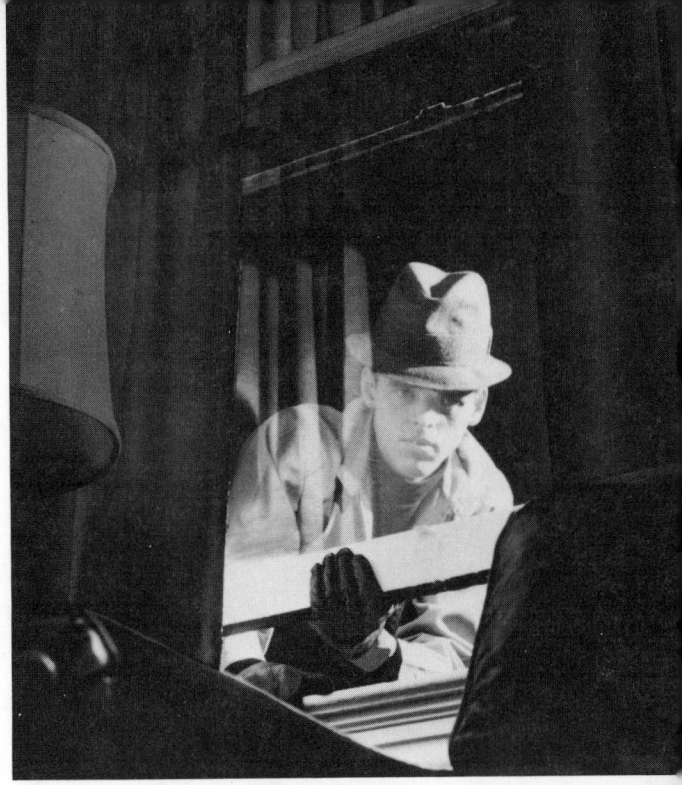

Install a Burglar Alarm

Here's how to select an alarm, and instructions for a complete alarm system

YOUR TELEPHONE RINGS, but goes unanswered because you are in the shower or away from home. Ten minutes later a stranger rings your doorbell. If you answer, he pretends to be looking for a friend in the neighborhood. If you do not answer the door, he will soon be inside, calmly taking his pick of your valuables.

Let's face facts. Lights left burning in an unoccupied house may discourage a wandering amateur housebreaker, but only the din of a burglar alarm upsets the pro.

The chance of your home being burglarized increases every year. Why be one of the victims when a good burglar alarm costs so little and is so easy to install.

What type of alarm? Many different kinds of burglar alarm systems are available. Each type has advantages and disadvantages. So investigate all available systems carefully before deciding which is best for your particular needs.

Those simple little alarms that fasten directly to doors deserve only passing mention here since they offer minimal protection at best. They may be adequate for apartments, or in other homes where there are few avenues of entry.

More reliable systems include photo-electric devices, ultrasonic alarms, switch and break-wire systems, and those that automatically telephone the police or anyone else of your choosing. A telephone system is the most expensive, but it may be the only wise choice for an isolated rural home where ordinary alarms would not be heard by neighbors or passersby.

A typical photo-electric unit costing $100 or more can protect only a limited area because triggering of the alarm depends on the breaking of a light beam by the intruder. Perhaps this is all the protection you need. However, bear these points in mind. First, give preference to a system that utilizes an invisible infra-red beam and place the two units (light box and receiver) where the prowler cannot see them readily. If he spots the boxes, he can determine exactly where the light beam is whether it is invisible or not; he can then either crawl under or step over it. Secondly, consider only a unit having a *modulated* light source because only this type will work in lighted as well as dark areas, and because it cannot be frustrated by the light from a burglar's flashlight.

alarm systems: see home security sensors
aliphatic resin glue: see adhesives
alligatoring: see painting, house

Below: Alert DC-6 alarm with blinker lens removed to show prewired, mounted electronic assembly. Right: A circuit tester helps you check switches. Tape a flashlight bulb socket to a dry cell. Solder stiff wires to socket; one serves as probe, the other contacts cell bottom. Touch probe and cell terminal to switch leads. Bulb lights if the switch is properly closed.

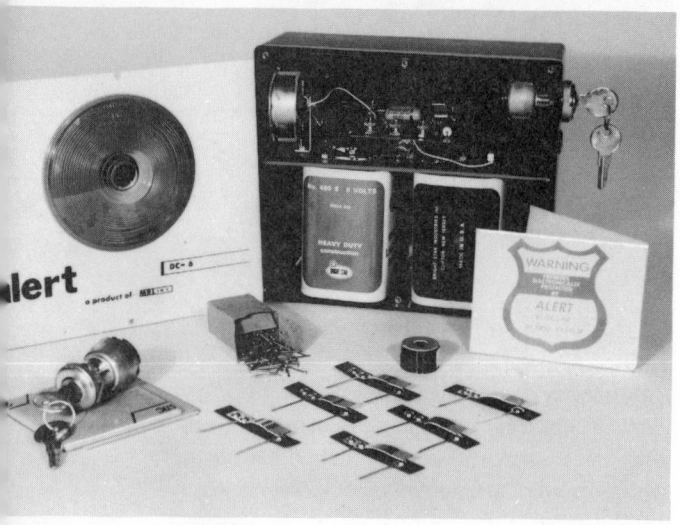

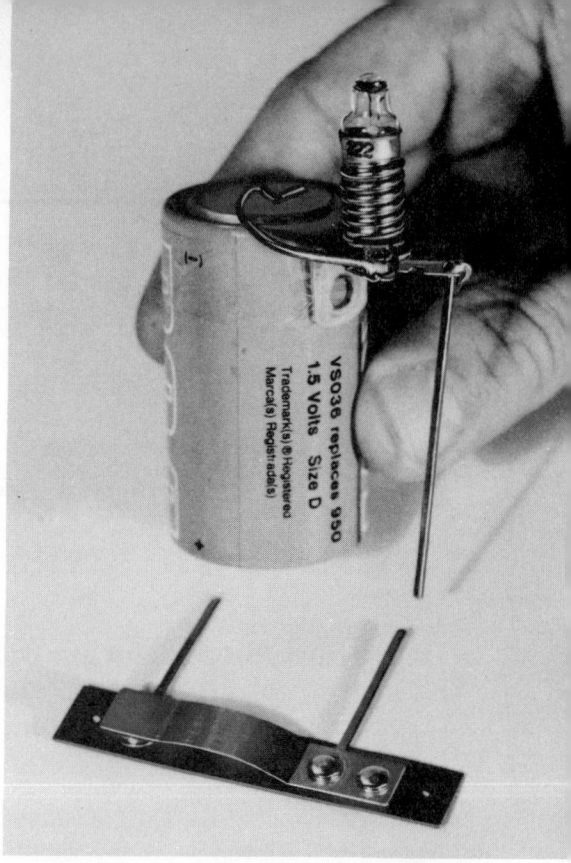

Finally, remember that the light beam must be where pet dogs and cats cannot intercept it.

One of the newest types of alarms utilizes ultrasonic sound to trigger the alarm. Such a unit consists of a single box placed in a strategic position from which it sends out a sound "pattern" that is inaudible to the human ear. The same unit also serves as a receiver. When an intruder steps into the sound area (about 100 square feet), he disturbs the pattern and sets off the alarm. These are good provided there is no air turbulence in the sound area. Cats and dogs will activate the alarm, as will air currents created by heating or air-conditioning systems. Incidentally, dogs and cats *can* hear the sound even though you cannot, and they may not enjoy it.

If you have no wandering pets, and all you wish to do is protect one room and perhaps a staircase to the second floor, either the photo-electric or ultrasonic system may be a good choice. Both are quiet, efficient, and least troublesome to install and maintain.

Perhaps the best choice for an average private home is a switch and break-wire system. Such a system can guard every possible avenue of entry into the house, even protect the henhouse and mailbox if you wish. Some models can also protect against smoke, fire, flooding and freezing. Finally, these systems are relatively inexpensive—only $20 to $40 for a typical basic unit.

The major disadvantage of a switch and break-wire system is that it cannot simply be plugged in for instant operation. You must run wire around the house to the various door and window switches. Also, you should check the switches periodically to make sure they are clean and that they make good contact. These are minor disadvantages considering the degree of protection these systems provide.

Compare the relative merits of switch and break-wire alarms made by different manufacturers. They are not all alike. Some give only an audible alarm, others simultaneously turn on a red light visible from the street. Some are primarily intruder alarms, others can utilize special sensors to detect other home hazards of the types already mentioned.

Plan for security. Careful advance planning will ensure the installation of an uncomplicated, foolproof alarm system. Start by making a rough drawing of your floor plan; on it indicate all windows and doors that need protection. Cross out those windows that require no protection—for example, upper story windows that cannot be reached from fire escapes, trees or porch roofs (provided that you do not keep long ladders lying about). If you do not store valuable tools in the garage, this area may be left unprotected provided that you *do* protect any door leading from the garage into the house.

Next, decide where you should locate the master control unit containing the alarm horn. If the system you select makes only an audible sound, it can be placed wherever it is best heard by neighbors, and where you can conveniently reach it to turn it on and off. If the system also turns on a signal light, place the box in the corner of a window, facing the street, so that the light will be visible to passersby.

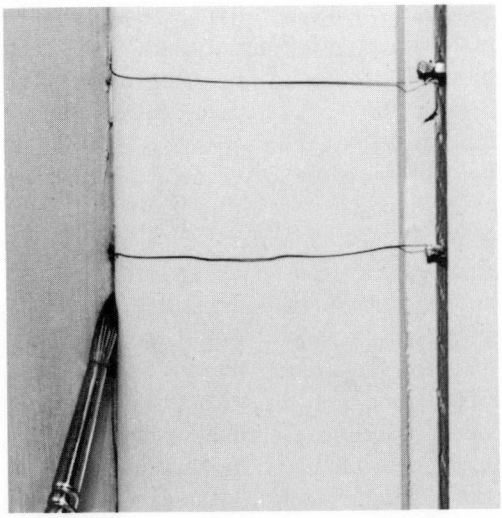

As can be seen here, switch installed on a door jamb is virtually invisible. Wire has been pushed into crevice between the door jamb and a cupboard wall, then held in place with small dabs of clear cement. Hair wires can be hidden with trim paint.

If placing the entire master control box in a window is inconvenient, remove the front panel from the master box and mount it alone in a window, then lead the wires from the flasher bulb back to the master control. A good way to make a connection in the control box is to make a plug from the base of an extra bulb that fits the original bulb socket. Break off the glass part of the bulb, remove the filaments, and drill through the base contact with a $^1/_{16}$ inch drill. Poke a wire through this hole and solder the end to the base terminal. Solder another lead wire to the outside of the bulb base. Attach your flasher leads to these wires, and simply plug into the original bulb socket.

Use of the front panel, with the flasher light, as a separate, remote unit has another advantage besides eliminating a bulky box in the window. You can hide the master control box wherever you wish, making it harder for an intruder to find it and tamper with it.

Using the floor plan as a guide, trace the best wiring route while you study the house itself for problem areas. The wire should not be run across or along electric power cables. Remember that you must route a singlewire loop to and from the control box so that it makes a *series* circuit through all the switches.

The fine "hair" wire (only 0.003 inches in diameter) is virtually invisible when properly installed. It is fairly delicate, so handle it carefully. In extensive wiring jobs, especially if you have to lead the wire from one floor level to another, your wiring job will be much easier if you substitute a heavier insulated wire for those stretches where concealment is no problem. Use telephone or other low-voltage wire readily available from any electronics supply shop.

The wire may be run through the attic or basement wherever convenient. In rooms, run it along baseboards, mouldings, window and door frames—wherever it is least visible. Planning the best wire route should be done with deliberation and care to avoid unnecessary back-tracking. To fasten the wire in place, just drive a small brad in part way, give the wire a twist around it, and tap the nail in all the way. Be careful with the hair wire; nailing down too hard may break it. In some places you may find it easier to glue the wire in place with small dabs of transparent glue; hold the wire in position with pieces of paper masking tape until the glue dries.

The accompanying illustrations show how the wire is attached to switches mounted in ordinary doors and sliding glass doors. Similar placements work with windows. Just cut the wire where it passes a switch, sandpaper the enamel coating from the hair wire, wrap around the switch terminals. For a really trouble-free job, add a touch of solder to each connection.

You need switches only on doors and windows that are opened and closed frequently. If some windows are rarely or never opened, you can protect them *without* using switches. Simply run the wire over the window and across the frame so that it will be broken if an intruder opens the window or breaks the glass. If you have inside screens, the wire can be threaded through the screen mesh where it will be virtually invisible. When the wire breaks, the alarm will sound.

Horn location. Alarms of this kind have the noise-making horn mounted inside the master control box. This is not really the best place for it in many applications. If the control box is hidden in a closet or cupboard, the sound will be muffled. In any case, the sound will be not as loud *outside* the house as it should be.

There is a simple solution. Remove the horn from the box and place it where it can be heard best, running a double-wire lead from the master control box to the horn.

Power in the *Alert* system is supplied by two six-volt batteries housed inside the control box. Other makes of alarms use ordinary flashlight cells. There really isn't much difference in operation except that the bigger batteries will keep the horn blaring for up to eight hours instead of half an hour. Only you can shut off the sound, by use of a key switch on the side of the master control box. The intruder cannot stop the alarm by simply closing a window or door he has opened. Once it is started, only the key will turn it off.

By-pass switch. But how are you going to get into the house without setting off the alarm? You can't unless you install a by-pass switch lock that inactivates the switch on your main entry. This tumbler-type lock is mounted on the door, or in a wall near the door, and is connected to the door switch terminals. This is an extra-cost item, but hardly expendable. When you turn the key in the lock, that door's alarm switch is inactivated permitting you to enter. You need not use this by-pass when leaving your home because the alarm system has a built-in delay (about 45 seconds) that lets you get out of the house before it becomes operative.

Think like a burglar. After you have installed and tested your alarm system, go outside and study the house as a burglar might. Is there any way that you could frustrate the alarm system—for example, by breaking a small pane of glass and reaching in to bridge the window switch with a length of wire? Have you missed protecting any avenue of entry, such as a basement window? Can the warning light be seen from the street? Can the horn be heard by your neighbors? Did you place the warning stickers where would-be intruders will see them?

Install a Burglar Alarm

About those stickers. Most burglars will leave a house alone if they are warned that an alarm system is in use. However, in some cases you should not use such warnings. If you live in a remote area and must rely on a warning system that automatically telephones the police, you should never advertise your security system. In this case you want the burglar to stick around until the police have time to respond to your call for help.

When your system is "go," tell your neighbors what the noise and signal light mean. You may wish to leave a duplicate cut-off key with a trusted neighbor so that the alarm can be turned off in your absence. Finally, let your police department know what kind of intruder protection you have.

Other applications. As mentioned before, some switch and break-wire alarm systems can also be fitted with special sensors to detect smoke, fire, basement flooding and freezing conditions.

Note that a typical switch and break-wire system can be used in other ways, and in other places, without the use of special sensors. With it you can guard your boat, camping trailer, car, henhouse, or even use it as a safety device around the swimming pool. In the latter case, make a "fence" around the pool area with the wire; anyone running toward the pool will break the wire and sound the alarm.

You may want to add a double-pole double-throw switch near the control box so that you can use the alarm system conveniently as a swimming pool safety system when you are at home, and as an intruder alarm when you are absent.

The system is also a good vandal detector. For example, the demolition of roadside mailboxes by juvenile marauders plague many a suburban community. A switch and break-wire alarm can be used to detect night time vandals. Just disconnect the house alarm wiring from the alarm box terminals and substitute a hair wire loop running to the mailbox. Wrap the wire around the flag, and run it through the holes in the mailbox latch. Anyone who twists the flag or attempts to open the box will break the wire and set off the alarm. If you do not want to tip off the vandals with an audible alarm, disconnect one wire leading to the

Break-wire, shown above, is best for sliding doors which are infrequently opened. A small nail stuck into door handle holds a wire loop that will break and sound the alarm when door is opened. Avoid slack in the wire which would defeat this purpose.

For sliding doors used more often, cement *a switch near the top of vertical channel so that it is closed by door edge. To prevent shorting, use clear adhesive tape to insulate hair wire leads from door frame.*

horn. Place the alarm box where you will see the light go on—perhaps the best place is near the TV set.

It is just as easy to detect fourfooted vandals. A break-wire fence around your garden will alert you to marauding deer. A simple switch system at the henhouse may tell you when that pesky skunk is on the prowl for eggs.

We are all properly concerned about the rising incidence of "crime in the streets." Yet, statistically, the largest number of crimes are committed *off* the streets, as burglaries of home and places of business. In this area, we can create some alarming situations for uninvited guests. J.H.

See also: ELECTRONICS.

By-pass switch can be weatherproofed with cover designed for outside sockets. A cover also camouflages switch, and can be padlocked for added security during extended absence from home.

WHERE TO FIND IT

Burglar alarm kits are available from electronic supply houses, such as Lafayette or Allied, and from some local burglar alarm installation companies. Check the Yellow Pages.

The unit described here is Lafayette's moderate-cost Alert DC-6. It includes 12 contact switches and 750 feet of wire, but a by-pass switch lock (recommended) is extra. The switch allows you to enter the house without triggering the alarm. Write to Lafayette Radio Electronics, P.O. Box 10, Syosset, Long Island, New York 11791. A fire sensor for the DC-6 is available from the equipment's manufacturer, MRL, Inc., 7227 Lee Highway, Falls Church, Va. 22046.

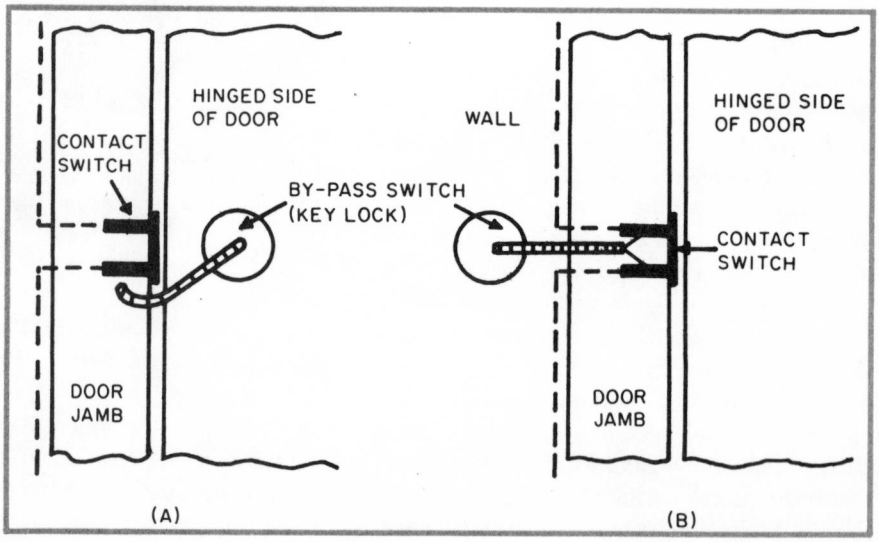

Place the by-pass switch that enables you to enter house without triggering alarm near or on your most used door. Installation is simplest on door (A); the contact switch is shorted by connecting cable. Switch mounted on wall (B) involves more work but eliminates a dangling cable and jutting wires.

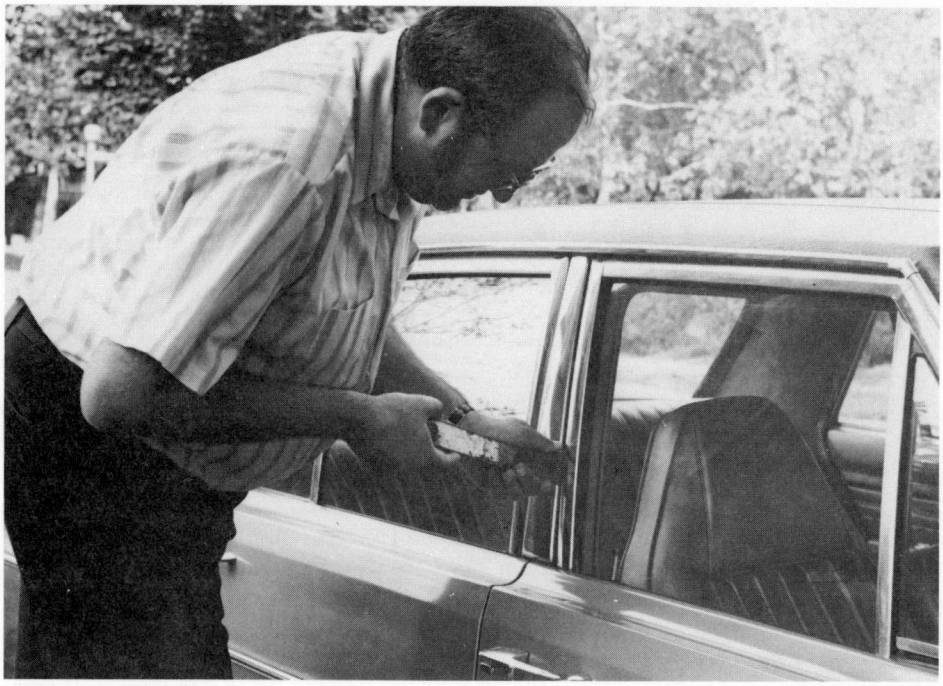

Install a Burglar Alarm in Your Car

Shrill alarm sounds whenever trunk, hood or doors are tampered with

TWO HOURS of work and a modest investment can put a theft alarm in your car that will sound whenever anyone tampers with the doors, trunk or hood. It will keep on sounding until you turn it off with a key.

In addition, the switch key on the fender next to the driver's door tells a would-be thief: "Careful. This car is wired for sound. Try something easier."

Unike some other alarms, this one cannot be silenced by a piece of tape holding down a trip switch or by the reclosing of an opened door. Turning it off requires either a key, or a hard yank on the right wires. And, if the wires are concealed, no thief will want to take the time to find them while the siren is churning out its loud, shrill warning.

How it works. The schematic diagram shows how the siren and locking circuits work (also, see "Electronics"). M1, an electronic siren module, in conjunction with speaker SPKR, comprise the *siren.* The positive voltage input is fed through S1, a key-lock switch, to the module. R1 is simply a dropping resistor for the module which works best with a 6- to 10-volt input.

The negative battery connection to the

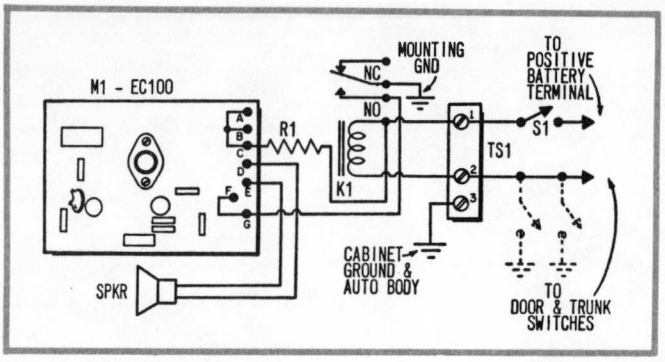

Noisemaker of the Auto Siren Sentry is the Eico EC 100 module (M1) that drives the speaker. Relay K1 keeps siren sounding even if car door is reclosed.

siren module is made through normally closed pushbutton switches, like those used to turn on courtesy lights when a door is opened (these switches are indicated by the dotted lines in the schematic).

Trace the circuit through. Note that when a door is opened, the associated switch connects terminal 2 of terminal strip TS1 to ground—completing the power connection to the module and the siren "sounds off." Also note that when terminal 2 is grounded relay K1 is energized, pulling down K1's armature or wiper contact. When the moving contact touches this normally open terminal (#2) it parallels the door and trunk switches and "permanently" grounds the relay and the module's ground connection —the siren keeps sounding even if the door is closed (opening the switch). The only way K1 can be released—to turn off the *Auto Siren Sentry*—is by interrupting the positive battery connection by opening key switch S1.

Protecting the user. Since key-switch S1 is mounted on the fender—and you want it there for all to see—it protects the user against the embarrassment which might be caused by the siren going off as he attempts to leave the car (which will happen if the alarm switch is mounted inside the car). After the user leaves the car, the alarm is set by turning S1 to *on*. Before getting into the car, the driver then turns S1 to *off*. Naturally, if S1 is mounted inside the car the alarm will sound whenever the driver enters the car. Mount the key switch out on the fender for your own peace of mind.

Construction. Actually there isn't much involved in building the *Auto Siren Sentry*. The siren module is an Eicocraft Siren Module Kit—type EC100, which can be assembled in a matter of minutes. There is but a handful of components which are mounted on a pre-punched and "component position marked" printed circuit board. However, assemble only the board itself, do not make the external connections given in the instructions; the *Auto Siren Sentry* uses a simpler external wiring than that given with the module.

After the module is completed, connect a 10-inch length of black wire to terminal *G*, loop the wire under the board and solder the end to *F*. Connect a one-inch length of bare wire to *C*. Connect a bare-wire jumper from point *A* to point *B*. Then connect two wires of the same color to *D* and *E*, the speaker terminals. Note that the board shows the battery conncetion to *A* and *B;* ignore these instructions. In the *Auto Siren Sentry* the positive battery connection is the short bare wire at *C* while the negative battery connection is the black wire going to *F* and *G*.

After all cabinet holes are cut in the main section of a 3 x 5 x 7-inch aluminum cabinet, mount the siren module as shown in the photographs, with the bottom as close as possible to one side; use stand-offs between the board and the cabinet to avoid shorting the printed-circuit wiring. The stand-offs as well as the necessary mounting hardware are supplied with the module.

The speaker is a three-inch waterproof type. The speaker specified in the Parts List is supplied in a metal cabinet having an integral gimbal bracket. If the speaker is installed as shown, in an aluminum cabinet, place a piece of perforated phenolic board in front of the speaker, to prevent possible damage to the cone. (If desired, the speaker can be used in the cabinet supplied.) Mount the speaker cabinet near the radiator, facing outwards, and connect the speaker leads from the module to the terminals on the speaker cabinet.

The wiper contact on K1 is *automatically grounded* when the relay is mounted in the cabinet—the wiper contact is connected directly to the frame of K1.

While only a three-lug terminal strip is required if the speaker is mounted in the aluminum cabinet, we show a five terminal type in the photographs to illustrate the arrangement when an external speaker is used. The speaker would connect to the two terminals shown unused. To reduce the possibility of wiring errors, place the battery connections on opposite ends of TS1, as shown, with at least the switch terminal in between.

Install the *Auto Siren Sentry* on any convenient surface under the hood. Just make certain the alarm doesn't project above hood line or you won't be able to close it.

Installing the switches. Any existing door switch automatically becomes part of the *Auto Siren Sentry* when the wire from terminal 2 of TS1 is connected to the courtesy light circuit. These switches are the self-grounding type, always switching the ground lead of the courtesy lights: therefore, when you look at these switches you will see only *one* connecting wire. All other switches which may be added should be of the same type, self-grounding, with their leads connected to the wiring of any of the original door switches. Additional switches for the hood, trunk or rear doors can be purchased from your car dealer at nominal cost.

The key switch should be installed so some smart "cooky" can't jump the terminals. If the switch is installed in the part of the fender that faces the tire anyone can reach under the car and jump the terminals, making the alarm inoperative. Install the switch on part of the *double fender.* Part of each fender, near the door, is shielded by the sides of the firewall, and access to the space between the fender and firewall is only through a small area which is exposed when the door is open. Place the switch so that its terminals are in the concealed space.

Positive grounds. The circuit shown is for cars with the more common *negative* ground battery. If your car uses a positive ground battery simply reverse the connections to siren module terminals C and G.

Six-volt systems. If your car uses six-volts, eliminate R1—use a direct connection from terminal 1 of TS1 and use the alternate six-volt relay specified in the parts list. H.F.

See also: ELECTRONICS.

PARTS LIST — Construction Time: 2 hours

K1	S.p.d.t. relay (Potter and Brumfield RS5D—12VDC, Allied 41D5504—P&B RS5D-6VDC—Allied 41D5896 or equivalent)
M1	Siren Module EC 100 or equivalent
R1	10-ohm, 5 watt resistor
Spkr	Weatherproof speaker (Lafayette 44C-5201 or equivalent)
TS1	Terminal Strip
	3 x 5 x 7 inch aluminum chassis box
Misc.	Wire, solder, mounting hardware, solder jugs, etc.

Burglar-proof Your Car's Tape Player

This alarm requires only four components, and you can install it quickly

MOST of the fancy tape player lock-alarms are useless—they are too obvious, too easily bypassed, and are often stolen along with the tape player. Our AutoAlarm sounds a car's horn continuously if anyone removes the tape player. And once triggered, the horn can be turned off only by the AutoAlarm's switch.

All it takes is a few dollars worth of experimenter's components to throw together an AutoAlarm that will give you just about as much protection as you can get because it doesn't *look* like an alarm. Tucked away in the glove compartment or under the seat, a single wire runs to the tape player's case—a wire that looks as if it's an ordinary ground wire.

The entire AutoAlarm is assembled directly on the back of a SPST slide switch. The assembly can then be installed in any small metal or plastic cabinet. Silicon Controlled Rectifier SCR1 can be just about any type rated at 25 PIV (peak inverse volts), 5-Amps or higher, such as the HEP-R1220.

To identify the SCR leads, lay it flat on

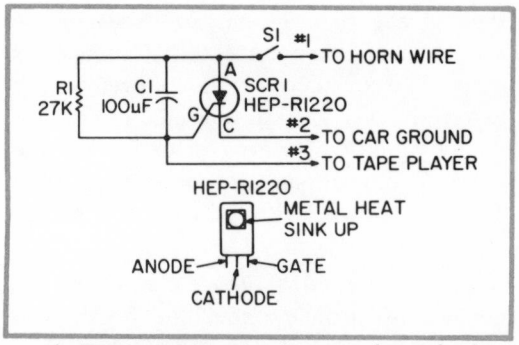

This simple circuit can be wired quickly. Switch S1 is closed for normal operation.

PARTS LIST	
C1	100-uF electrolytic capacitor 15 VDC or better
R1	27,000-ohms, 1/2-watt resistor
SCR1	HEP-R1220 or equivalent
S1	SPST slide switch (alarm off)
Misc.	Metal or plastic cabinet, wire, hardware, solder, etc.

the table so the side with the metal rim (around the mounting hole) faces up; the side *without* a rim should be against the table. The SCR leads will now conform to the layout shown.

No wiring precautions are necessary other than to doublecheck that the C1 polarity is correct; its positive terminal connects to SCR1's anode (A) terminal.

The other figure shows how to connect the AutoAlarm. Note that AutoAlarm wire #2, from SCR1's cathode, must connect to the car body (ground) while the #3 wire also connects to ground *but* through the tape player's case. Wire #1 connects to the horn control wire which generally enters at the bottom of the steering column (sometimes in the engine compartment, sometimes under the dash).

How it works. There is a positive voltage from the car battery across a horn button when it is open. By closing the horn button, the circuit is completed and the horn will sound. This positive voltage is applied to SCR1's anode. The SCR's gate is grounded through the tape player's case, so the SCR is normally off. When the tape player is removed from its mount, the AutoAlarm's #3 wire is disconnected from ground. The SCR gate is no longer grounded, so current can flow through R1 to the gate. The SCR turns on, effectively shorting its anode to its cathode. This means the horn control wire is now grounded, so the horn will sound.

Once the horn is sounded it can only be turned off by opening switch SW1.

To make it easy for the thief to trigger the AutoAlarm we suggest that the #3 wire be 22 or 24 gauge stranded—thin enough to be easily broken when the player is removed. The #1 and#2 wires should be 18 gauge stranded. H.F.

See also: ELECTRONICS.

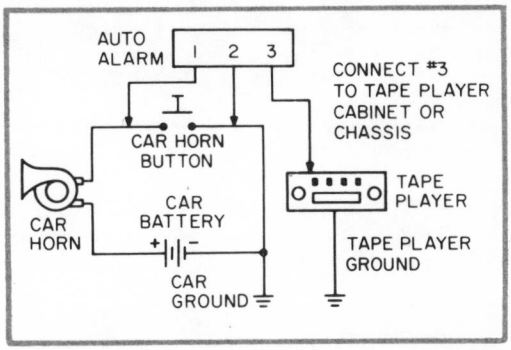

Intermediate solenoid found on most autos in place of horn in our simple diagram does not alter operation. Connect #1 to button. Remember, the curved side of electrolytic capacitor symbols, such as C1, represents the terminal that must be connected to the negative voltage (with respect to the plus capacitor connection). In this circuit, it means the negative terminal of capacitor C1 must be connected to the gate terminal of Silicon Control Rectifier SCR1 at left.

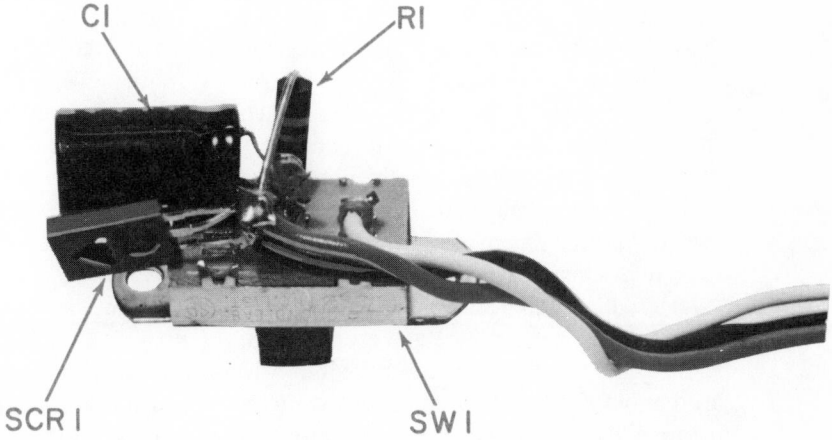

Here you can see just why we say, "Build it fast." And a simple three point installation means you install it fast, too! Count 'em, just four components and some wire make up this protective device that can save you a lot of grief over a lost, expensive player.

Interrupting the light from an ordinary bulb activates this alarm driver. Connect it to the Magnum alarm, and you've got a combination that will stun any burglar!

Light Sensor Alarm

This system's photocell "eyes" can detect an intruder's shadow as he passes an ordinary light bulb

YOU NEED PROTECTION? Don't pay the mob! Take the money and build the *Light Sensor,* an unusual burglar alarm you can construct in a few hours which will give protection for years to come.

The *Light Sensor* is a solid-state, battery-operated, light-activated intrusion burglar alarm system that's different from other light-alarm systems in use today. As a starter, there isn't an obvious light-beam that a burglar might notice and try to avoid. Neither is a special light source required—any common 117-vac lamp will do. And to top it off, the *Light Sensor* requires so little power that a single low-cost battery will operate it for months.

How it works. Perhaps the best way to explain the operation of the *Light Sensor* is to compare it to the human eye in a stationary position, looking at a light. All is fine as long as the light isn't interrupted, but let an object pass between the light source and the eye, and at that instant the light level reaching the eye is reduced, so the eye signals the brain to sound an alarm. Add to the alarm as many as three more such eyes and you have a system that compares to four tireless guards that cannot sleep or be diverted in any way.

Protection need not stop here. You can add as many closed-circuit protection switches as desired for both window and door protection, such as magnetic reed switches, pressure-sensitive switches, lead foil (used for glass-breakage detection), and any other suitable closed circuits, all of which must be wired in series and connected to one of the remote inputs, J1 through J4.

Putting it together. Today's burglar alarms need not have that typical "plain-Jane square-box" look as did the alarms of yesterday. You can go modern and build yours in a LMB CO-3 cabinet to match the author's model. Since housing or circuit layout isn't critical you can, if you wish, build your alarm in any suitable enclosure and use perfboard for the circuit wiring.

A printed-circuit board is available, with or without components.

If a printed-circuit board is used, just follow the component layout diagram, mount all parts on the board, and solder in place. Care should be taken when installing the semiconductors to insert the leads in the correct holes. Heat-sink each lead during soldering.

Lock switch S1 can be replaced by a lower cost switch, such as a standard toggle, hidden in an out-of-sight location so that it will not be obvious to an intruder.

Photocell mounting. Remote pickup *eyes* PE1-PE4 can be constructed in a variety of shapes to meet almost any specific requirement. Constructing the eyes is easy—just glue the photocell in one end of a light-tight paper or metal tube of the desired length, bring out the leads through spaghetti, and seal the end with either shrinkable tubing or electrical tape.

Sealing of the tubing is necessary to reduce the light leakage to the back end of the photocell that would cause a loss in sensitivity. It is very important that the *dark* resistance of the photocell be as high as possible for proper operation of the remote eye.

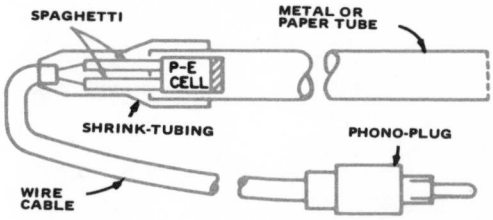

Construction details for a remote eye. Electrical tape can be used instead of shrink tubing to seal the end.

If the distance from the light source to the remote eye is great (over 25 feet) then the tubing should be 6 to 18 inches long. A 3- to 6-inch tube is suitable for shorter distances. The correct length of tubing can be determined by experimenting with different tube lengths and various light sources.

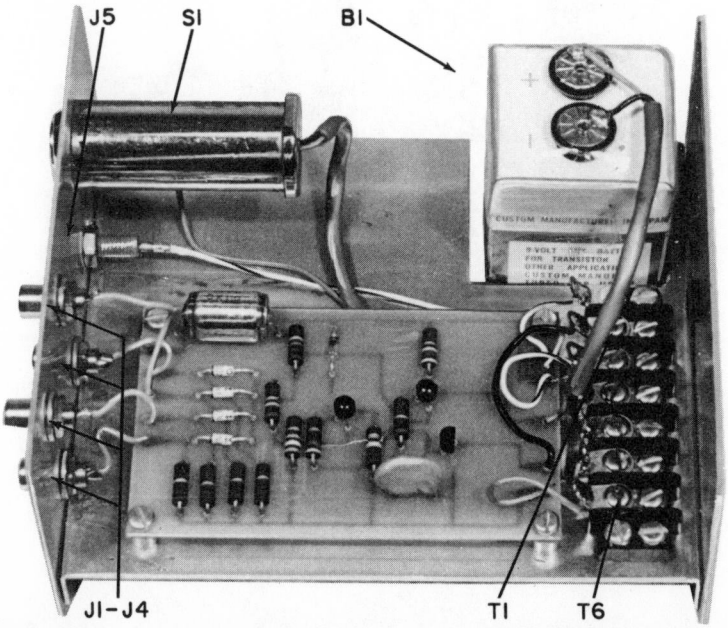

The circuit layout isn't critical, so the components could be mounted on perfboard and put in any convenient housing. Jack J6 is hidden by lock switch S1.

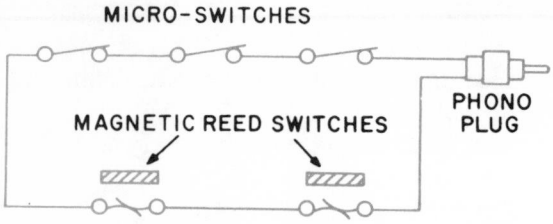

Doors and windows can also be protected with the Light Sensor by wiring normally closed switches in a closed circuit.

To simplify mounting of the remote eye, the photocell tubing can be assembled in a small mini-box with a two-wire cable connected to the photocell at one end and to a phono plug at the other.

If a low-wattage light source is used, or if the distance from the light to the photocell pickup is great, then the more sensitive CL603AL photocell should be used. If the distance is small, then use the less sensitive CL603A cell. These two photocells are far from the only suitable ones. You may find that most similar types of cells will work just as well.

Setting up the alarm system. The alarm unit can be placed in almost any convenient location, although it should not be placed in front of any of the remote eyes. Short all four input jacks J1-J4 and connect the battery to the alarm. Turn key switch S1 to the *on* position and monitor the voltage at the meter jacks J5 and J6, with a voltmeter set to the 10-VDC range. The voltage reading will represent the minimum reading obtainable under a non-alarm condition, and should be between one and five volts with all inputs shorted. Remove one of the jumpers from ground,

The remote pickup "eyes" can be built in a variety of ways, with the tube exposed as at left, or enclosed in a casing as shown at right.

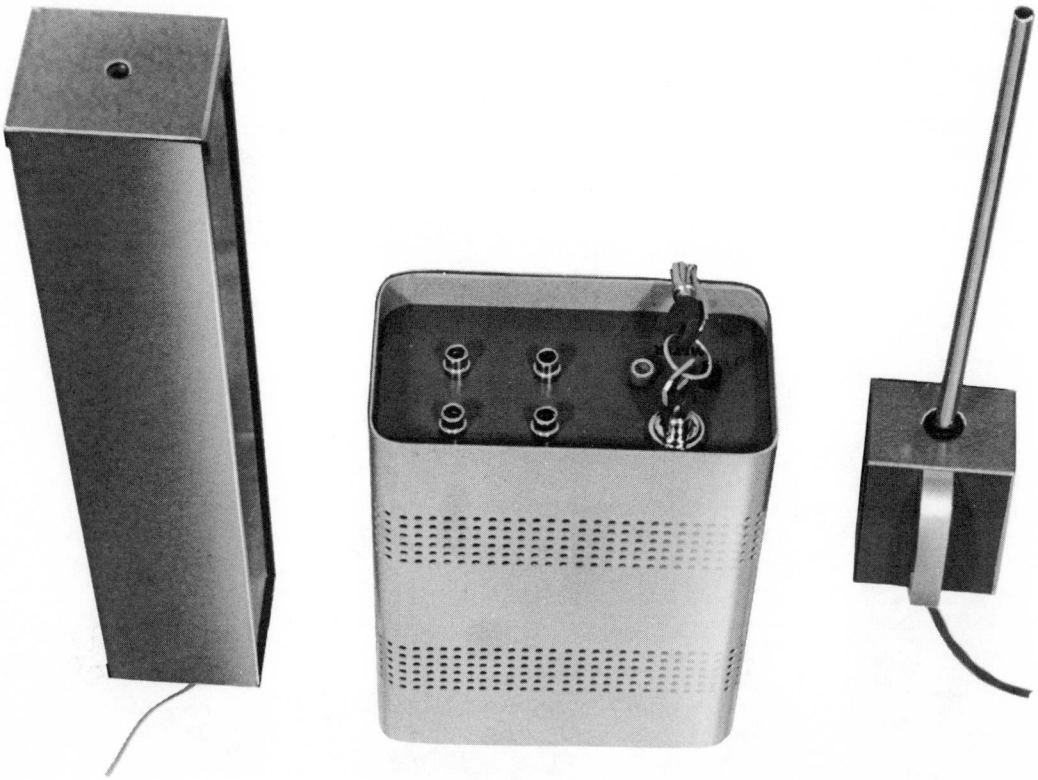

Light Sensor Alarm

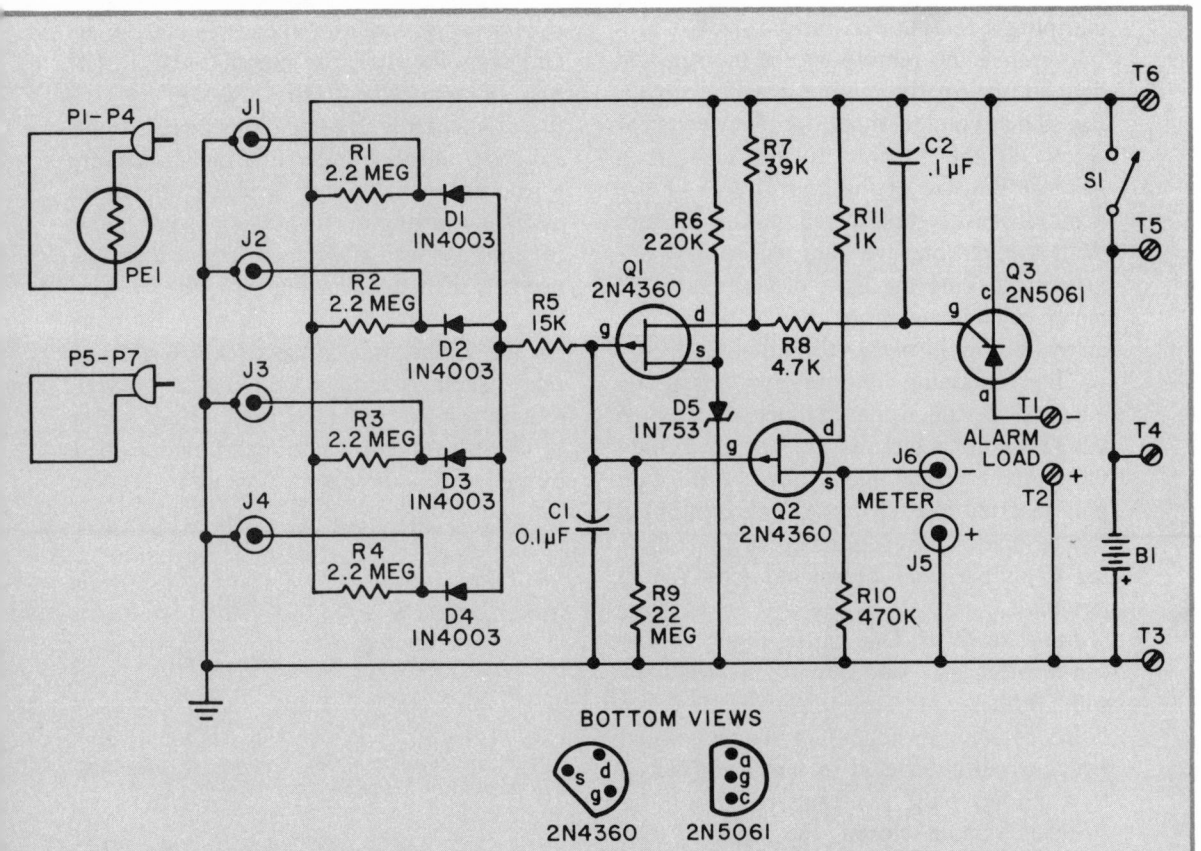

PARTS LIST

B1	9-volt transistor battery (Eveready 276 or RCA VS306)
C1	.01-uF, 600-volt polystyrene capacitor (Mallory)
C2	.1-uF disc capacitor
D1-D4	Silicon rectifier (Motorola IN4003 or HEP-156)
D5	Zener diode (Motorola IN753 or HEP-Z0214
Q1, Q2	P-channel field-effect transistor (Fairchild 2N4360)
Q3	.8 amp 60 PIV silicon-controlled rectifier (Motorola 2N5061 or HEP-R1002)
R1-R4	2,200,000-ohm, 1/2-watt 10%
R5	15,000-ohm, 1/2-watt 10%
R6	220,000-ohm, 1/2 watt, 10%
R7	39,000-ohm, 1/2 watt 10%
R8	4,700-ohm, 1/2-watt 10%
R9	22,000,000-ohm, 1/2-watt 10%
R10	470,000-ohm, 1/2-watt 10%
R11	1,000-ohm, 1/2 watt, 10%
PE1	CL603AL or CL603A (see text) Clairex Photocell
P1-P4	Phono plugs
P5-P7	Phono plugs with shorting wire
J1-J4	Phono jacks, chassis-mount type
S1	Lock switch
Misc.	Six-terminal barrier strip, LMB type CO-3 cabinet, wire solder, hardware, PE-cell housing (see text), etc.

and plug a remote eye into the jack. Carefully adjust the remote eye at the selected light source for the minimum voltage reading. This voltage must be five volts or below. If the reading is too high, then increase the size of the light source or use a more sensitive photocell in the pickup. With the remote eye plugged in and adjusted, blocking the light should cause the meter to indicate more than 6 volts. The alarm is now in *alarm* condition.

The remaining remote eyes must be adjusted in the same manner. If any of the J1-J4 input circuits are not used, then the unused inputs must have a shorting plug inserted in each jack. A shorting plug can be made from a photo plug by soldering a jumper wire between the two plug terminals.

Input switches. One of the input circuits can protect all your doors and windows with either pressure-sensitive switches (such as Microswitches) or magnetic-reed switches, all connected in series and wired to a phono plug. As long as all of the switches remain closed, the alarm is set. If only one of the switches opens, the alarm is then latched in the *alarm* condition and will remain so until reset with the key switch.

Alarm sounder. When it comes to choosing the type of audible alarm that may be connected to the *Light Sensor,* it's dealer's choice. By far the cheapest and simplest alarm sounder to connect directly to the unit is a Mallory *Sonalert* solid-state audible warning device, which is just great for inhouse use. If a much louder alarm is needed, then hook up the *Magnum.*

Low-voltage alarm bells may be connected to the unit by using a low-current relay, such as a Sigma 11F-1000-G SIL, to control the bell's current. Other types of alarm sounders could also be controlled by the relay—the choice is yours! C.D.R.

See also: ELECTRONICS; HOME SECURITY SENSORS.

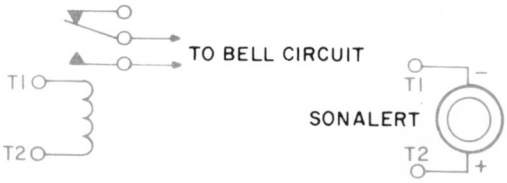

▲ *For an audible alarm, connect a relay and bell circuit, or a Sonalert, to T1 and T2.*

▼ *Placement of parts on printed-circuit board. Drill holes in corners for mounting. The board is available, with or without parts—see parts list for details. The foil pattern is exact size, and can be used to make your own printed-circuit board.*

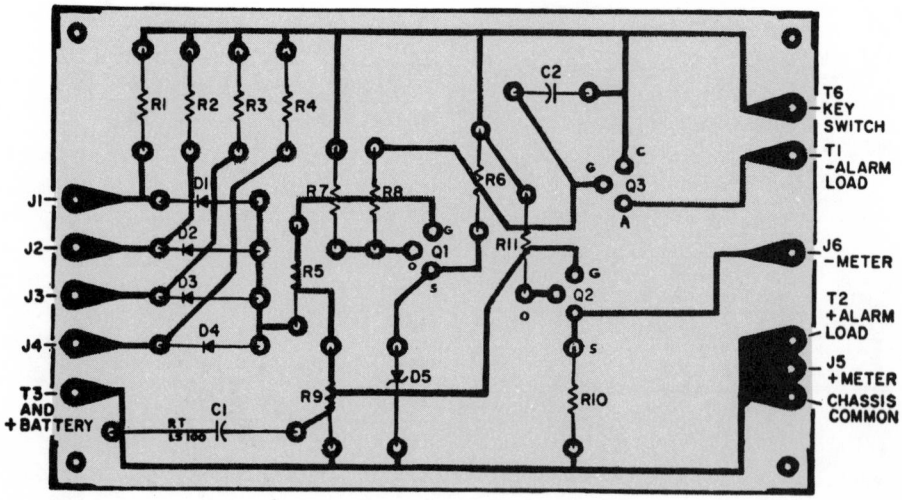

This is the utimate in charging systems—an alternator with built-in voltage regulation.

Maintaining Alternator Output

This job is advanced for a novice, but an experienced weekend mechanic can handle it

VIRTUALLY ALL CARS built in recent years (Volkswagen a notable exception) have AC generators, commonly called alternators.

The alternator electrical system represents a high achievement in obtaining the most electrical power from a minimum draw on engine output. It has been termed the ultimate electrical power source for automotive use.

The alternator offers the potential for longer battery life in addition to its primary advantage—higher output. The higher output is due to the comparatively low weight of the rotor and coil assembly allowing greater pulley ratios for higher rpm. The result, of course, is higher output—even at engine idle. Maintaining the advantage an alternate gives your electrical system is just a matter of knowing the alternator and keeping it in top tune.

Construction. All alternators consist of a stator, which corresponds to the generator's field circuit, and a rotor, which corresponds to the generator's armature. The only essential difference between the two is the method used to convert alternating current to direct current. Alternator construction can be seen in the accompanying illustrations.

In generators, as you've seen, brushes are used to pick the alternating current off a commutator, converting that current to direct. Alternators, however, employ silicon rectifiers or, for short, diodes. Don't be confused by the fact that alternators also contain brushes because they are used for a different purpose than in a generator. Alternator brushes supply field current to the rotor by connecting two slip rings mounted concentrically on the rotor shaft.

The rectifier in the alternator is a chemical disc that changes alternating current to direct current since it permits current to

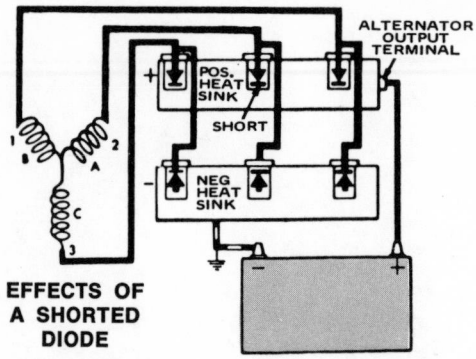

Shorted diode will allow current to flow in both directions. It will flow back to the A winding instead of to the battery.

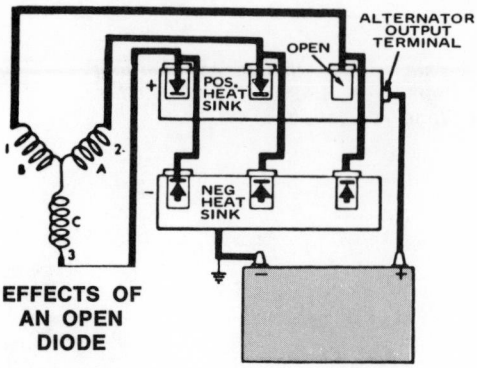

Open diode will not let current flow in either direction. The circuit is not complete through the B winding to battery.

The diode, also called rectifier, converts the AC output of the alternator into DC by permitting current to flow only one way.

flow in one direction only. In other words, the rectifiers used in alternators have a low resistance to the flow of electrical current in one direction and a high resistance to the flow of electrical current in the other direction.

This low resistance allows current to flow from the alternator to the battery, but the rectifier's high resistance prevents a return flow from the battery to the alternator when battery current exceeds alternator output, as it does when the engine idles.

Both alternator and generator have regulator units, but the makeup of each is different. One difference is the absence of a circuit breaker (the cut-out relay) in the alternator regulator.

In the generator's regulator, as you've seen, the circuit breaker connects and disconnects the battery and generator at the proper time. Since the alternator is self-rectifying, though, allowing current to flow only in one direction—toward the battery—there is no need for a circuit breaker. The constant, steady flow of current from the alternator to the battery allows the battery to maintain a full state of charge.

Another difference is the absence of a current regulator. The alternator cannot overcharge so long as the voltage regulation is correct, so there is no need for other than a voltage regulator.

The simple requirements of the alternator for regulation hastened the development of the fully-electronic voltage regulator.

Now used on virtually all cars with alternators, the fully-electronic regulator has no vibrating contacts and is not adjustable. Either it works or it doesn't, and it usually does.

On most cars, the fully-electronic regulator is either a plug-in to the alternator or built into it.

The service information in this article on voltage regulators, therefore, refers to the vibrating contact type used through the 1960's.

Maintenance. The alternator is no harder to tune than the generator. If trouble is apparent, you don't usually have to replace the entire unit. The unit breaks into two parts—the stator and rotor—allowing you to replace the one that is giving the trouble.

In many cases, you don't even have to replace one of those major components. A common problem, low output, is normally traced to either of two things: a slipping fan belt or defective diodes (rectifiers).

Fan belt tension is critical with the

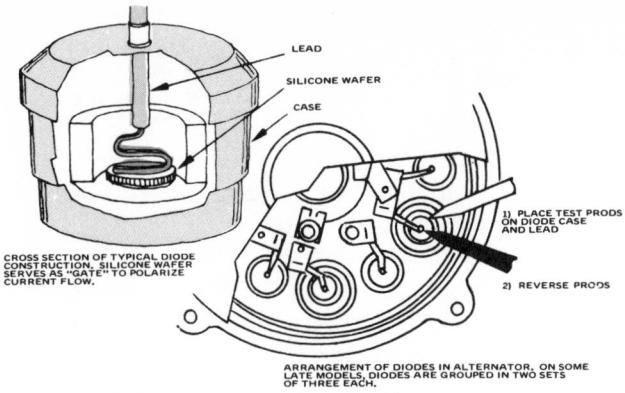

◄ Top: Testing diode requires a 12-volt test lamp with battery built in or a third connector for car's battery. Test prods should be touched at points shown in illustration, then reversed. Test lamp bulb should light in only one direction. If it fails to light in either connection, or lights in both connections, at least one diode in a group is defective. Center: Defective diode replacement is not for the weekend mechanic, as special tools to press out and install are necessary. Bottom: Alternator rotor should be checked for internal ground—a defect—with diode test lamp, as shown. If lamp lights, stator is internally grounded and should be replaced.

▼ Alternator output test requires an ammeter and voltmeter, connected as shown, and a fully-charged battery. Carbon pile is a load-adjusting rheostat, but you can also load battery by turning on accessories and lights. For this test, disconnect battery cables and alternator connections. On some GM Delcotron alternators, field terminal has "2" below it; on all others, the letter "F" is used. When fully loaded, alternator should put out within three amps of specifications. If five amps or more below specifications, bad diode is indicated.

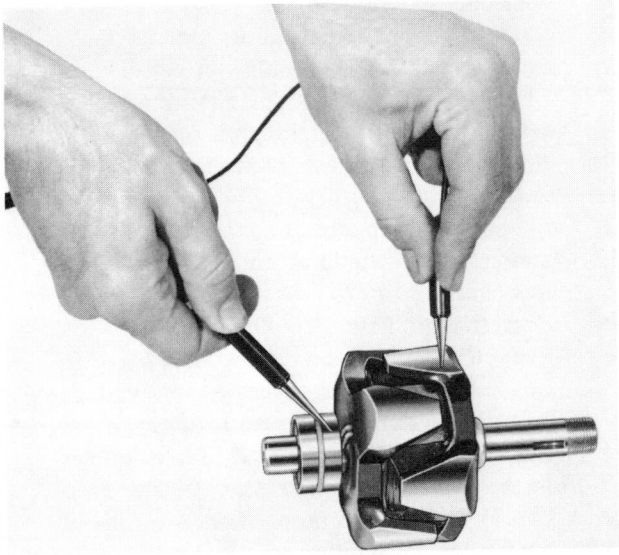

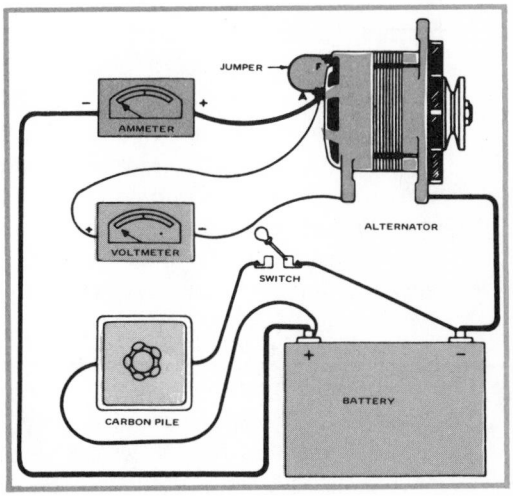

alternator. Always make sure the belt is in good condition and adjusted to specification.

The one precaution you must keep in mind when working with the alternator is guarding against reverse polarity. Reverse the polarity of the alternator or the battery for even an instant and you stand a chance of burning out the rectifiers. To prevent accidental grounding, furthermore, you should always use insulated tools when working in the area of the alternator.

Following adjustment of the fan belt, turn your attention to the regulator. Make sure all connections at this unit are tight. Follow this by checking the condition of the regulator points. If you find they're burned or pitted, you'll have to replace the regulator. Now, check and tighten all connections including those to the ignition switch, the ballast resistor, the regulator and the conducting surfaces of the fuse and holder.

Unscrew the brushes from the alternator and inspect them for wear. If worn, replace them.

In some cars, the brushes can be removed from the alternator with the unit in the car. This is done by unscrewing the external cap screws to which the brushes are attached. In other cars, the unit must be removed from the car to reach the brushes, which can then be unscrewed.

If it becomes necessary to take the unit apart, remove it from the car and split it open, separating the stator from the rotor. Test the rectifiers first. This can be done with a commercial diode tester, although you can also use any continuity tester, such as an ohmmeter or a test lamp that plugs into household current. The test connections are illustrated.

If a diode is defective, it must be replaced. This requires special tools and should be left to a professional shop.

Next inspect the stator wiring carefully for breaks. To be absolutely sure there are none, you should test from the stator leads to the stator core with a 110-volt test lamp or other suitable tester. If the lamp lights, the stator is grounded and should be replaced.

Finally, test the field windings in the rotor part of the alternator. This is done with an ammeter hooked to the alternator battery output terminal while turning the rotor shaft by hand. The correct field current draw should be recorded on the meter. This reading differs from car to car, so check your service manual.

The above description tells you what to do if you are not getting output from the alternator. However, there are things a faultily adjusted or malfunctioning alternator can cause—most can be checked on the car.

Low charging rate. A low charging rate is indicated when the ammeter or trouble light in your car begins to show discharge at low engine speed and idle. It is also indicated if a battery gets run-down.

Look at the fan belt first and make sure it's properly adjusted. Then check the battery terminals where high resistance could be causing the trouble. Remove the cables and clean the terminals and posts. Make sure the ground cable is clean and tight.

Finally, check at the alternator for loose connections. If the trouble still persists, replace the brushes in the alternator since poor contact between brushes and slip rings is a major factor for a low charging rate. As a final tuneup procedure, remove the alternator from the car and check the stator. Open windings cause an unsteady low charging rate.

If the ammeter trouble light flicks on and off at all speeds and you get a run-down battery, which indicates low voltage output, check the regulator first. To do this, hook the negative lead of a voltmeter to the battery's negative post and the positive to the positive post. Connect a jumper wire from the ignition terminal to the field terminal on the regulator and then start the engine. The voltmeter should read about 14 to 15 volts for a 12-volt charging system. If not, the regulator is faulty. Try adjusting the regulator points; if that does not increase the voltage output, get a new regulator.

But if the regulator does check out, go to the alternator and tighten all connections. The trouble could also be a shorted rectifier or grounded stator, so check them as well.

High charging rate. It is possible for the alternator to throw out too much charge. An over-charge condition will show up by acid salts on the battery and the battery beginning to use too much water. Check the regulator first; if it's set too high, adjust the points. If this doesn't help, don't scrap the regulator yet.

First remove the unit and clean its mounting surface. A poorly grounded regulator could be causing the problem. If not, the problem is either that the regulator points are stuck or that there are open windings in the unit. If so, replace the regulator.

If the battery is using too much water or a lot of acid salts begin to form, it could also mean that the regulator points are oxidizing. The cause could be a loose or dirty ground connection, so clean the mounting surface and tighten all attaching bolts. Now, test the regulator. If the meter shows a high voltage, set the points.

Finally, check and adjust the regulator air gap to specification as given in your car's manual. To do this, connect a test lamp between the regulator ignition and field terminals. Insert the proper wire gauge (one of 0.48 inch). Press the armature plate down. The contacts should open and the test lamp should dim.

Now, insert a larger wire gauge in the same position (usually one of .052 inch). Depress the armature plate. The upper contact should be closed and the test lamp should remain lighted. If the air gap doesn't check out, adjust it by bending the upper contact support until you get the right openings and test readings.

Another reason for oxidized points could be shorted field windings in the rotor pole. In this case, the rotor has to be replaced.

Again, excessive use of water by the battery and acid salts on the battery are indications of another condition—burned regulator points. The trouble is probably a regulator set too high or shorted field windings in the rotor pole. In the former case, adjust the points—in the latter, replace the rotor.

Mechanical problems. An alternator that is noisy is one that is either loose on its mountings or one that has internal problems. First check the mounting bolts and make sure the alternator is tightly connected. The drive pulley could also be causing the noise, so ensure that it is tight.

If this fails to stop the noise, remove the alternator from the car and break it open. Inspect the rotor fan blades. If bent, replace the rotor. Now test each rectifier for a short. If this doesn't stop the trouble, the problem is a sprung rotor shaft, worn shaft bearings or open or shorted windings in the stator and a rubbing rotor pole.

In the event of a sprung rotor shaft, replace the rotor. If the problem boils down to worn shaft bearings, you can have them replaced too. If, though, the stator windings are shorted and the rotor poles are rubbing, you'll have to replace the entire alternator.

If the battery keeps running down for no rhyme or reason, it indicates that the regulator points are stuck closed. This was probably caused by a poor ground connection between the alternator and regulator. Replace the regulator and make sure the new unit is properly grounded so the trouble doesn't recur. P.W.

See also: ENGINE; ELECTRICAL, AUTO.

How to Make Screens and Storm Windows

Do the job yourself with inexpensive aluminum components and a few simple tools

Completed screen is hung from brackets at top and held by hook and eye fasteners at the bottom.

ONE EASY and satisfying way to save money on home maintenance and improvement is to make your own interchangeable window screens and storm sashes using maintenance-free aluminum construction materials that are available at any large hardware store. Only a few simple hand tools are needed.

The following discussion applies primarily to the making of full-size screens for installation on conventional double-hung windows. But screens for any other type of window can be made as easily, following the additional tips provided at the end of this article. Surprisingly, constructing storm sashes is even more of a breeze than making the screens. The only important point to bear in mind is that you need one type of framing material to hold screening, and a different type for glass (see diagram). The corner locking pieces and hanger units are identical in each case.

To avoid wasting material, rough-measure your window height and width to determine whether the six- or eight-foot lengths of framing material will be more economical. Re-measure the windows just outside the blind stops more carefully when you are ready to cut the framing to proper size. Make the vertical and horizontal sections all ⅛-inch shorter than the actual window measurements to avoid an over-tight fit. After removing the U-shaped spline that locks in the screening, mark 45-degree angles at the measured points so that the edge forming the channel accepting the spline becomes the shorter of the two sides. Cut accurately along the 45-degree lines using a hacksaw. If you plan to make many screens and/or storm sashes, the construction of a simple miter box (see photo) will save much time and ensure precise cuts. De-burr the cut ends with a file or sandpaper.

To assemble the frame, push a corner lock into each end of one short side, add vertical members to the exposed portions of the corner locks, and finish off by pushing on the other end piece to which corner locks have been added. Check all corners to make sure they form good right angles. The frame is now ready for addition of the screening if the screen area is six square feet or less. A cross brace should be added to larger screens, as shown. Just notch back two ends of a length of framing material to form ⅝-inch lips to overlap the basic frame. Drill a hole

ammunition: see reloading
amplifiers: see high fidelity systems
anemometer: see wind gauge
animal toys: see handicrafts
animal tracks: see wildlife

in each lip to accept a #6 ⅜-inch aluminum sheet metal screw, and smaller pilot holes in appropriate positions on the frame. Note that the screening is *not* attached to this brace.

During the following operations, make certain that the weave of the screening runs parallel to the frame channels, and try to cut carefully between two adjacent screen wires to help keep the screening square. Ordinary household shears can be used to cut the screening.

Start by aligning the selvedge edge, or a pre-cut straight edge, along one long channel so that the screening just covers the channel opening. When this edge is pressed into the channel later, it will fit down against the inside edge of the groove *only*; do not allow it to run across the bottom of the channel. While holding the screen in place, cut about two inches up an adjacent side, then snip a small triangular bit of screening off the corner to avoid bunching inside the channel.

Use an ordinary putty knife to press the selvedge or pre-cut edge into the groove. This is easier if you lay a strip of ¼-inch thick plywood above and below the screen as shown. Try to obtain a neat right-angle bend. Lock this edge of screening in place by inserting the proper length of spline which has been square-cut to run the full length of the channel. Tighten the spline by tapping a length of ¼-inch thick plywood laid atop the spline. To avoid dents, slightly round the edges and ends of the plywood.

Before cutting and locking in the other edges in the same manner, place some scraps of aluminum framing, or wood scraps of the same thickness, under the screening to keep it from sagging during the finishing operations. Cut the screening along the two short edges so that the edges can be shaped neatly along the inside walls of the channels. Lock in place with splines, and then complete assembly of the fourth side in the same manner.

MATERIALS FOR SCREENS

	Reynolds No.
Aluminum screen framing complete with spline:	
6 ft. lengths	6020
8 ft. lengths	6021
Corner locks (4 per frame)	7210
Hangers (2 units per frame)	7215
Aluminum screen cloth	
Small hooks with screw-eyes (2 each per frame)	

Aluminum screens and storm windows are assembled in about the same way, but screen uses a different frame member (left) than the storm window (right).

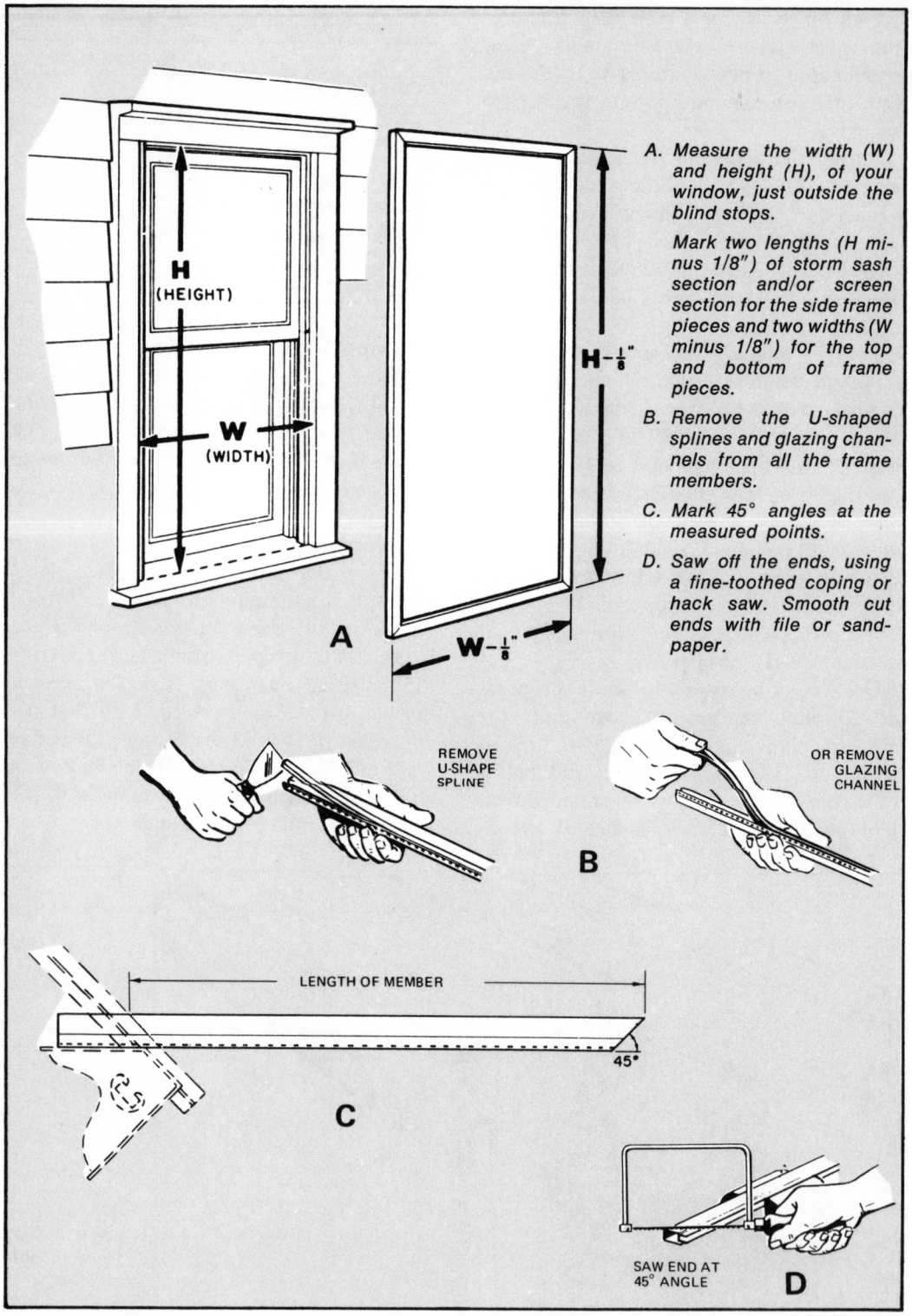

A. Measure the width (W) and height (H), of your window, just outside the blind stops.

Mark two lengths (H minus 1/8") of storm sash section and/or screen section for the side frame pieces and two widths (W minus 1/8") for the top and bottom of frame pieces.

B. Remove the U-shaped splines and glazing channels from all the frame members.

C. Mark 45° angles at the measured points.

D. Saw off the ends, using a fine-toothed coping or hack saw. Smooth cut ends with file or sandpaper.

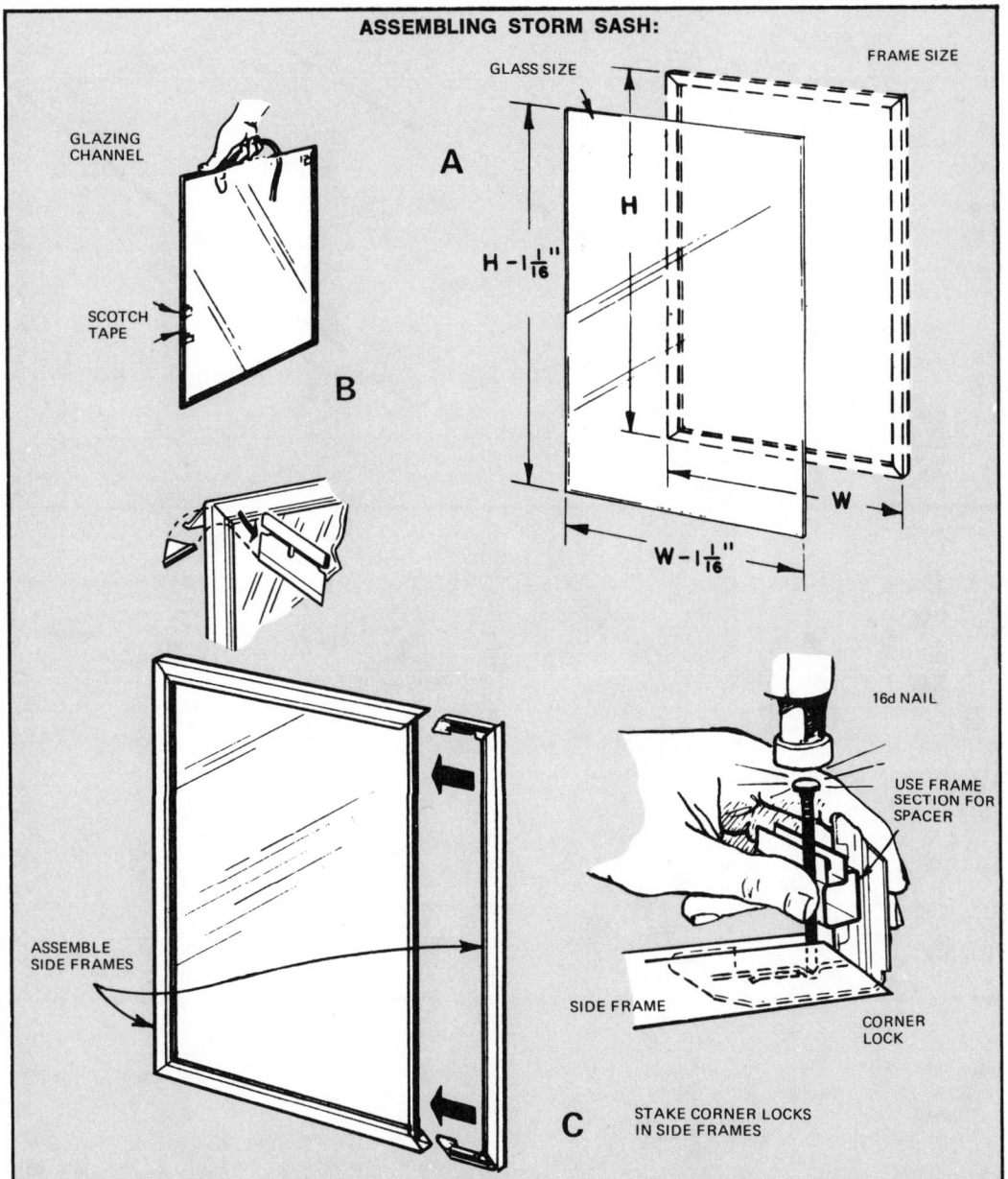

A. Order glass 1-1/16" less than the frame size, in each direction. Use single-strength glass for small (up to 9 sq. ft.) panes; double-strength for large (over 9 sq. ft.) panes.

B. Starting at one corner, fit glazing channel around edges of glass. Make pie cuts at corners.

C. Insert the corner locks into the two side frames. Stake corner lock in place with nail mark—just behind the edge of the corner lock web.

Center end frame members over top and bottom edges of the glass, so they will match with side members.

Add side frame members (with corner locks already in place) to complete assembly.

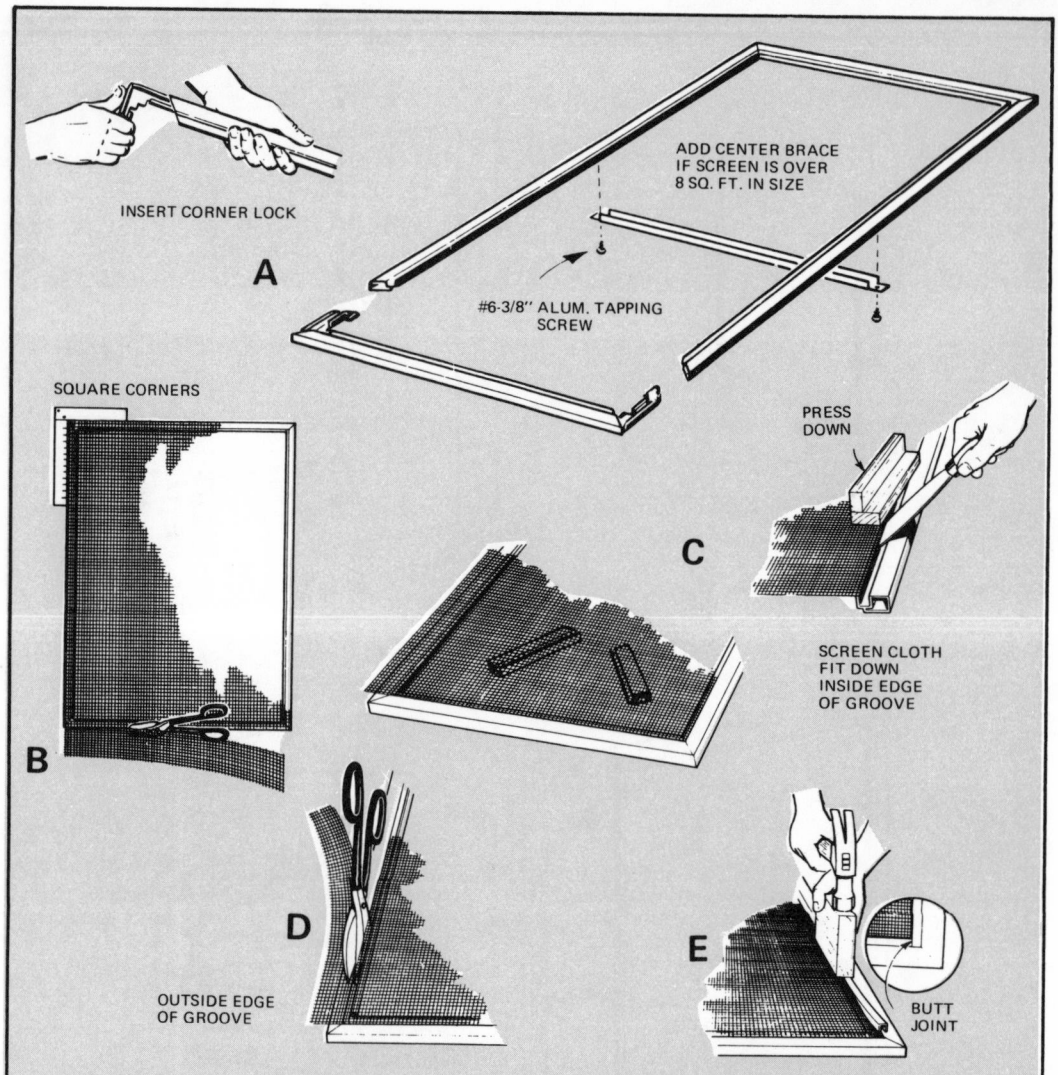

A. Insert corner locks into the two short frame pieces. Slip the two long frame pieces onto one of the end pieces. Finally add the other end as shown to complete the frame.

B. Cut screening to outside dimensions of frame. Cut carefully between two screen wires to keep screening square.

Place frame on table and scatter scraps of frame section in the center area to hold screening level with top of frame.

C. Line up screening with the outside edge of the screen groove, at the side and end of the frame shown. Bend the screening into the side and end grooves.

CAUTION: *Screening is to fit down inside edge of groove only.*

D. After completing operation along one side (as in step above), cut off excess screen cloth along line even with outside edge of groove in other adjacent leg.

E. Cut U-shaped splines to length of spline groove; make butt joints at the corners.

Next, tap spline into groove (on one long frame piece) to hold screening securely.

In the same manner, form screen cloth on the two short sides, cut off excess screen cloth and insert spline. Then, complete fourth side.

A. Screw fasten the jamb hanging brackets into place, 1" in from the side (as shown) and with the back edges against the blind stop.

B. Position the top rail brackets flush with the top of the frame. Punch screw holes in the frame at top of slots with a 4d nail. Attach with sheet metal screws.

C. To install screens or storm windows, angle bottom edge out about 45° to engage top brackets; swing bottom end in.

D. Bottom hooks: Using a 4-penny nail, punch holes close to glass or spline groove 4" from each side. Screw in the hooks. Install the screen or storm window and position the screw eyes so the hooks hold the panel tightly in place.

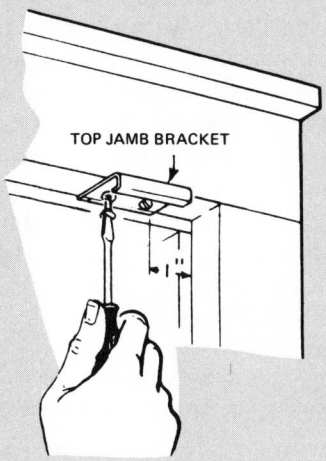

A.

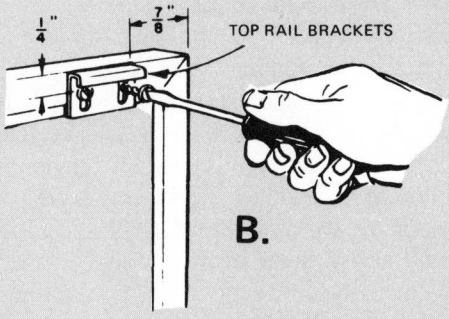

B.

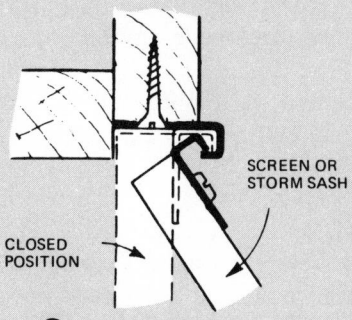

C.

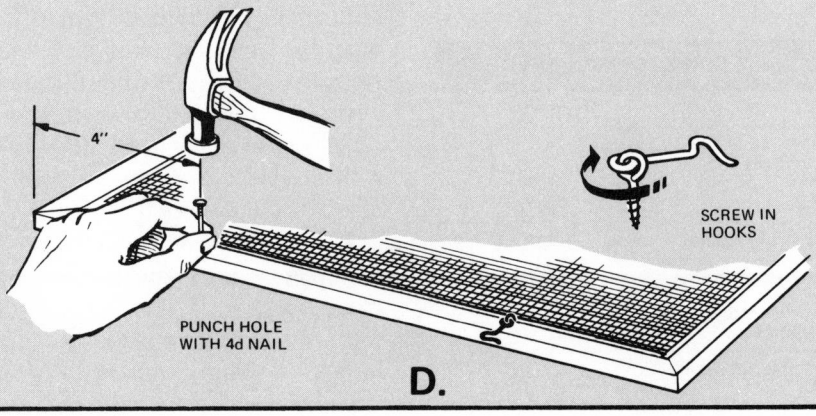

D.

Two screen brackets, used to hold the screen on the window framing, are attached to the top rail of the screen. Place these $3\frac{15}{16}$-inches from the ends of the screen, and flush with the top of the rail. Mark hole positions at the top of the bracket slots, and punch screw holes in the screen frame using a 4-penny nail. Attach the brackets with ⅜-inch self tapping screws. The other half of each bracket is attached to the window jamb, on the underside of the window casing and 4 inches from the side casings. Put the back edge tight against the blind stop. Fasten in place using ¾-inch wood screws.

Two hook-and-eye catches are used on the bottom edge of the screen. Place each 4 inches from a lower corner. Use a 4-penny nail to punch pilot holes close to the spline groove to accept the hook. After the screen is hung, locate proper position of the eye on the window framing.

Storm windows. Frames for storm windows are made in the same manner as those for screens, except that you use aluminum framing material shaped a bit differently; it has a glazing channel to hold the glass. Make the frame for a window ⅛-inch shorter than the width and height measurements just outside the blind stops, as before. Check the *outside* dimensions of the frame, and order glass measuring $1\frac{1}{16}$-inch less than these two frame dimensions.

MATERIALS FOR STORM SASHES

	Reynolds No.
Aluminum storm sash framing with glazing channel:	
6 ft. lengths	6041
8 ft. lengths	6042
Corner locks (4 per frame)	7210
Hangers (2 units per frame)	7215
Small hooks with screw-eyes (2 each per frame)	
Single- or double-strength glass	

Use single-strength glass for frames up to nine square feet in area, double-strength glass for larger panes.

Fit the flexible glazing channel (removed from the framing material before the metal is cut to frame size) around the glass, starting at one corner. At each corner, snip out a small pie-shaped piece from the front and rear of the channel to form a neat beveled turn. Insert corner locks into the two side (longer) sections of framing, staking them firmly in place with nail-formed indentations just behind the edge of each corner lock web. Now center the shorter frame sections onto the top and bottom edges of the glass, then add the longer side members to complete the assembly. The same types of hangers and hooks as used with screens are added to the top and bottom edges.

Half screens. You can save money on materials by making screens to fit only the lower halves of standard double-hung windows. You make the screen as before, but mount it differently. Install lengths of aluminum *channel* as sliding tracks on two sides of the window frame. Drill and countersink screw holes every six inches along the channel to accept ¾-inch aluminum wood screws. Before fastening the channels permanently in place, try inserting the screen. You will then see just how much you must notch out the top of each channel to permit insertion of the screen. *Important:* make the screen frame $\frac{3}{16}$-inch less than the opening between window blind stops to allow for the thickness of the channel. Insertion and removal of the screen is easier if the channel is lubricated with products available at gasoline stations or hardware dealers.

Basement windows. A storm sash and/or screen is fitted on the inside of a basement window if the window opens outward, and on the outside in the case of an inward-opening window. Measure the opening inside the window frame, then

➤ *Join adjacent screen frame members by simply pushing them on angular corner locks. Deburr the cut ends before joining them.*

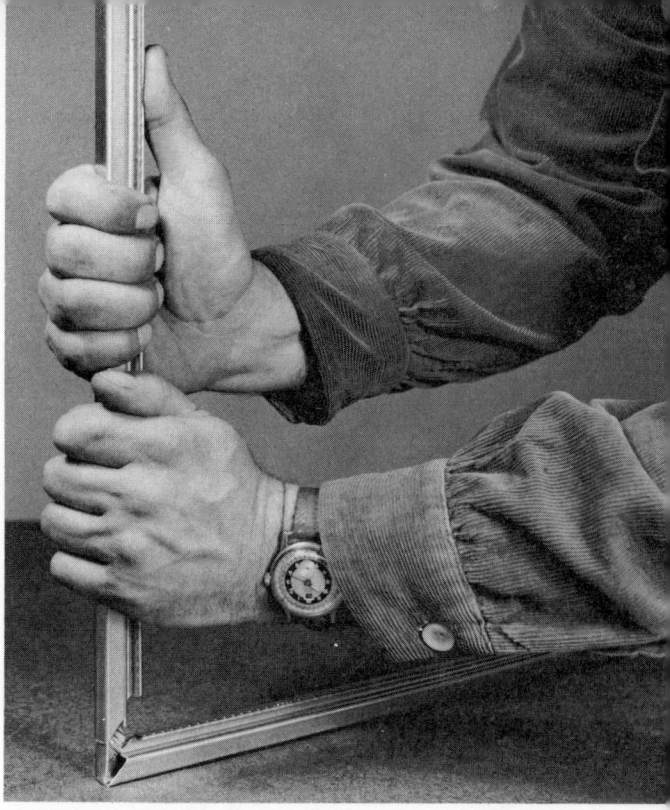

▲ *Make a 90-degree corner jig by nailing two strips of 1/4-inch thick plywood on working surface. This will improve accuracy and lighten your work load.*

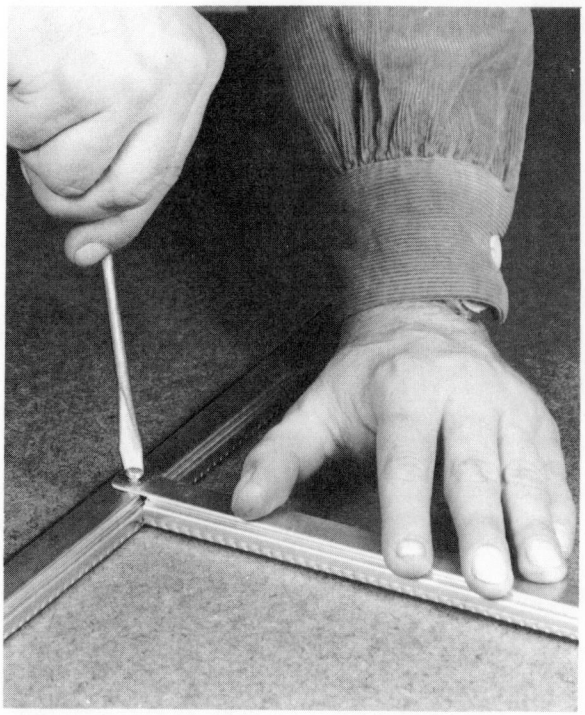

➤ *Screens greater than six square feet in area require cross braces. Use a framing section notched back 5/8-inch from each end and fastened to the frame as shown. The brace is attached on the back of the frame. Add the brace before the screening is installed, and do not fasten the screening to the brace.*

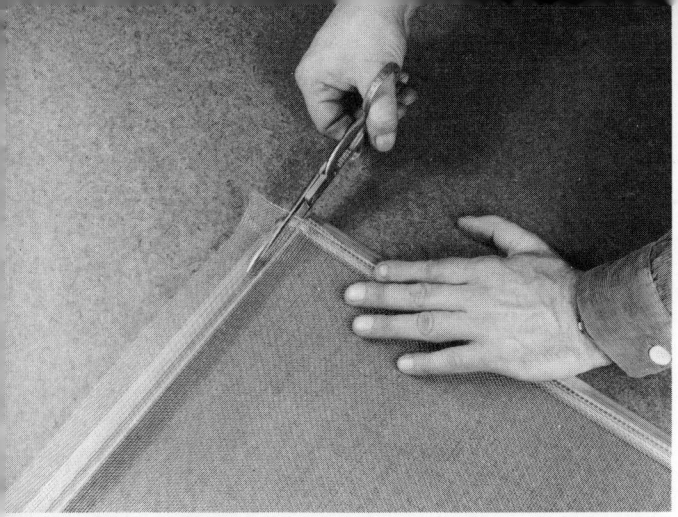

Align selvedged side of screening so that it just covers one long groove. Cut about two inches along the adjacent side and snip off a little of the corner so the screening will fold into the grooves without bunching. Cutting can be done with kitchen shears.

Press screening into groove with a putty knife so that it runs close to the bottom of the groove, but no further. Strips of wood 1/4-inch thick laid under and on top of the screening make it easy to fold neat 90-degree bends in the screening.

Spline locks screening into groove. Hammer a 1/4-inch thick length of plywood laid over the spline to drive it home. Round the edges of the plywood slightly to prevent it from marring the spline. Note that the spline is straight cut, not beveled.

How to Make Screens and Storm Windows

➤ ***Punch screw holes for screen brackets with a 4-penny nail, then attach the bracket with 3/8-inch self-tapping screws.***

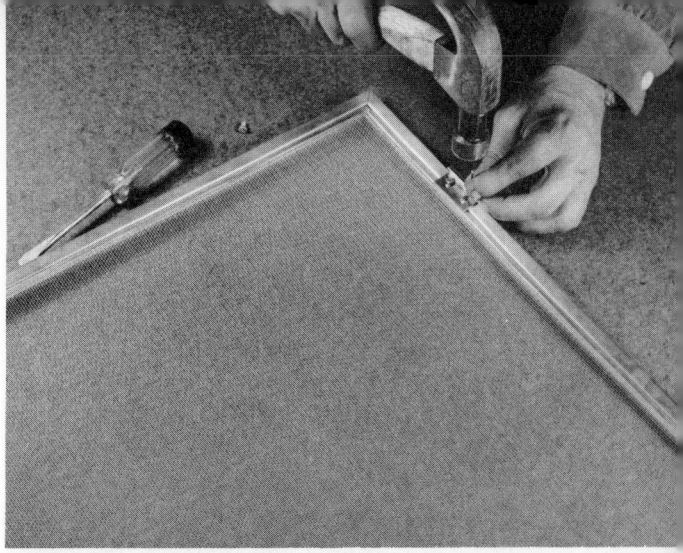

▲ ***Small hooks on bottom rail of screen engage with screw eyes fastened to window frame to hold screen in place. Screw the hooks into pilot holes made with a 4-penny nail.***

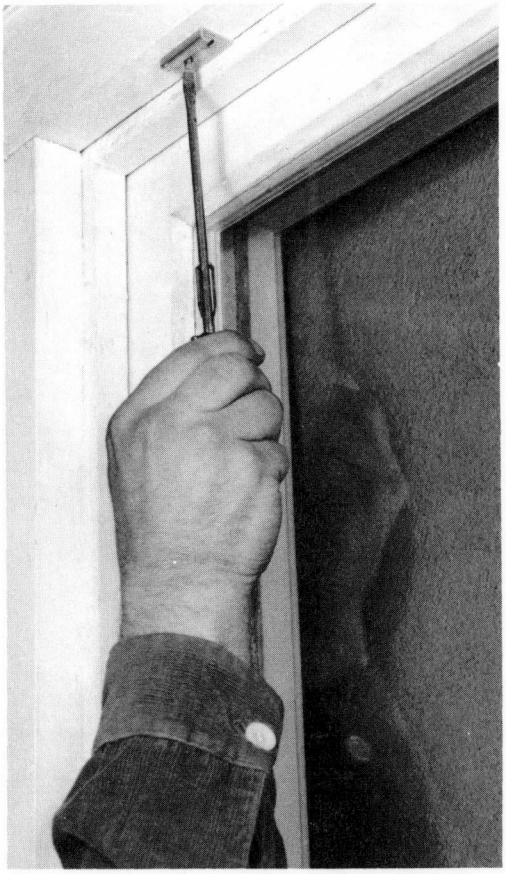

◄ ***Jamb brackets on underside of window casing engage screen brackets. They are attached with 3/4-inch wood screws.***

add ¾-inch to each dimension to provide a ⅜-inch overlap on all four sides of a *wooden* basement window frame. If you have metal window frames, they probably have holes for attaching screens or storm sash. Use self-tapping screws and clips made from 1 x 1 x 1/16-inch aluminum angle iron to install the storm sash on metal frames. Use round-head wood screws on wood window frames. Attach a strip of felt or rubber tape weather stripping around the edge of the storm sash between the sash and metal window frame. Frames for metal basement windows are made in the same manner as those used for casement windows.

Casement windows. Determine the width of a casement window storm sash by measuring between screw holes you will probably find on the sides of the window frame. For height, measure from top of the crank mechanism to the top of the window frame, then add ¼-inch for overlap at the top. The completed storm sash, or screen, is held in place with angle clips made from 1 x 1 x 1/6-inch aluminum angles. Use self-tapping screws to fasten these to the edges of the frame. Be sure to use felt or rubber stripping between the screen or storm sash frame and a *metal* window frame to prevent acceleration of corrosion that occurs when dissimilar metals are in contact.

Awning windows. If your awning window opens outward, fit the storm sash or screen around the blind stop on the inside. It may be necessary to fit a wood filler strip on the window sill to clear the crank. Drill a hole through the wood for the crank.

Measure the width of the window opening just inside the blind stop and cut the top and bottom sections of the frame ⅛-inch shorter than this dimension. Measure the height from the top of the wood filler strip to the top of the window opening, just inside the blind stop. Make the side pieces of the frame ⅛-inch shorter than this measurement. Attach a strip of felt or rubber weather stripping along the bottom of the sash. Attach the sash or screen with screws passing through the side sections of the frame into the blind stop.

One final tip: measure the width of your window opening at three different positions (top, middle and bottom) and use the shortest dimension if there are differences. Also measure the vertical distance on both sides of the window to be sure that they are the same. J.H.

See also: GLASS; SCREENS; STORM DOORS AND WINDOWS; WINDOW; WINDOW REPAIR; WINDOWS.

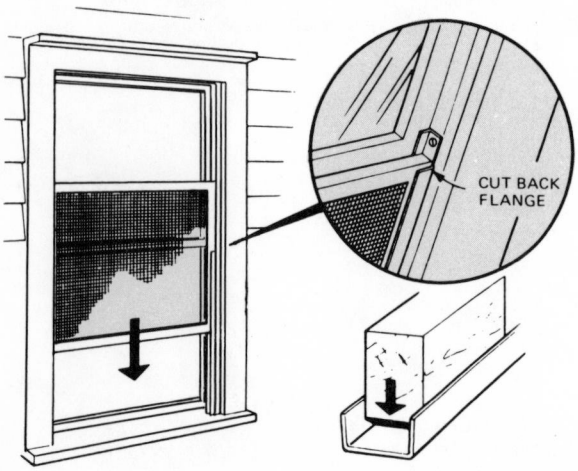

Half screens for standard double hung windows may be installed using aluminum channel (Item #6010) as a sliding track. Drill and countersink screw holes every 6" along channel on 3/4" aluminum wood screws. Cut back flange on one side to insert screen. Spread track slightly if necessary. Attach channel to blind stop flush with the inner edge. Make screen frame 3/16" less than opening between blind stops. Lubricate channel with products available at gasoline stations or hardware dealers.

Casement windows usually have screw holes drilled along sides of frame for installing screens or storm sash on the inside. Measure for width of storm sash between inside edges of holes at sides. For height, measure from top of crank mechanism to frame at top (see sketch). Add 1/4" for overlap at top. Hold completed sash in place with angle clips (made from 1"x1"x1/16" aluminum angle) and self-tapping screws. Whenever aluminum storm sash is installed on a metal frame, be sure to use a felt or rubber strip between them.

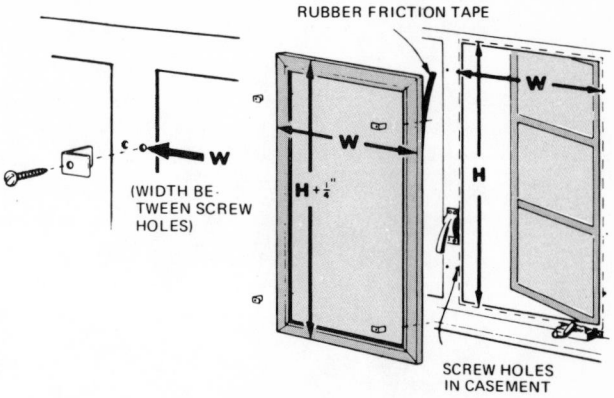

Awning windows which open out are fitted with storm sash or screens around the blind stop on the inside of the house. Usually it is necessary to fit a wood filler strip on window sill to clear the crank. Drill a hole through the wood for the crank.

Measure width (W) of opening just inside of the blind stop and cut the top and bottom sections 1/8" less than W. Measure height (H) from top of wood strip to top of opening just inside blind stop. Length of side pieces equal H minus 1/8". Attach a strip of felt or rubber along the bottom of sash. Attach sash or screens with screws through the side sections into blind stop.

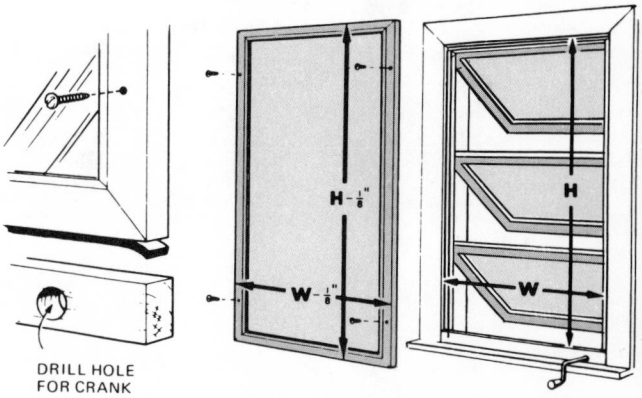

Basement windows are fitted with storm sash outside if they open inward or inside if they open outward. Measure the opening inside the window frame. Add 3/4" to height and width for a 3/8" overlap on all four sides of wood frames. For metal frames follow instructions on casement windows. Holes are usually provided in metal window frames for attaching screens or storm sash. Use self-tapping screws and clips made from 1"x1"x1/16" aluminum angle to install the storm sash on metal frames or round head wood screws on wood window frames. Attach a strip of weather stripping, felt or rubber tape, around the edge of the storm sash between the sash and metal window frames.

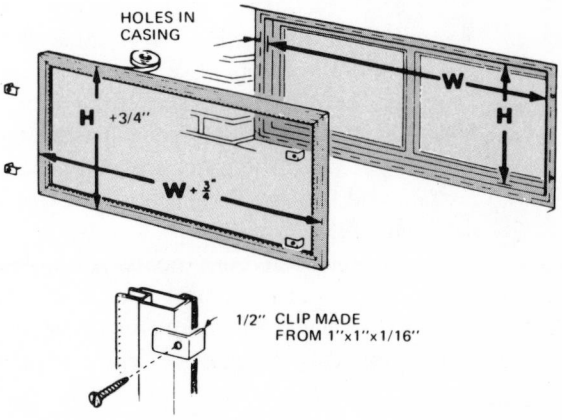

Maintaining Your Aluminum Boat

That hull is tough and corrosion-resistant, but choose an antifouling paint with care

RECENTLY a man said that he wouldn't have an aluminum boat because they just wouldn't hold up in his area. Not too long ago he said the same thing about fiberglass boats and plywood boats. His father swore that the auto was just a passing fad, and that the Wright brothers would never get off the ground.

Of course, aluminum boats got a bad reputation in the early post World War II days when a lot of unknowing—or uncaring—builders bought up surplus aircraft aluminum and turned it into boats. The aircraft alloy contains copper; in salt water, the aluminum in the alloy, being less noble than copper, erodes.

Now, the alloys developed for marine use will last indefinitely in salt water. These alloys are the only ones that the major aluminum producers will furnish to a boat builder, and they are the same as the alloys used in many outboard motor parts. Of course, the surface of unpainted aluminum will corrode. The bright, silver finish turns greyish when it oxidizes. This surface corrosion inhibits further corrosion, however, and has no effect on the durability of the metal.

If a boat is car-topped or trailered to the water for each use, there's no need for a paint job to protect the metal. If the boat is to be kept in the water for any length of time, the bottom should be painted to inhibit marine growth and other fouling. This is true of any boat made of any material.

The secret in providing a good, long-lasting paint job on aluminum is to provide a clean surface. Use a solvent wash of the ordinary petroleum type, an inhibited alkaline cleaner, or an alcohol-phosphoric acid cleaner.

Once the surface is clean, you can apply your paint. Many marine paints available for topside or antifouling use can be applied directly to the metal; for others, a priming coat of zinc chromate is needed.

While it is possible to use a copper-bearing antifouling paint on aluminum, this paint must be applied over a heavy coating of zinc chromate in order to prevent galvanic corrosion, which would result from copper and aluminum in contact whenever the paint is scraped or damaged so the aluminum is exposed to the water. Aluminum producers now discourage the use of copper-bearing antifoulants.

Another type of bottom paint that must not be used is the mercury-bearing type, as the mercury forms an amalgam that will destroy the aluminum.

The tributyl tin oxide antifouling paints have been used most successfully with aluminum. The TBTO paints do not react with aluminum in any way, and they are available in hard racing finishes and soft leaching finishes from most major marine-paint manufacturers. If this paint is scratched so that bare aluminum is exposed, the leaching action continues to provide a measure of protection to the exposed metal.

If an aluminum boat strikes a submerged object with considerable force, the metal isn't likely to rupture. Samples were subjected to impact testing of an informal nature—a .38 Police Special revolver bullet at eight feet—and the metal was not punctured.

Of course, it is possible for an aluminum hull to be punctured or torn open by a hard, sharp underwater object; the same is true of boats made of other materials. Fortunately, aluminum boats now offered have built-in flotation, in the form of Styrofoam or polyurethane foam, so the boats will not sink if holed or swamped.

Small abrasions and dents can be repaired by gently hammering the surface to flatten it as much as possible. Any remaining depressions can be filled with epoxy putty after they have been cleaned thoroughly with one of the compounds mentioned above in connection with painting.

If you are handy with tools and are not too concerned with appearance, you can put an aluminum patch over a hole. The patch should extend at least two inches on each side of the hole or rip, and it should be riveted around its perimeter with rivets spaced about one inch apart. Bed the patch in sealant before riveting.

If damage is major and welding is needed, the boat should be returned to the manufacturer or to a welder known to be expert with aluminum Marine aluminum alloys are heat tempered. Too much heat in the area of a weld destroys the temper and leaves the metal brittle. Any flexing at or along the weld could then crack the hull.

No single material is best for all boats; all materials have their advantages and limitations. Whether a boat is good or bad depends on design and the quality of construction. It doesn't make sense to reject a good material on the basis of what was true in a few cases years ago. T.B.

See also: BOATING; MAINTENANCE, BOAT; PAINTING; PAINT.

How to Erect a Rooftop Antenna

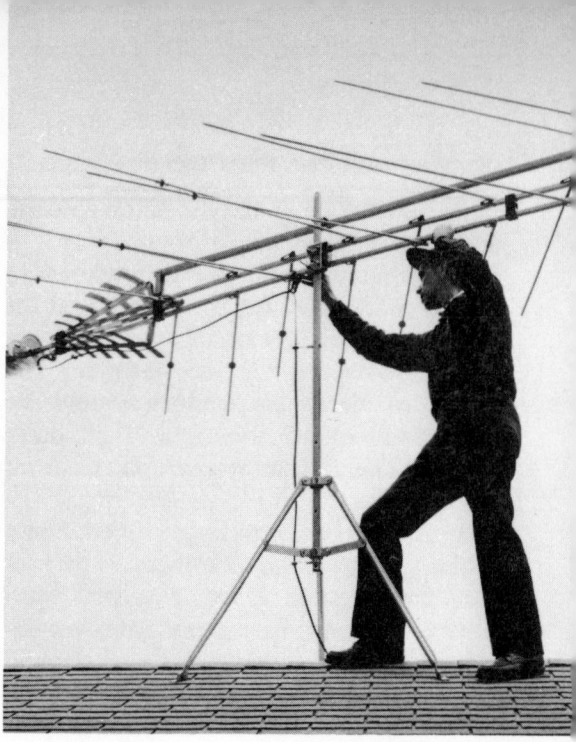

Putting an antenna on your roof is easier than it looks, and it can give your TV set and FM radio a sharp boost in performance

DON'T LET ANYONE pressure you into sinking a lot of money into a mile-high mast antenna that may blow down in a storm. And don't think that an antenna is too tough a job to handle yourself. There's no need to hire a high-priced workman to do a job you can do yourself by following the guidelines shown here. A solidly installed rooftop antenna will let you sleep at night without worrying about high winds, and you'll feel better in the pocketbook.

So when you decide it's time for a new or stronger antenna, do the job yourself. A good quality antenna, when installed the do-it-yourself way, will cost less than the cheapest model installed by a "pro." This is one of the repair jobs that the man of the house can handle.

Start off with a good roof (good shingles and joists), a few tools, and the roof mounting antenna. The antenna you buy will probably come with a pretty good mounting base; but for a top-notch, really wind-resistant job, spend a few extra dollars for a small antenna tower. The one shown here cost a little over seven dollars.

With screwdriver, pliers, and crescent wrench in hand, all you do is select the right tower for your particular receiving area. This depends on the kind of signals you wish to receive (UHF, VHF, FM, etc.), distance from the transmitter, and the obstructions in between. Your local TV shop will probably give you pretty good advice on just what kind of antenna and tower you need.

Here to stay. A rooftop tower has many advantages over a mast. It's easier to install, it has a much better appearance, it's more secure, and you eliminate vibrating guy wires that run endlessly from the mast to your house. Very few rooftop antennas blow over during severe storms, so they prevent additional damage to your roof. Should the boom or any of the elements be damaged they can be reached with no trouble at all.

Only a few holes are needed to install the tower on your roof. Before you get started, check and make sure that your antenna will be no higher than other installations in your neighborhood. If necessary, check the local city ordinance for TV antenna installations. Some cities have very exact requirements and even a per-

antifouling paint: see maintenance, boat
antifreeze: see cooling systems, auto

mit fee. Better to be safe now than sorry later.

Small TV towers come in lengths of 18, 30 and 36 inches, as well as 5- and 10-foot lengths. While they are sturdy and cost little, a tower mounted on a 1½ to 2 story home should provide adequate reception even in a fringe area. If you're really out in the cold, a hi-gain Yagi-type antenna will help to put you in the ball park.

Selecting a site. Once on the roof, select a likely spot for a three-legged tower. We'll help you out by recommending dead center on the roof peak (you get a ground-plane effect this way that will help reduce local r.f. interference somewhat); just count the total number of shingles and divide by two to reach *ground zero.* Mounting the antenna to one side of the roof is possible, but less effective.

Make sure you're clear of tree limbs, etc., and in the line of sight of some TV stations. At all cost, keep away from power lines of any description.

In an extreme fringe area you can mount the tower on the highest part of your roof. But if you've got more than 10 ft. of antenna skyward (extending above the tower), it will have to be guyed properly. Under normal circumstances, however, guy wires shouldn't be necessary. A good rule of thumb is: a five-foot mast extended out of a 30- to 36-inch tower; a 10-foot mast extended out of a 5- to 10-foot tower.

If you're mounting the tower on a flat surface (with no peak), simply center it by using the roof corners as a guide. A friend can hold the boom at approximate dead center while you take sightings from alternate corners.

Mounting tower and mast. Before securing the three-legged tower, check that all three legs are located *over* a roof joist (i. e. supporting beam). The towers have adjustable legs and hold-down feet so this is possible. You can locate the joist by tapping lightly over the surface of the roof.

▲*Brush roofing compound on screw heads and bases of stand-offs to seal roof against water penetration.*

◄*Use long screws to attach tripod feet to roof joists. Note that mast is clamped into two rings. Each ring has three locking bolts so that mast can be adjusted to precisely vertical position.*

The first solid thump indicates you've got a beam where you need it.

Temporarily place the legs of the tower on the corresponding joists. Place the two adjoining legs (i.e. the two that form the base of the triangle) in the direction where winds are strongest. It's usually north winds or northwesterlies that cause most problems, but it pays to make sure for your particular area.

Level the tower before securing (lagging) to the joists. A carpenter's level will prove to be a worthwhile investment, but should one be lacking, place the boom (or even the free mast) on the tower and sight it against house outlines and other reference points. When using a level, level the tower and mast in two opposite directions.

Now you can secure the legs to the joists using the supplied screws. Be sure to place at least two screws in the base of each supporting leg. If they don't go directly into the joist you will have to sound out the joist's location again. Probably a shift of ¼-inch is all that will be needed. Make sure that all screws are flush with the tower feet and as tight as possible.

If your combined tower and mast is short enough so that you can reach near the top of the mast, install the mast first so that it is perfectly perpendicular, then clamp on the antenna. If your tower plus mast is too high, fasten the mast to the tower long enough to plumb it, then loosen only one screw in each clamp just enough to free the mast. Attach the mast to the antenna, and remount as a unit.

Antenna up and away. Remove the antenna from the packing carton and prepare it for mounting. Most TV antennas can be unfolded in minutes because the antenna rods lock into position automatically. Simply push or pull the elements into the correct configuration and snap them in place. You'll find it easier to assemble the antenna on the roof, if you have a *flat* roof. If you have a pitched roof, prepare the antenna on the ground and hoist it up with a length of clothesline. Then, if you drop a nut or washer, it can't go rolling into the rain gutter. More important, you won't lunge for a sliding part and end up in the gutter yourself.

If you have a fairly complicated antenna, like the one shown here, you can work with it more comfortably if you screw the support base that comes with the antenna to a scrap of plywood and mount the antenna on the mast. You can move it about easily, study its space requirements (it's a biggie, measuring almost 14 feet!), and make the lead-in wire connections on the ground. As we said before, the base that comes with this antenna is fairly good, and it can be attached to the roof many different ways—on a flat roof, on the side or peak of a pitched roof, or on the eave of a pitched roof. But as we also said, you get a *better* job if you opt for a heavy-duty tower.

To connect the 300-ohm lead-in wire to the assembled antenna, use either small eyelet connectors or form an eyelet with the bare wire. Place the lead tip under a lock washer, tighten the wing nut, and place some electrical tape over the antenna terminals. This will insulate the antenna connections from corrosion due to wind and moisture. Before making the terminal connections, take care to thread the lead-in wire through rubber or other strain-relief devices you may find on the antenna.

If your antenna has a fairly long boom, two brace supports angled from the boom to the mast will add strength. The antenna shown here has an extra boom brace that clamps to the mast and runs parallel with the antenna boom, so no extra braces are needed. Place standoffs on the mast to keep the lead-in cable taut and away from the mast.

If you live close to the transmitters of the channels you want to receive, a relatively simple and inexpensive antenna will suffice. If you live in fringe area, a more elaborate antenna is worth the extra price. This is especially true if you want to pick up UHF channels, which are much harder to pull in than VHF channels. You can buy separate VHF and UHF antennas and mount them one atop the other on the same mast. Or you can obtain a combination antenna that is designed to pull in both VHF and UHF, plus FM radio signals.

The antenna used to illustrate this article is a good example of a combination antenna. It has 39 elements and a boom length of 163 inches. The maximum ranges in miles are: VHF, 185; UHF, 90; FM, 100 miles. A signal lead-in cable brings the signals down into the house. To obtain maximum signal strength, the antenna must be pointed in the direction of the transmitters; if the antenna is even a few degrees off target, TV picture quality can suffer. The easiest way to determine the proper orientation is to tune in various TV channels and have someone evaluate the picture quality as you slowly rotate the antenna mast.

If you have separate VHF and UHF antennas, and perhaps a third antenna for your FM radio, you will need separate lead-ins for each. If you have a combination antenna, the same lead-in does all the work. Just be sure to follow the manufacturer's instructions, and use the hardware provided (cable standoffs, for example) to lead the cable down along the mast and along the rooftop to the point where it enters the house. The cable should be reasonably taut to prevent flopping around in a strong wind, but not so tight that strain is put on connecting points. Standoffs are especially important if you use a conventional twin-lead cable (the flat kind); if you use the more expensive coax cable (round type with shield) to cut down pickup of interfering signals from the local

▲ *Use carpenter's level to make sure mast is vertical. If mast is short, you can install it before putting on the antenna. If the top is out of reach, place antenna on top of mast before placing mast in tripod.*

▼ *Screw the base that comes with the antenna to a piece of plywood. This will hold antenna while you are working on it. The base can be used to mount the antenna on the roof, but a tripod tower is recommended.*

environment, the cable can be taped to the mast. The flat, twin lead should be twisted into a loose spiral, not laid flat, to help cancel unwanted signals generated in the lead-in.

If the lead-in must run along the roof (this would not be necessary if you mount the rig at a gable), use standoffs about every four feet to keep the cable from touching the roof surface. After the tower legs and standoffs are in place, smear roofing cement on screws and around the bases of the standoffs to prevent water leaks.

Bring the antenna lead down the side of the house, again using standoffs every few feet. Try to keep the cable away from metal rain gutters and downspouts, power lines and other obstructions. Bring the cable into the house through a window, or through siding using an insulating ceramic tube. Waterproof this installation also.

Where the lead-in reaches your TV set, you will add a signal splitter that separates the VHF, UHF and FM radio signals so that they can be directed to the proper terminals on the TV set and to the radio equipment. The splitter will probably be part of the antenna package, and the simple installation directions are included.

Do you need an antenna rotator? If all the TV channels you can reasonably hope to pick up are pretty much in the same compass direction from your home, you probably wouldn't have much use for an antenna rotator. But turning the entire antenna system full circle by remote control from your living room is a definite boon if the transmitters of desired TV stations lie in distinctly different directions. Also, a rotating antenna will help you bring in many more distant FM radio stations, if the antenna is also used to pick up radio signals. You may also find that even when TV channels come pretty much from the same direction, a slight off-target orientation of the antenna can help clear up fuzzy pictures resulting from temporary atmospheric or other signal-messing interferences.

The rotator you buy will include full directions for installation. The kit will include a motor housing you install between the tower and the antenna mast, a low-voltage power cable having from 4 to 8 leads, and a control unit to place near your TV set. The power cable is coded so that you should have no difficulty making the proper terminal connections at both ends. Use more standoffs to lead the cable along the roof and down the side of the house.

Be sure to leave a 1½- to 2-foot loop in the *antenna lead-in* (not the rotator power cable) where it passes the rotator. This loop slack is necessary to prevent binding of the antenna lead-in when the mast turns. Use a standoff above and below the rotator to help keep the antenna lead-in clear. Place the lower standoff in position before you tape the rotator power cable to the mast so that the standoff clamp doesn't cut into the thin insulation of the power cable and cause a short circuit.

Rotator mechanisms have either a north or south starting position. Check the manufacturer's directions for setting the proper starting position. Before you leave the roof, have someone operate the rotator from your living room as you watch to see that all cables are free from possible binding.

This completes your antenna installation. *Almost!* There's just one more thing to do. Add a good lightning arrester with a proper earth ground! You have spent a good deal of money on your new antenna rig, not to mention the hundreds you have sunk into that color TV set; so why risk ruining everything, including your home, by neglecting the installation of a good but very inexpensive ground wire? Your dealer can provide the necessary items, plus complete installation directions. J.H.

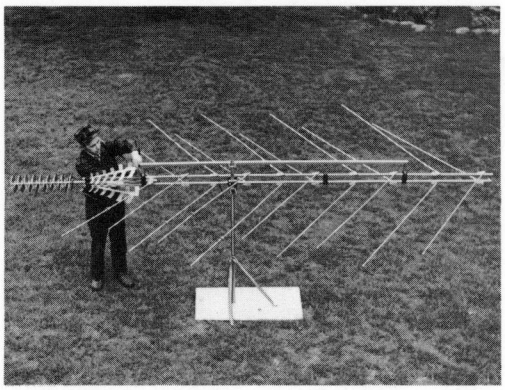

Unfold antenna elements and assemble them. It is easier to do this job on the roof, if it is flat. If the roof is pitched, assemble the antenna on the ground and pull it up with a length of clothes line (top left).

Make lead-in connections before mounting the antenna. Waterproof the connections and make sure the lead-in cable passes through the flexible strain relief tabs. These are the black tabs sticking down from the boom (top right).

Clamp the antenna to the boom and spray all nuts and bolts with a rust preventive to protect them from corrosion. Note how lead-in passes through strain relief tab at left (above left).

Use stand-offs along mast, rooftop and wall to keep lead-in cable away from house structure. Pull the cable taut, so it won't flap in a wind, but not tightly enough to strain connections (above right).

The rooftop antenna in place (at right.)

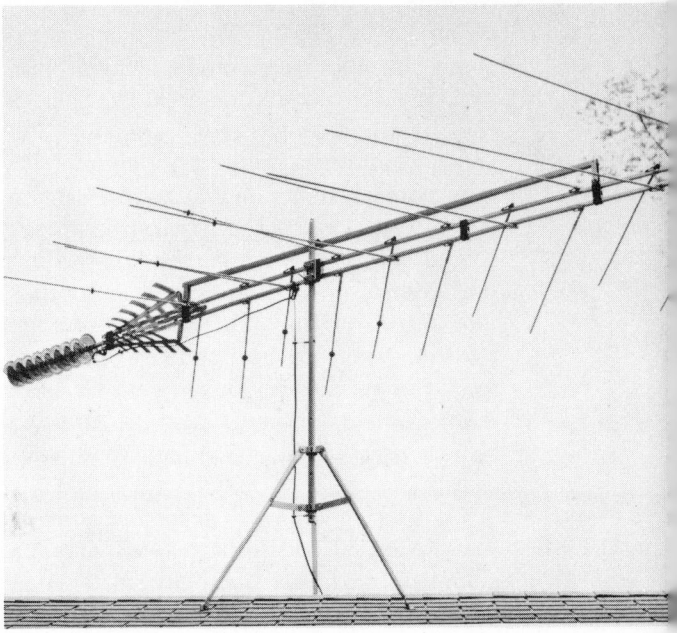

Citizen's Band Radio Antenna

Your CB radio gear will only work as well as your antenna. Here's how to pick one out and how to choose a location for it

EVERY MESSAGE you send or receive on your citizens band radio must pass through the antenna. This makes the antenna you mount on your car, boat or home base and the location you choose for it both vital factors in the way your CB radio works.

On an automobile, your choice of a location will be: the cowl, the roof, the rear deck, the bumper.

For a mounting which requires no drilling into the vehicle, your best bet is the bumper mount. This mount is held in place by a strap or chain link, it holds tight, it works well, it requires the use of a full length (102 inch) whip and a spring.

A popular mounting place for CB antenna seems to be the "rear deck," just behind the rear window and on the left side. Mounting here, while not so good as roof top mounting (insofar as optimum results), seems to be popular because of the fact that a full-length whip can be used. Also, trunk lid mounts can be mounted here without drilling any holes in your chariot.

Roof-top mounting is best from an electrical point of view because an antenna mounted here will radiate the signal equally well in all directions. This is opposed to the other mounting spots which beam their maximum signal diagonally across the car (an antenna mounted on the left rear will produce its best signal towards the right front fender). A big problem with the roof top is that you are forced to use a shortened whip unless you feel like smacking your antenna on tree branches and garage doors. Another problem is that of getting the coaxial cable from the rig to the antenna, because you must go through a complicated "snaking" maneuver to get the cable up the door post and under the headliner. The shortened whips generally do not perform as well as full-length whips.

The cowl mounting location is directly in front of the driver's door, in the spot normally used for the car's regular radio antenna. This is a good spot, although it hasn't proven to be very popular with CB operators, probably because it means relocating the broadcast antenna. Combination antennas which will work on both broadcast radio and CB may be used here, although these also haven't caught the fancy of CB'ers.

You can put a full length whip on the cowl if you want, although most CB'ers seem to prefer a medium length whip here.

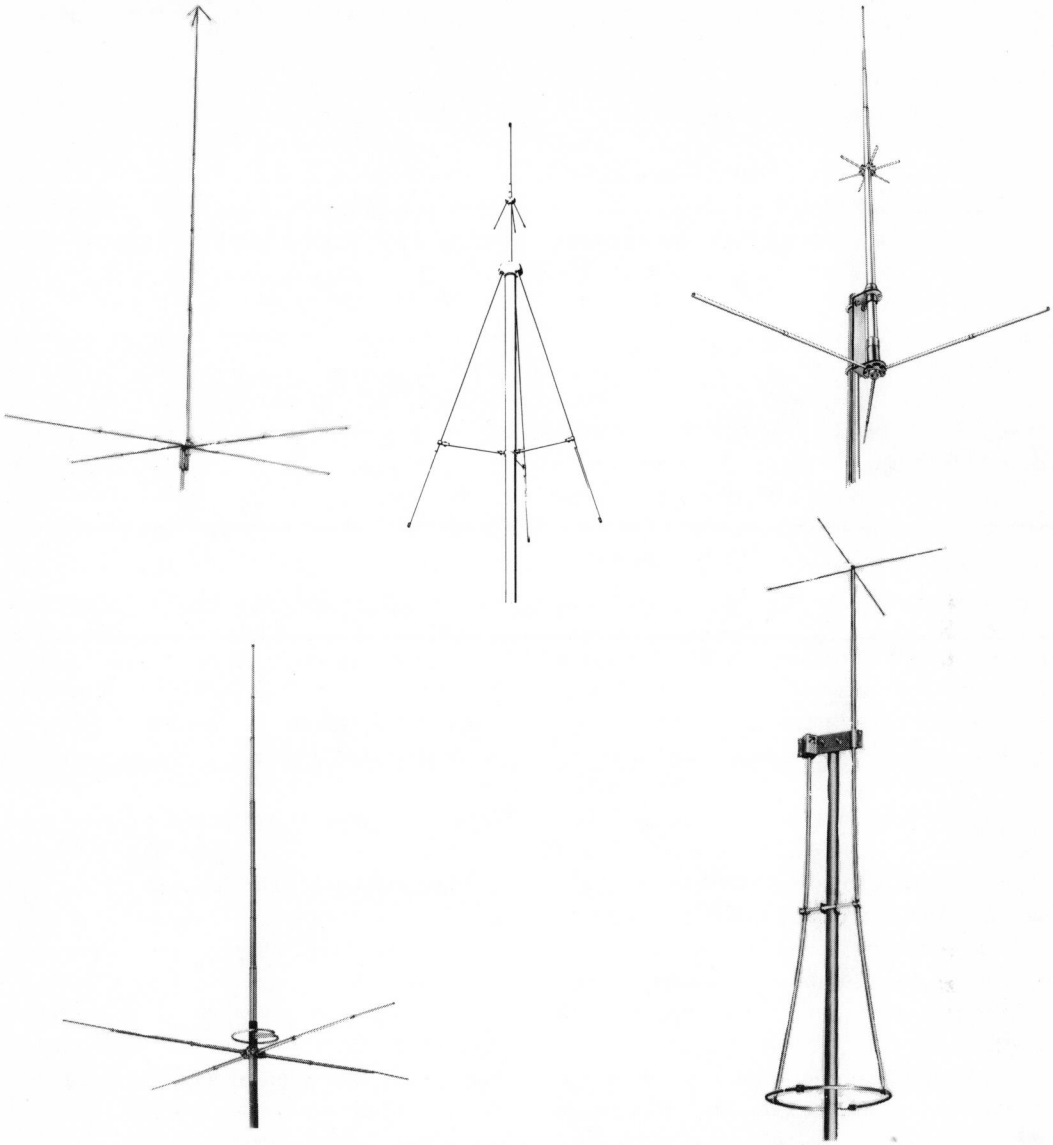

▲ *These typical citizens band radio antennas are intended for stationary installation at home base. They are omnidirectional.*

The reason for placing the CB antenna here and relocating the broadcast antenna is that the CB rig will probably be closer to the left side and it will be easier to make the run over to the left side mounting.

If you've got a car with an unusual shape, you'll probably want to use your imagination to find the best mounting spot for your antenna. Put a full length whip on the roof of a red VW and the bug'll look like an upside down jelly apple.

Call it a whip, a beam, a coolinear, a ground plane, or even a stick or a *sky hook;* it's still a CB antenna, the hunk of metal that radiates your CB signal into the air and receives signals from other stations. Some are elegant and extravagant, others are nothing more complicated than a thin steel rod.

Which one for you? That's what you will have to decide for yourself. Following is some background on the various types available, what they do, and who makes them. Somewhere, there's one which will do the job at your station.

Base station antenna fall into two general categories, those which are *omnidirectional* (also known, incorrectly, as non-directional) and radiate the signal with equal strength in all directions; and those which are designed to concentrate the signal in one direction, they are usually called *beams*.

Within these two general groupings there is the wildest assortment of unusual looking contrivances to come along since the plumber's nightmare.

Notice the word used, "beam," because that's the name for an antenna which is able to do these electronic tricks. While using two Hy-Gain CLR-2 antennas in the co-phaser hookup isn't a true beam, as the word is commonly used in CB, it is a clever way of achieving the same effect.

There are a number of actual beams available however, and, depending on their design, they each produce varying degrees of gain in one specific direction. As an example, one manufacturer has a gigantic monster of CB beam (it's actually two five element beams placed side by side) which will boost your signal to the point where it is actually equal to over 100 watts in the direction it is aimed. The antennas are ganged.

Where size is a problem—on a vehicle, for example—why not shorten the rod so that it won't be so lethal? Since an antenna can't be just arbitrarily snipped off to any random length and still be expected to resonate on a given frequency, something was done to get the thing shorter while still keeping it working on 11 meters. The method of shortening the antenna was by the insertion of a "loading coil" right in the whip itself.

Using loading gimmicks on a whip to cut down on its size will also cut down on its efficiency. Since it is known, however, that the higher a CB antenna is from the ground, the better the range it will deliver; the fact that the shortened whip will not only be centrally located for better pattern distribution, but also high for maximum distance coverage, compensates for the loading losses.

Top loading whips (those shortened whips with the loading coil at the top of the whip) have better signals, as a rule. Problem with them is that the loading coil at the top makes them slightly top heavy and subject to bending when you drive at high speeds. On the other hand, move the loading coil down to the bottom of the whip and you get an antenna which is stronger mechanically, but less effective from an electronic standpoint. To make everybody happy, several models of loaded whips now have their loading coil in the center of the whip.

The accessories offered to CB operators are varied.

The field strength meter is an inexpensive gem that tells plenty about any CB system. It acts like a miniature receiver that picks up your transmitter signal and reads its strength, much as an S-meter does. Since the instrument picks up the signal after it leaves the antenna, it takes into account every link in the chain—transmitter, coaxial cable and antenna. Place a field strength meter near a newly-installed antenna; you can make transmitter tuning adjustments for maximum output by viewing the meter for an increase. Once you see a peak, use it as your reference for future troubleshooting. Some field strength meters have a magnetic base, so

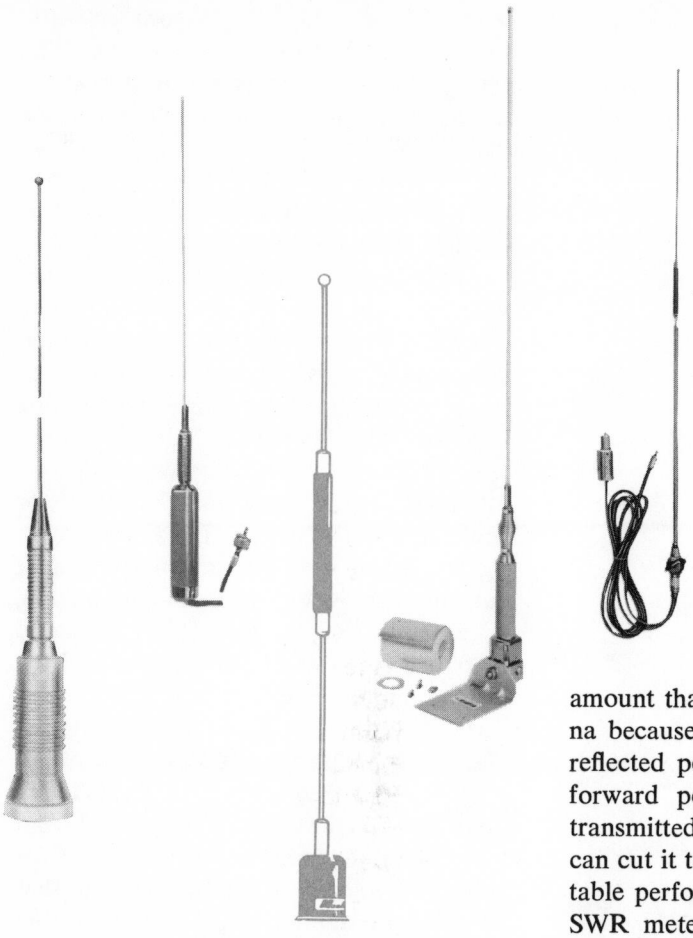

Antennas for mobile citizens band radios come in a variety of designs. Shown here, left to right, are a whip antenna, two relatively short antennas intended for mounting on a car roof or deck, a mobile home antenna and a cowl antenna. The cowl antenna can serve both a citizens band radio and a standard AM FM broadcast receiver, so it can use the cowl location of an ordinary automobile antenna.

you can place them on a dashboard. You'll have a continuous and positive monitor of output power each time you press the mike button. Another handy model has a nine-inch telescoping whip antenna and earphone. That earphone enables you to hear and check the quality of your modulation while transmitting. These meters, incidentally, need no batteries because they're driven directly from on-the-air signals captured by the antenna.

The SWR indicator is an excellent accessory that should be owned by any CBer who wants a better electronic view of his rig. SWR, which means standing wave ratio, is a measure of how much power is sent to the antenna, compared to the amount that bounces back from the antenna because of impedance mismatch. Since reflected power acts to cancel and reduce forward power (that's the part actually transmitted), you want lowest SWR. If you can cut it to less than 2:1, you have acceptable performance and good efficiency. An SWR meter inserted in the coaxial cable tells the figure. When the meter indicates too high, your transmitter is poorly tuned, the coaxial cable isn't 50 ohms or something's amiss with the antenna or its installation. In a base station, high SWR could mean the antenna is too close to a mass of metal (maybe a rain pipe running down the house). Broken antenna elements or shorted cable can do the same.

SWR meters are available as separate instruments. They have coaxial connectors which permit insertion into an antenna line where they monitor output full-time, if you wish, without robbing more than a snippet of power. SWR instruments, incidentally, are fine companions to the field-strength meter. When you tune a rig and watch an SWR meter for the lowest possible re-

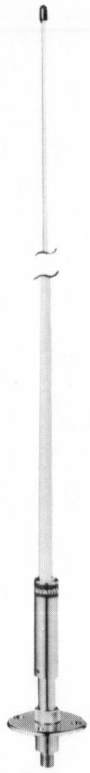

▲ *A CB antenna designed for marine use.*

▼ *Automobile bumper mount for CB antenna.*

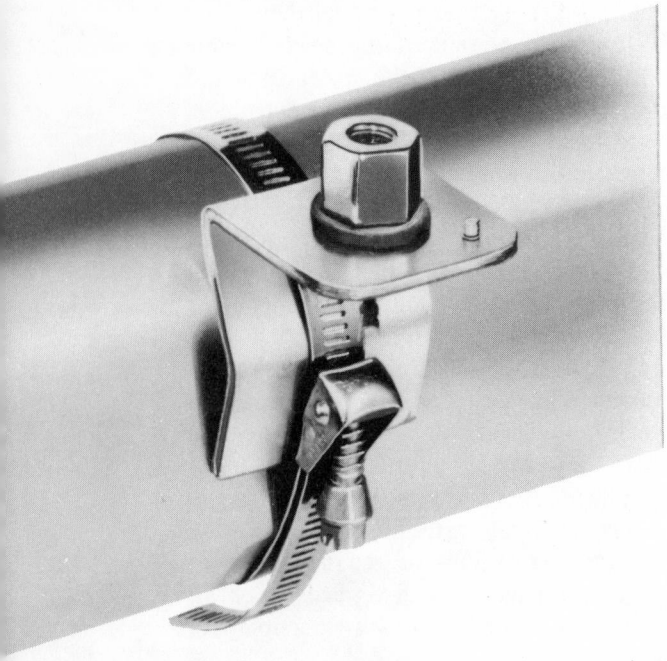

flected power, there's a chance you may be reducing the forward power, too. (This should be equivalent to the doctor killing the patient to lower his fever!) But if you make SWR adjustments while simultaneously viewing a field strength meter, you can't be misled. When SWR drops, field strength should increase.

The instruments described above are invaluable, but they have one limitation. They read relative, not actual output power. If you wish to read the actual number of watts emanating from your rig, look into an inline wattmeter. Your system may be tuned for highest power and lowest SWR, but a weak tube or transistor could be cutting the maximum power the rig had when it was new. The wattmeter answers this one. It has direct-reading scales calibrated in, say, 0-10 watts and 0-100 watts.

The dummy load is a low-priced accessory, this gadget was called a "phantom" load back in Teddy Roosevelt's day. In some manuals and instruction sheets today we're told to construct a dummy load from a No. 47 pilot lamp and tune the rig for maximum brightness. The problem is that the filament within the lamp is something of a radio-frequency coil and, worse yet, changes resistance at different degrees of heating. The lamp, therefore, is not a true load for CB, which should be 50 ohms (sometimes indicated as 52 ohms to agree with coaxial cable ratings, but you can ignore the small difference). Several manufacturers offer an accurate dummy load in the $1.50 to $3 class. Two advantages over the lamp are a non-inductive load whose value won't change with power, and adequate shielding to prevent any escaping signal from causing undue interference on the air. Thus you can make adjustments to your rig without radiating an illegal signal. Another reason to own a dummy load is that it checks your other test instruments. Almost all CB test gadgets are designed to operate into or out of a 50-ohm impedance. If your various measurements somehow appear out of whack, you can always install the dummy load (in place of the antenna, for example) and be assured of an accurate 50 ohms.

Here are three small items fitted with coaxial connectors for easy attachment into the antenna line. Lightning arresters protect against lightning strikes. It has an internal discharge gap which helps shunt static charges to ground before there's damage to equipment. To do the job, though, you must provide a good electrical ground and connect it to the terminal supplied on the arrester.

Coaxial antenna switches form another helpful group of antenna accessories. There's quite a variety, depending on the functions you want. Simplest is the two-position model which connects your transceiver to one of two antennas at a flick of a switch. This is handy when you have both a beam and a conventional non-directional antenna. The switch may also work in reverse; it can connect one of two transceivers to one antenna line. Cost of these switches runs from about $5 for the two-position type, up through six-position models for about $10. Price varies with number of positions, styling and wattage rating (though the standard CB rig may not run more than 4 watts RF output).

Antenna matching is also a matter for accessories. Manufacturers design transceivers for an output of 50 ohms, coaxial cable for 50 ohms and antennas for 50 ohms. Connect all together and, *voila!* There is a perfect impedance match for maximum efficiency. Well, not completely. Sometimes a line presents an odd impedance because it's upset by an antenna which may not be operating at 50 ohms. A good example is mounting a 50-ohm antenna on a vehicle, where interaction with the car body may cause impedance to drop to 30 ohms or so. Although the mismatch is not serious in most cases, an antenna matcher inserted in the line is available to anyone who wants to tweak the last particle of power from his transmitter. To use one of the many matchers on the market, you'll need an SWR meter to adjust the matcher knobs for lowest SWR.

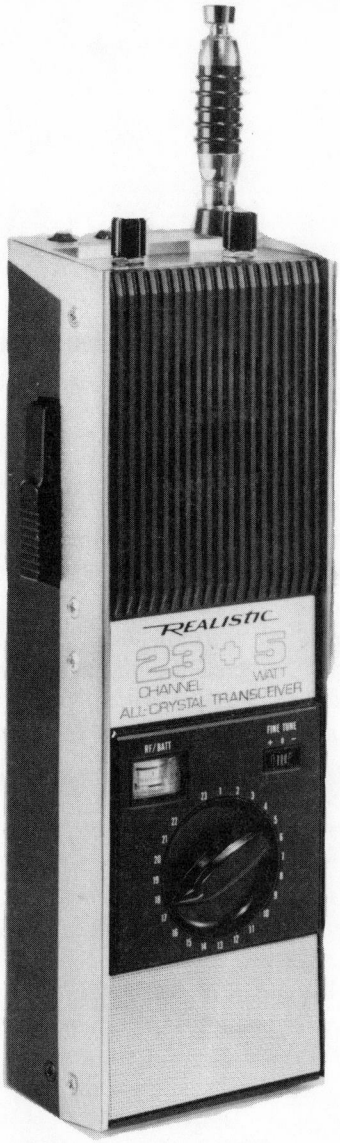

A hand-held citizens band transceiver with telescoping antenna.

See also: CITIZEN'S BAND RADIO.

Pollution Control Systems

Neglect of these devices can lead to poor performance, increased engine wear

DETROIT'S EFFORT to curb automobile-caused air pollution has spawned a wide assortment of underhood gadgetry.

Examples include positive crankcase ventilation (popularly called PCV), the air injection system, the thermostatically controlled air cleaner, a carburetor solenoid designed to keep the critically tuned engine from running on after it is turned off, and systems that retard ignition timing at low engine speeds ("vacuum choppers").

The first of the antipollution systems was PCV. It was introduced in the early 1960's to replace the road draft tube. With the road draft tube, gasoline fumes in the crankcase were purged to the atmosphere. PCV instead reroutes the fumes from the crankcase back into the engine via the carburetor intake, and from there into the combustion chamber for burning.

The most widely used PCV systems are these: 1) Fresh air is drawn from the air cleaner through a hose into an otherwise closed oil filter cap. The air circulates through the engine, picking up fumes and exhaling them into the PCV valve. The PCV valve regulates the flow of the fumes through a hose into the carburetor air intake (at the carburetor base). Here the fumes mix with the incoming air-fuel charge and go into the combustion chamber for burning. 2) Fresh air is drawn through the filter built into the oil filler cap. This filter usually is made of wire mesh. The air flow through the engine from this point is the same as the first type.

The PCV valve is a spring-loaded device that regulates flow according to manifold vacuum (as vacuum drops, the valve opens further). Clearly, the fumes that flow through the valve deposit soot on its working parts, and the valve in time will plug. The valve normally must be replaced once a year, although this interval can be extended by periodic cleaning with an appropriate solvent.

There is more to servicing PCV than replacing the valve, or even cleaning it. The PCV system should be checked at every available opportunity, for on many cars it will need service at least four times a year, and preferably every two months, particularly as the car ages.

The ventilation system does not change with the age of the vehicle, so its maximum capacity for handling crankcase fumes is fixed. But as the engine wears, more and more unburned fuel blows by the piston rings into the crankcase. A worn engine can deposit three to four times as much unburned gasoline into the crankcase. Therefore, it is important to keep the ventilation system clean and operative, to handle the increasing loads imposed by engine wear.

If the system is poorly maintained, the

antique finish: see finishing, wood
antique furniture: see furniture, used
antique radio: see radio
antique secretary desk: see desk

blowby fumes will condense in the crankcase and dilute the oil, increasing engine wear. The buildup of pressure in the crankcase from the fumes actually can be sufficient to blow engine seals. As a result, suddenly the engine will start to leak oil from everywhere.

More blowby has another effect: it agitates the oil, breaking some of it into droplets, which will mix with the crankcase fumes and be blown out the inlet breather (if the pressure is high enough) or drawn through the PCV valve into the engine. The engine will burn rather large quantities of oil, particularly at higher engine speeds, when blowby reaches a maximum.

PCV service is also important for two other reasons. 1) Most new car warranties require at least periodic replacement of the PCV valve, and some require frequent checking and cleaning of the valve. 2) The engine is designed to run smoothly with a clean and properly functioning PCV system. If the system malfunctions, the engine performance will be affected; rough idle is one ailment common to engines with malfunctioning PCV.

To check out the two common PCV systems, proceed in this manner. With type 1, run the engine at idle, remove the hose from the air cleaner and place your finger over the hose end. You should feel vacuum. Note: Some PCV systems of this type have an additional filter of wire gauze in the end of the hose. If you just try to pull off the hose, without removing the filter first, you will damage the molded end of the hose. Take off the air filter cover, remove the regular element and check for the presence of this gauze filter. If it is there, clean it and refit after checking the entire system.

If you feel vacuum at the end of the hose, proceed directly to the PCV valve. On most cars, it can be pulled out of the rocker cover. Shake the valve and if it rattles, it is all right. Just clean it with special solvent, using the procedure discussed later in this section. If the valve doesn't rattle, try cleaning it, and if cleaning doesn't work, install a new valve.

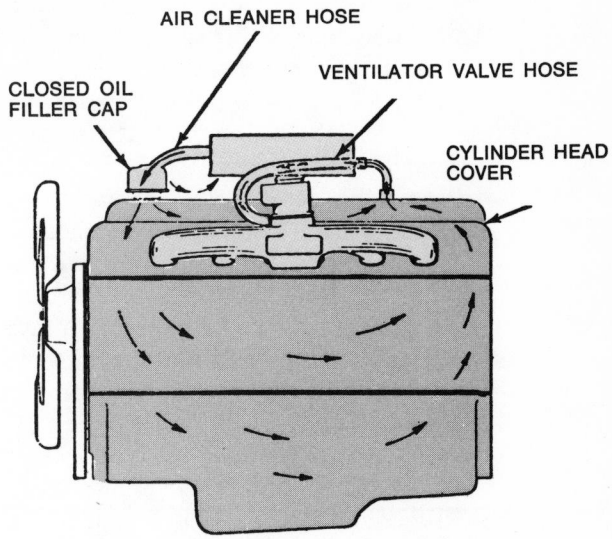

SIX-CYLINDER ENGINES

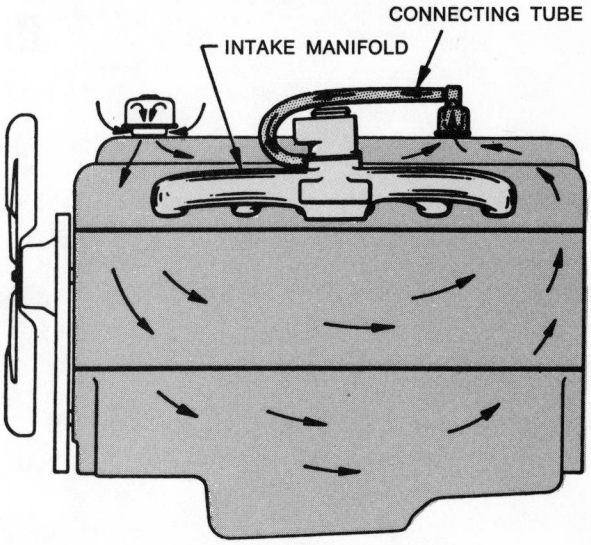

Above is most common type of PCV system. Fumes are drawn from crankcase into intake manifold for reburning. Below is another type of system. Only difference is that a filter is built into the oil filler cap.

If you do not feel vacuum at the end of the hose disconnected from the air cleaner, pull off the oil filter cap, and again run the engine at idle. Place a piece of paper over the oil filter tube and within a few seconds it should be sucked against the tube. If this happens, the hose to the air cleaner is plugged, probably because of contamination from heavy blowby fumes that are backing up through the system and/or plugging somewhere else in the PCV system. Replace the hose. If the engine is old, there is not much you can do about the cause of this condition except check the PCV system frequently.

At this point, let's introduce the checking procedure for the type 2 system. Remove the oil filler cap and look at the wire mesh filter. If it's dirty, clean it in solvent and let it air dry (or blow it dry with compressed air). Then make the same test as with the type 1 system, using the piece of paper over the oil filler tube with the engine idling. From this point, the checking and service procedure for both systems is the same.

If the paper is not sucked against the oil filler tube, disconnect the PCV valve from the rocker cover or engine valley cover (wherever it is mounted). Or if the valve is mounted at the carburetor, disconnect the hose connection at the rocker cover or engine valley cover.

With the engine idling, place your finger over the end of the valve or hose, and you should feel vacuum. If there is none, check the hose for plugging. If the hose is good, remove the valve completely and check for vacuum at the carburetor base. If there is vacuum here, the valve is plugged and must be cleaned or replaced.

If there is no vacuum at the carburetor

If possible, disconnect hose at air cleaner, run engine and feel for vacuum at end of hose.

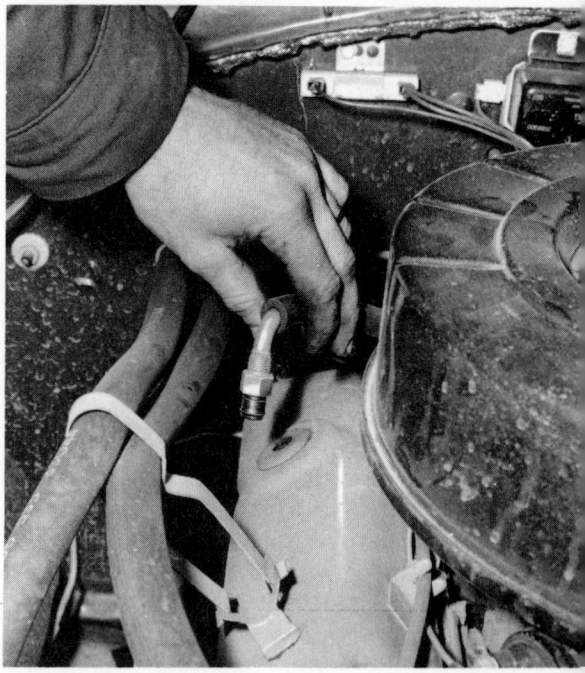

If there is vacuum at other end of system, check at PCV valve. On most cars, valve sits in grommet in rocker cover. Just pull it out.

base, the carburetor vacuum passage is clogged. Remove the carburetor and clean the passage by dunking the lower end in solvent and cleaning the neck with a small drill bit. Select a drill bit that will not remove any metal, and hand turn the bit through the neck. Even if the system checks out, the valve should be cleaned. The best way is with one of the special cans of solvent designed for the job. Such cans have a tapered spout for insertion into the valve.

With the engine off, disconnect the hose or valve at the rocker cover or engine valley cover (as you did to check for vacuum). By leaving the vacuum side connected (at the carburetor base), the solvent will be drawn through the valve, cleaning it, when you run the engine.

Insert the solvent can spout into the open end of the PCV valve, and work it back and forth against the spring-loaded plunger while squirting a few shots of solvent into the valve interior. Note: if the valve is mounted on the carburetor,

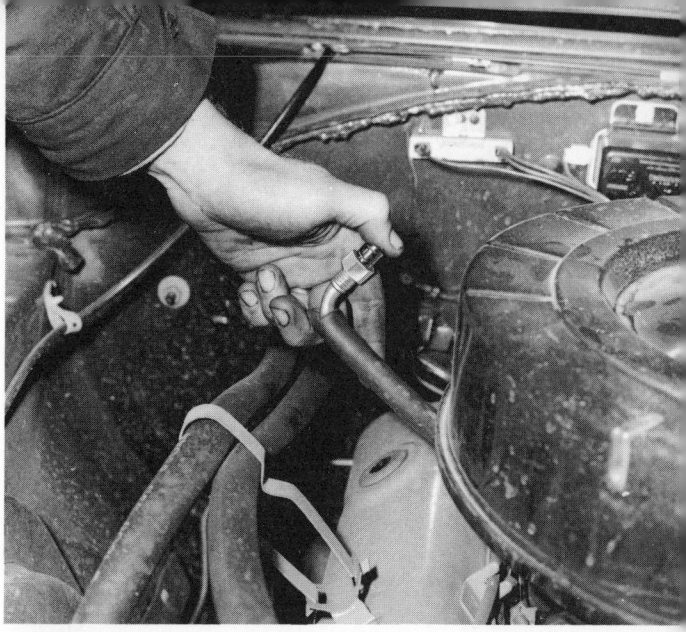

With engine running, feel for vacuum at end of PCV valve.

If there is no vacuum at end of PCV valve, place paper tag on oil filler cap neck (cap removed, engine idling). Paper should be sucked against neck and held by crankcase vacuum.

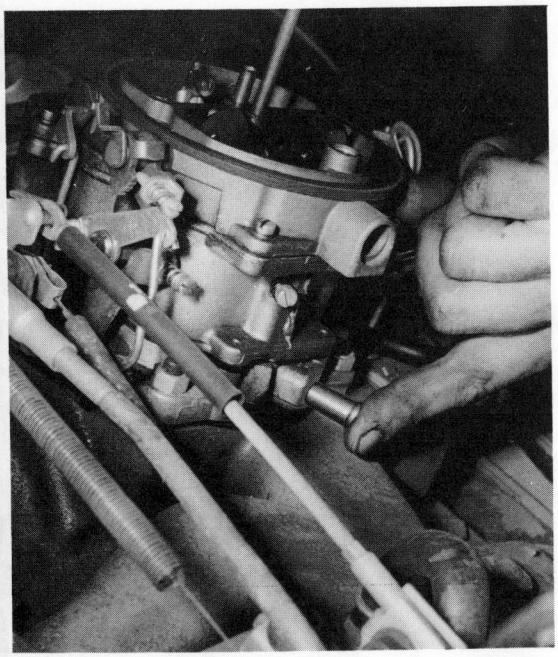

If there is no vacuum anywhere, check hose neck at base of carburetor. If vacuum is weak with engine running, neck may be clogged. Clean with a small drill bit.

and merely squirting solvent into the hose doesn't clean and free up the valve, disconnect the hose at the other end and work the solvent in against the spring-loaded plunger.

Now start the engine and let it idle. Squirt a few more shots of solvent into the valve, reconnect it and let the engine run for a few more minutes to evaporate the solvent. PCV puts a tremendous strain on the regular air filter in most PCV systems which have the hose connected to the air cleaner. So check the air filter element frequently as part of your PCV checkout.

Two of the newest anti-pollution systems, exhaust gas recirculation and evaporative emission control, also are among the most widely used.

Virtually all cars since 1970 have been equipped with evaporative emission control. EEC eliminates the vents in the fuel system; when the engine is shut off, fuel vapors that would otherwise evaporate into and pollute the atmosphere are trapped inside.

In the typical EEC design, the vapors are trapped in a charcoal cannister. When the engine is started, a valve opens, permitting engine vacuum to suck the vapors out of the canister. The vapors then flow into the cylinders for burning.

All evaporative emission control systems use a gas gap with pressure and vacuum valves to prevent damage to the gas tank, and to permit gasoline to flow. As gasoline is drawn from the tank, a vacuum void is created, which if not filled with air would soon result in cessation of fuel flow. Additionally, the vacuum might cause collapse of the gas tank. To prevent this, the gas cap vacuum valve opens, and air flows in to fill the void. If gasoline expansion creates pressure, the pressure valve opens to relieve it, preventing rupture of the tank. Yes, the fuel system is vented when either of these valves opens, but when the system has to be closed—when the engine is off—it is.

Service of the evaporative emission control system is limited to checking hoses and connections, and replacing the foam filter in the base of the charcoal canister once a year (see illustration). Always replace a hose with one designed for the EEC

▲ *PCV valve can be cleaned with special solvent, as shown. If solvent fails to free up valve, it should be replaced. Good preventive maintenance practice is to replace valve once a year, and clean with solvent six months later.*

➤ *Foam filter in base of evaporative emission control charcoal canister is easily pulled out for service.*

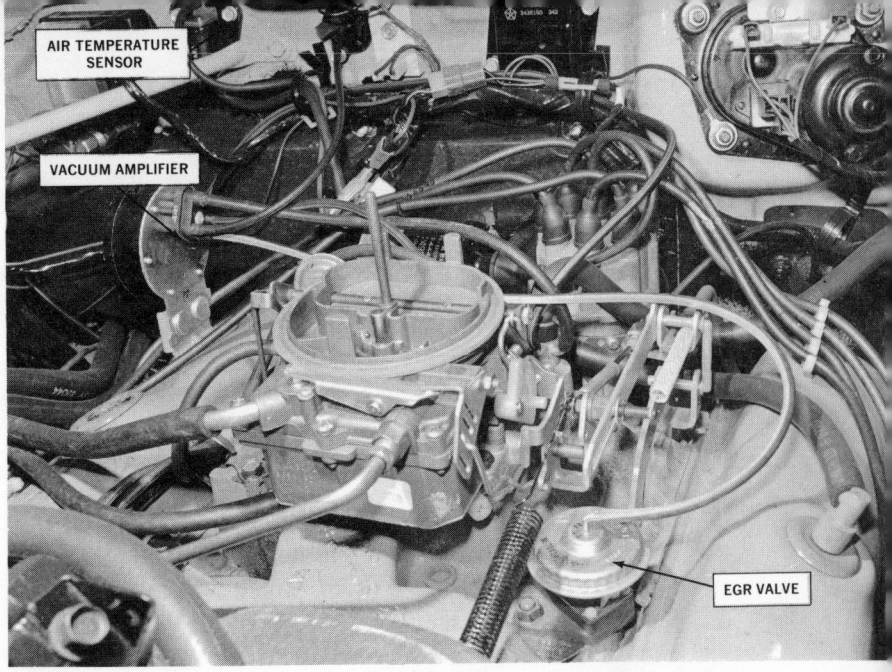

This is one of Chrysler Corp.'s exhaust gas recirculation systems of the type that uses a vacuum amplifier for a vacuum signal from the carburetor Venturi. On most models, a coolant sensor in the radiator top tank is used rather than the air temperature sensor shown here.

system, for one that is not may be prematurely deteriorated by the fuel vapors.

If you ever replace the gas cap (either because it is lost or to switch to a locking design), be absolutely certain you have a cap designed for the EEC system. Failure to use a cap with pressure relief and vacuum valves not only will defeat the system, but if you mistakenly use a non-vented cap, would cause the gas tank to collapse. Just because a cap fits the fill neck doesn't mean it is the right type.

The exhaust gas recirculation system first appeared on 1972 California-bound cars, then was installed nationwide in 1973, to control oxides of nitrogen, another major air pollutant.

Oxides of nitrogen are formed in the cylinders when combustion temperatures reach peaks. The injection of a small amount of exhaust gas back into the combustion chamber reduces the peak temperatures.

Injection of exhaust gas is regulated on most cars by a vacuum-operated flow control valve, the EGR valve. The vacuum control on the valve is somewhat different from car to car. In one Chrysler Corp. design, the vacuum is tapped off the venturi portion of the carburetor air horn. This provides the control that Chrysler wants for certain engines, but the vacuum signal is not strong enough to operate the valve. The weak signal is fed into a "vacuum amplifier," which is a mechanical version of a transistor. It works as a form of relay to control a stronger vacuum supply and it is the stronger vacuum supply that actually moves the EGR valve.

Some other Chrysler products have no EGR valve. Instead, calibrated jets permit exhaust gas to flow from the exhaust crossover passage in the intake manifold into the air-fuel passages of the intake manifold, just under the carburetor.

Naturally, the pumping back of some already burned gasoline causes a bit of deterioration in engine performance, so the car manufacturers have designed systems that cut out the exhaust gas recirculation when it might cause problems: at idle, when it could cause engine stalling; at very low outside air temperatures, when it could cause driveaway problems; at very high coolant temperatures, when the reduced performance could contribute to overheating; at full throttle, when performance is needed for passing.

The sensors that defeat the system are not used on all cars. Their use varies according to the needs of different engines.

A basic check of the exhaust gas recirculation system should be made as part of a tuneup. On Chrysler products without the valve, remove the air cleaner and hold the choke and throttle plates open. Using a flashlight, inspect the jets visually through the carburetor air horn, and if they are open, all is okay. If not, remove the carburetor, unthread the jets and clean in solvent. Warning: the jets are nonmagnetic, so be careful not to let them fall into the intake manifold during removal or reinstallation, for you will not be able to get them out with a magnet. You'll have to pull the intake manifold and shake them out.

On all other cars with the valve, you can make a basic check when ambient air temperature is about 70 degrees or above. Warm up the engine and let it idle. Snap open the throttle to about 2000 rpm and watch the external shaft on the EGR valve. It should move visibly. Repeat the test if necessary to confirm movement, which is slight. If there is definitely no movement, either the valve is defective or there is a poor hose connection. All hoses should be checked for looseness and deterioration, and replaced if necessary, as a routine matter. If the valve is defective, the simplest procedure is to replace it, although it theoretically can be cleaned. Of course, a defective EGR valve is only a problem in states that check exhaust emissions.

Exhaust gas recirculation systems have a somewhat different effect on each cylinder, so if you wish to check the engine power balance, you must first disconnect the vacuum hose to the valve, and plug the hose end. On Chrysler products with the calibrated jets, you cannot do a power balance test unless you temporarily plug the jets in the intake manifold. Because of the obvious difficulty this entails, compression and vacuum gauge tests would appear to be the only ones you should make prior to tuneup. P.W.

See also: AIR CLEANERS; ENGINE; PARTS REPLACEMENT, ENGINE.

GM's exhaust gas recirculation system has an easily identifiable valve.

All about Antiquing

Follow these steps to achieve a professional-looking result on a piece of furniture—whether it's an old relic or brand new

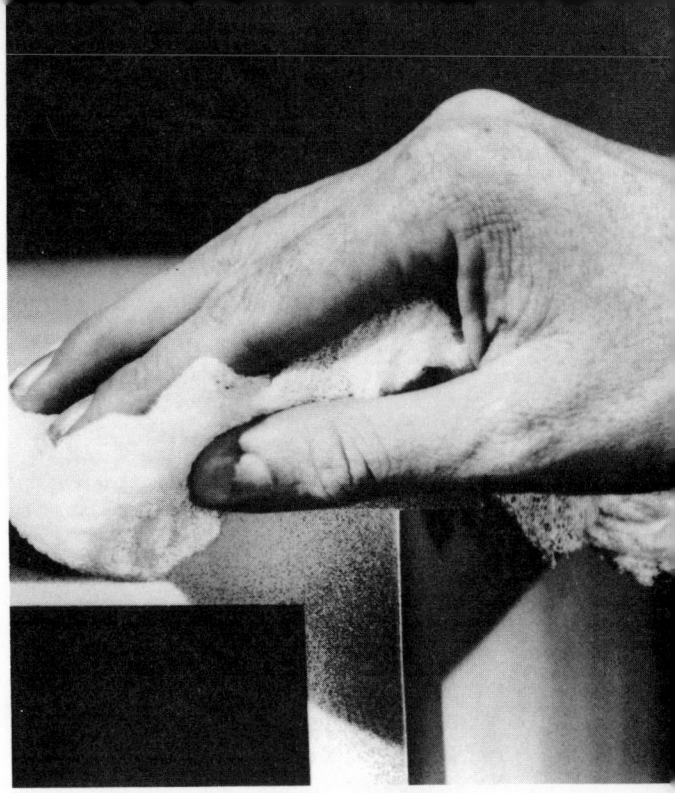

ANTIQUING is definitely "in" the home scene these days and thanks to the magic of the new antiquing kits now available it's possible to make an old piece of furniture that you've had lying around the basement or attic look brand new—or give a new piece you've just purchased the charming appearance of age.

There are several steps you can take to assure a professional-looking result. First of all, be sure to remove all handles, knobs or other hardware as it is far easier to work on a smooth surface. It is not necessary to remove old finishes, varnish or enamel, unless you want to reduce the surface to the bare wood. In that case a paint and varnish remover will do the job.

Cleaning is done by scrubbing all surfaces with tri-sodium phosphate, ammonia and water, or an abrasive household detergent using a small brush—such as a toothbrush—to get into hard-to-reach areas. Wash off all traces of the cleaning agent with clear water and allow the surface to dry.

Sanding. The final results of your antiquing job may depend on whether or not the piece of furniture you are working on is sanded properly. To obtain the best results you should use three different grades of sandpaper, starting with the coarsest of the three, and applying the finishing touches with the finest one. You can make the sanding process—which insures adhesion of the paint—much easier by using a wooden block covered with the sandpaper, coarse side out. Any deep cuts or abused areas need not be sanded smooth, as they will absorb more of the toner, producing a "distressed" effect.

If you want to fill any scratches or mars, a plastic wood filler will accomplish this job, and these areas can be sanded smooth after thoroughly dried. If you wish, these fillers can be colored to match the natural wood tones of the furniture and chalk like color mixtures can be bought with the filler at most stores.

When all sanding is completed, dampen a cloth with mineral spirits, and clear all the surfaces of dust.

Undercoating. Once the piece is dry and clear of all dust you may apply the undercoating. Read the label instructions care-

antivenin: see snakes
anvil cloud: see camping

fully, making sure that the coating is stirred thoroughly so that there isn't any pigment collected at the bottom of the can.

If you use a spray-gun to apply the paint, you should add two tablespoons of mineral spirits to thin the mixture enough to insure an even flow of paint. Remove all drawers and doors, place them on a flat horizontal surface—to avoid streaking—and you're ready to begin.

Use a flat, wide brush for the larger surfaces, painting one side of the piece of furniture at a time. By applying long, even strokes with the grain of the wood you will produce the best results. For any piece with prominent legs, turn it upside down and paint the legs first, followed by the top and work downward.

Only enough undercoating to cover the surface well should be applied, letting it dry for about twelve or twenty-four hours. Then sand lightly, and you're ready for the toner.

Above: Applying first coat of paint to the piece of furniture. Allow to dry. Right: Apply second coat of paint. Use flat, wide brush for larger surfaces, paint one side at a time.

Applying toner. After you have stirred the toner thoroughly with a wooden paddle, read the label instructions carefully, applying a thin coat of the toner in the same manner as suggested for the undercoating. Be sure to pay special attention to any carved trim and crevices, painting them first to allow more absorption of the toner. Let the color toner set for ten to thirty minutes before beginning to rub.

Rubbing. Here you can use your imagination along with a cheese cloth, dry brush and steel wool. Just be sure to step back and check your progress every so often to make sure you aren't overdoing it.

Rub large, flat areas in long, even strokes, starting with a light touch and apply more pressure as you go along. If you discover you've allowed the toner to set too long, simply dampen your rub cloth with mineral spirits. If the reverse is true and you haven't permitted the toner to set long enough, you can apply another coat and wait again.

The difficulty in rubbing intricate carved trim can be overcome by using a cotton tip in those hard-to-reach areas. After rubbing, allow at least twenty-four hours for the paint to dry thoroughly.

If you want to add a protective coat of

clear varnish, it can be applied as soon as the toner has dried. But if you wish to wax the surface, it is best to allow the paint to dry for at least a week before applying.

Special effects. After the coat of toner is applied, there are several methods which can be used to achieve interesting special effects:

Grain. For a wood grain simulation, use a dry brush for your rubbing. Place a small amount of toner on a piece of tin foil or glass, touching the tip of the brush lightly in the color. Apply in long, even strokes, with the grain of the wood but in irregular lines.

Splattern. For this artistic touch use a stiff bristle brush, such as an old toothbrush. Dip the ends of the brush into the paint, and "spring" the bristles with your finger to throw a fine spray of toner over the undercoated surface. Check the desired effect by practicing on a piece of paper first, remembering that too much toner on the brush could result in splotches.

Water stained wood. This interesting and traditional look is accomplished by first rubbing the toned surface, then splattering it with mineral spirits. The toner spreads out in the spots where the liquid has fallen, creating an authentic water stained look.

Marble. Apply a relatively heavy coat of toner to your surface, then lay a large piece of wrinkled, clear plastic lightly on top of the area. Pat the plastic lightly with a cloth, making sure wrinkles and air bubbles are in evidence. Then pick up the plastic quickly and carefully, but be sure not to drag it. Similar effects can be achieved by using a feather, a sponge or burlap, or a combination of these materials.

Tortoise shell. The best way to create this effect is to work on one small area at a time. Applying a heavier than usual amount of toner glaze, tap the surface lightly with your fingertips, changing the angle of your hand each time. A similar effect can be accomplished by tapping the surface with a short bristle brush, beginning in the center of the area and working toward the edges.

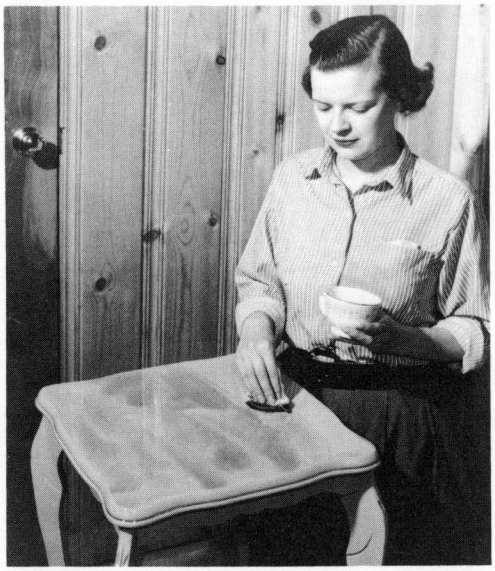

Applying toner for final glaze. Paint any carved trim or crevices first to allow for more absorption of toner.

Distressed. If your piece of furniture isn't naturally worn, this popular antiquing effect can be simulated. You can make your own scratches and mars simply by beating the surface with a heavy tool, or a burlap bag filled with chains. After sanding the scratches, apply the artists oil paint "raw umber" straight from the tube, rubbing off the excess paint vigorously.

Distressed paint. To achieve this effect you apply two layers of contrasting colors to your furniture, allowing each to dry thoroughly. Using a coarse grade of sand paper, lightly sand the surface until the initial color is in evidence. Do this only in those spots where normal wear would occur.

See also: ABRASIVES; FINISHING, WOOD; FURNITURE, USED; LUMBER; PAINTING.

Trouble-shooting Home Appliances

Here's how to do everything you can, depending on your tools and experience, to head off those costly visits by the repairman

THERE ARE SEVERAL steps you should consider before deciding what to do when an appliance breaks down or fails to operate in a normal manner. Whenever you are faced with such a situation, check-out the following pre-service program before deciding how to proceed. You may need to go no further to clear up your trouble.

Make certain there is a problem. Have you read the operating instructions supplied with your appliance so well that you are sure you know how to operate it properly and are entirely aware of what the manufacturer claims it will do? If not, read over the instructions carefully. In any case, the steps outlined below will help you spot unusual performance by localizing the problem.

Incorrect use? Maybe the person using your machine did not know how to handle it. Did she (or he) get careless? Did she expect too much? Did she overload the machine?

Is this a new operator who has not been properly instructed in how to use the appliance? (A young member of the family? a visitor? or a maid?) The same type of appliance built by a different manufacturer may have a different load capacity and/or methods of control. A user should be "checked out" on each machine.

External supply failure? An electrical appliance must have electricity, so make certain that there is power to the appliance; that the fuse hasn't blown, and that the plug hasn't pulled out of the socket.

A gas appliance must have gas. Make sure that the valve hasn't been shut off in the gas supply line.

An oil burner must have fuel. Be certain the tank isn't empty.

A water-using appliance must have the water turned on, an adequate supply of water, and the kind of water needed to do the job for which the appliance is designed.

Make certain that the temperature of the water at its points of use is within the range recommended by the manufacturer. For example: Dishwashers require water temperature in the tub within a 140° - 160° range, for each wash and rinse cycle.

You must be sure there is enough water available to operate the appliance. Both water pressure and condition of the supply are important factors and should be considered as a pair. These two control "flow rate" or gallons per minute (gpm). A low flow rate will not allow some appliances time to fill with enough water to do a good job.

Water quality such as pollution, hardness, and iron are important factors. Be sure that clean water is available. Polluted water can be a health hazard. This is unlikely with a public water supply, but you could still have pollution with an improper

appliance storage: see storage
archway: see concrete blocks
asbestos shingles: see roofs
asphalt shingles: see roofs
aster: see garden planning

plumbing connection. In the country, a well may easily become polluted. If there is any question, have your water analyzed by your local health officer.

Chemical impurities (as opposed to biological pollution) are also major problems. Mineral content such as calcium, iron, etc., will leave deposits on dishes, in clothes, and in the plumbing. Many problems of washability and poor flow are caused by "hard water."

Physical damage? Not a fault of the machine, this concerns damage done to an appliance in normally good condition, free of any failures. Examples are dropping, fire, flood, etc. This is a matter of judgment.

Is your machine worth fixing? Minor damage such as broken handles, dials, knobs, cabinet dents, and scratches should be easy to fix. Individual damaged parts can be ordered and you can replace them.

In case of fire or flood: clean out the machine thoroughly and bake the electrical parts dry at a low temperature (180°), in your oven for several hours. Check all contacts for cleanliness and all insulation for damage. Make sure that all connections are tight and see that all moving parts are operating smoothly.

Make certain that the gear box, crankcase, and such are properly lubricated and free of water and other impurities. Clean all sand, soot, and carbon deposits from all electrical connections and terminals. Remove all rust and protect the surface with a proper finish. Replace any questionable parts.

Operation failure? This is the machine-breakdown situation in which the appliance will not start, has suddenly stopped, or isn't working the way it should. After checking the external factors, you have decided that the trouble is within the appliance. Now you stop, look, listen, smell—and think!

The smell of burning insulation is a warning to turn off or disconnect your machine promptly. Then remove the cover and/or electrical part to check for burned insulation and smoke smudges. Once you find the part, it can be removed and replaced. It is usually less costly to replace burned out electrical parts than to repair them. If the insulation is burned off a connecting wire, the parts connected to this

Most appliances usually work. If one stops working, check simple things first. Is it being used properly? Is it getting enough water? Is it plugged in?

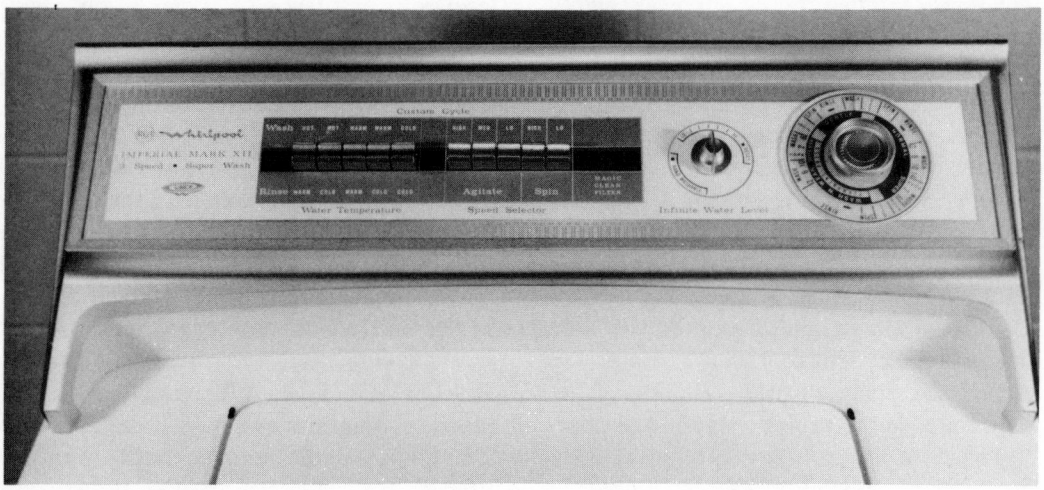

wire must be checked for "shorts" or "grounds."

Listening will tell if there are any unusual squeaks, rattles, bangs, or if your machine is "dead," assuming the switch is on.

If your appliance is inoperative, or partially so, the procedure is to use a volt-ohmmeter to check for a faulty circuit. Follow the electrical supply circuit until you come to a point where there is no reading. This indicates that there's probably something wrong between that point and the one tested just before.

Home appliance repairs. Rattles and similar noises are usually due to something loose that is vibrating or swinging out of place and hitting another part of the machine. You will have to listen and look for the offending part.

Look first for a foreign object such as a bottle cap, button, bobby pin, marble or a coin which may be floating, bouncing, rolling, or caught in a moving part of your machine. Once found, the remedy will suggest itself.

It may only be necessary to tighten some screws. However, the noise may be caused by a worn bearing which would have to be replaced. This is usually a special tool job!

Squeaks are that source of noise made by two surfaces rubbing each other or friction. It may be caused by two loose pieces of metal, which can be tightened. Lack of lubrication has a characteristic sound. Proper use of grease or oil will often remedy such noises. Another cause of noise could be a slipping belt, which usually requires a tension adjustment.

Looking carefully will often reveal a great deal about the condition of your machine. The broken control knobs previously mentioned might be binding against the escutcheon to prevent proper operation.

The door lid on many appliances operates a switch to shut off the machine while it is open. If the door is not closed tightly the machine will not start. A slight push to secure the latch may be all that is needed; however, a simple hinge or latch adjustment may be required.

A loose drive belt can be tightened; all machines have an adjustment for that. On some there is automatic tension adjustment; on others it is manual. This is usually evidenced by slow or erratic operating speed.

Keep all appliances clean. An abnormal collection of dust and dirt in a machine will certainly affect its performance. For instance, lint in your dryer can be a hazard; dust on your refrigerator coils will cause it to run too much.

A panel bulb or indicator light may be burned out. Your owner's manual may point out that it should be considered a "safety light," such as with freezers, and that as long as it was lighted everything was fine. So check it before you look further. Even the best bulbs have an end to their life sometime.

Water leakage is self evident. Once the source of a leak is located, replace the hose or tighten the clamp. Pump or tub leaks will require replacement of the part. Patching is *not* a satisfactory permanent repair.

Electrical testing. After you have checked the machine for mechanical problems the next step is to check the electrical system—both wiring and parts.

Electrical wiring and testing. Before trying to locate trouble in the electrical circuitry of an appliance you should know how to read a wiring diagram. This is the electrical map showing which parts are which and how they are connected to each other. There are many signs and symbols with which you will need to become familiar before you will be able to understand a diagram and use it intelligently. The table lists the symbols most commonly used.

APPLIANCE WIRING DIAGRAM SYMBOLS

(Note: S.P.S.T. means single-pole single-throw; S.P.D.T. means single-pole double-throw; N.O. means normally open and N.C. means normally closed.)

MANUAL AND MECHANICAL SWITCHES

S.P.S.T.

S.P.D.T.

S.P.D.T.
(2 Contacts on One Side)

Multi-Position

Push-Button (N.O.)
(Momentary Contact)

Push-Button (N.C.)

Push-Button
(Two-Circuit)

Timer Switch

Pressure Operated
(S.P.D.T.)

Centrifugal Switch

Master or Control Sw.
(Number of Positions
and Internal Contact
Operation as Required)

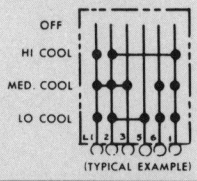

(TYPICAL EXAMPLE)

TEMPERATURE ACTUATED COMPONENTS

(Note: Symbols shown to be used for thermostats, bimetal switches, overload protectors, or other similar components, as required.)

S.P.S.T.
(Open on Heat Rise)

S.P.S.T.
(Close on Heat Rise)

TEMPERATURE ACTUATED COMPONENTS

(Note: Symbols shown to be used for thermostats, bimetal switches, overload protectors, or other similar components, as required.)

Temp. Actuated
(Close on Heat Rise)

Temp. Actuated
(Open on Heat Rise)

S.P.S.T.
(Open on Heat Rise)

S.P.D.T.

S.P.D.T.

S.P.S.T.
(Two Contacts)

S.P.S.T. (Adj.)
(Close on Heat Rise)

S.P.D.T. (Adj.)

S.P.S.T. (Adj.)
(Open on Heat Rise)

S.P.D.T. (Adj.)
(With Aux. "OFF" Contacts)
(Typical Example)

S.P.S.T. (w/Internal Heater)
(Close on Heat Rise)

S.P.S.T. (w/Internal Heater)
(Open on Heat Rise)

MOTORS

Note: Internal Motor Circuitry May Be Shown if Required.

Compressor Motor

Single-Speed Motor

Two-Speed Motor

Multi-Speed Motor (Show Internal Circuitry as Req'd)

(Typical Example)

Three-Speed Motor

Timer Motor

Single-Speed

Two-Speed

Three-Speed

LINES AND CONNECTIONS

Integral Conductor

Harness Wire

Crossover

Crossover

Shield

Permanent Connection

Terminal

Ground (Earth)

Ground (Chassis)

Plug Connector

Grounded Service Cord (3-prong)

Service Cord (2-prong)

Mechanical Connection

Terminal Board (Number and Arrangement as Required)

Multiple Connector (Engaged)

Male Female

LIGHTS

Incandescent

Germicidal

Neon

Fluorescent

COMBINATION DEVICES

Relay-Magnetic
(Arrangement of Contacts
as Necessary to Show Operation)

Relay-Thermal
(Arrangement of Contacts
as Necessary to Show Operation)

Timer (Defrost)

MISCELLANEOUS

Circuit Breaker

Coil (Solenoid)

Coil

NOTE: COILS MAY ALSO BE SHOWN WITH OPEN LOOPS AS IN THE EXAMPLES BELOW.

Coil (Solenoid)

Coil

Fuse

Heater or
Resistor

Humidistat

Relay

Use Symbols for Coil
and Switches and Show
Separately in Circuit.

Thermocouple

Transformer

Adjustable Component
(Arrow Drawn Through Component
at Approximately 45°)

Auto. Starter

Ballast

Bell

Buzzer

Capacitor
(Polarity Must
Be Correct)

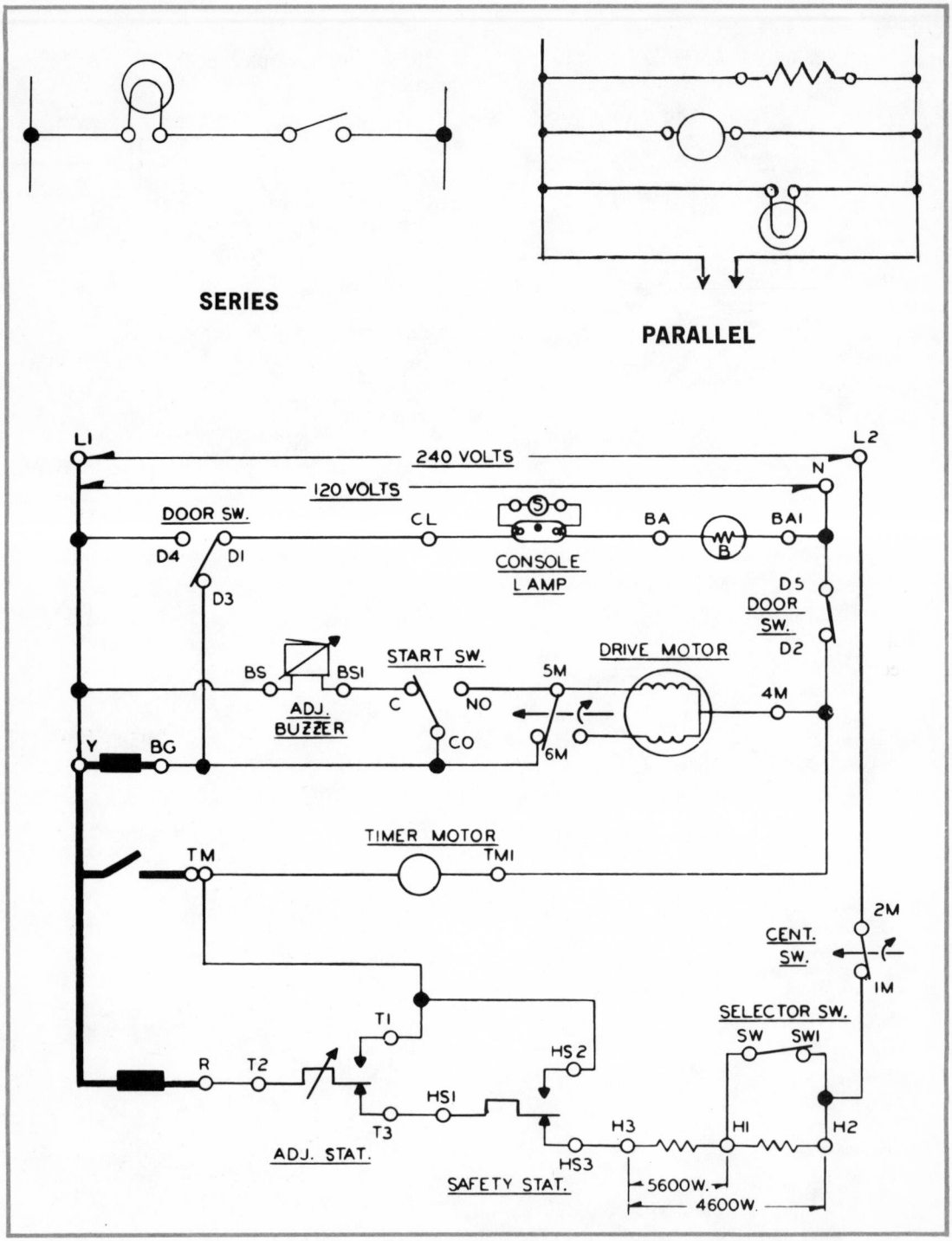

This typical wiring diagram is for an electric dryer. Every appliance complicated enough to require a wiring diagram has one attached in an out-of-sight location.

Switches and thermostats control the flow of electricity. Motors, heaters, lights, and solenoids use electricity to do work. A relay both uses and controls the current.

The two principal methods of connecting parts are "in series" and "in parallel." Most diagrams are a combination of these as shown in the electric dryer diagram.

The ways of wiring. A schematic wiring diagram shows, by symbols, the various parts that use electricity and how they are wired—electrically connected—to each other. This type of diagram is usually attached to an appliance and sometimes included in your owner's manual.

Don't let the size or complexity of a diagram, or the number of parts and wires worry you. Study it and follow each circuit, one at a time. Remember that there must always be a complete electrical path from one side of the input to the other.

Electrical failures. An electrical part may fail for either a mechanical or an electrical reason:

1. Switch parts may break, wear, or burn out.
2. Motors may develop bearing wear or "freezing."
3. A housing may crack.
4. A screw may vibrate loose.
5. Solenoid plungers may stick.
6. Contact points may stick and weld together.
7. A loose part may chafe the insulation or cut a wire.
8. A part may "burn out." That is, when it is overheated, a wire or a contact may melt thus breaking the electrical circuit. The part should be replaced.
9. A part may go "open circuit." That is, a wire or connection may break or a contact in a switch may fail to close. This can be repaired or replaced.
10. A part may "short-circuit." That is, an unexpected, unauthorized, or improper electrical connection may oc-

A volt-ohmmeter is the recommended tool for testing appliance electrical circuits.

cur within a part. This diverts the flow of electricity from its proper path, drawing an excessive amount of current. It usually causes a fuse to blow or an overload protector to function. The short will have to be cleared and the part repaired or replaced, depending on the extent of damage.

11. A part may "ground." That is, there will be an insulation breakdown between the current carrying and the non-current carrying parts of an assembly. The part may remain operating but the user will get a shock from the appliance unless metal parts of the appliance are properly grounded.

All built-in appliances have provisions for grounding to a water pipe or some such metal conductor to earth. Many plug in appliances are now connected with a special three-wire cord, one terminal of which grounds through a special wire in the household's electrical circuit.

Remember these basic electrical failures, then realize that one may cause another. For example, a wire might chafe against a frame, eventually wearing the insulation to a degree that will allow the bare wire to "ground" on the frame. This may cause a "short circuit" that could "burn out" a switch, causing it to go "open" and giving the user a "shock" in the process.

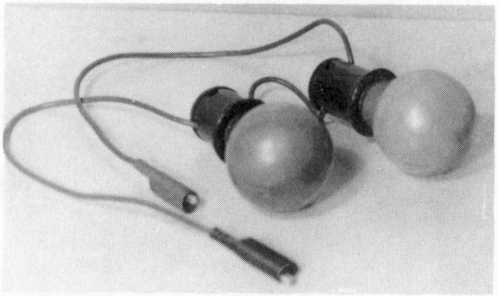

A test light with two 120-volt lamps in series can be used to test either a 120- or 24-volt line to determine if a circuit is live. Use 15- or 25-watt lamps.

Repairing connections. Most wires are attached to components with quick-disconnect-type terminals and connectors. A damaged terminal or connector should be replaced, soldering a wire to a terminal will work in a pinch but it is not recommended. This will not affect operation of the machine; but it will make things more difficult if the part has to be removed in the future.

Chafed wire insulation must be taped to protect it from being grounded and then the wire should be so positioned that the chafing won't happen again.

When disconnecting leads from the terminals, it is wise to make a sketch using a color code to remind you of the right terminals for each lead.

It often happens that the electrical supply cord breaks at the place where it connects to the attachment cap. This can occur through handling, aging (drying out), or accident. If the rest of the wire is all right and shows no signs of wear, cracking, drying out, etc., the best thing to do is to connect a new attachment cap.

Installing new cap on line cord. There is always more than one way to do a job, but when you attach a new cap to an appliance cord be sure to use an "underwriter's" knot. This is the approved means of providing "strain relief" so that any pulling of the cord will not tend to pull the wires from the screw terminals.

Using a test light. A great deal of checking can be done with a test light by connecting it to the terminals in parallel with the electricity-using part in question. If the bulb lights you know that electricity is available at the terminals of the part that is being tested and that any trouble is probably in the part itself. If the bulb does not light, you know that electricity is not reaching the part being tested; therefore, the trouble must be elsewhere.

When using a test light on a normal 115-volt appliance, a 115-volt bulb will do;

but when working on an electric range, dryer, or any other 230-volt appliance, you must install a 230-volt bulb. At the higher voltage this bulb will light normally and at 115 volts it will light dimly. A 115-volt bulb used on 230-volt appliances will burn out.

Caution. You must know the complaint or reason for service before starting to look for trouble. This will tell you where to start testing and trouble-shooting. When using a test light to trouble-shoot an appliance, remember the power is turned on and you can get a shock. Be careful!

When working on an automatic appliance in which operations are controlled by a timer, make certain the timer is advanced to the circuit in question.

If you have a "healthy respect" for electricity and what it can do, it would be smart to use an ohmmeter or continuity tester with the power *disconnected* from the machine.

A simple continuity tester will show whether a circuit is continuous between two test points and indicate that electricity could flow there. This tester should be accurate enough to prove circuit "completeness" when the bulb lights.

A good volt-ohmmeter is a big help in circuit testing and will do much more than a test light. If you have one, use it.

Some areas of testing in electrical circuits require sensitive instruments. You would be wise to have such work tested by your qualified service man. When you reach the point where the equipment you have won't do the job, it is best to call for help from someone who has the special tools.

Who does the job? If, after having satisfied yourself that the trouble is not of a simple and observable nature, you still wish to continue further toward finding it yourself; you must answer some questions: Do you have the equipment to continue? Tools? Ability? Parts?

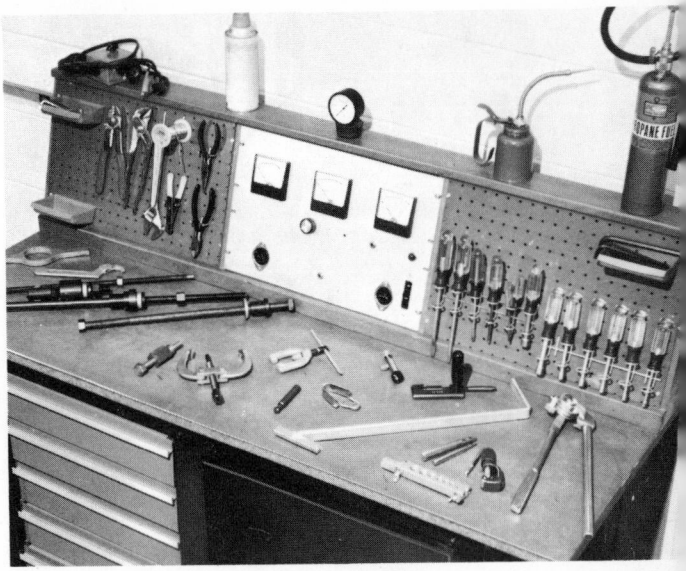

An appliance repairman's workbench.

If you reach a "yes" decision, read carefully the basic information on the type of appliance you wish to repair. Also restudy the owner's manual for that appliance, supplied by the manufacturer.

Locate the wiring diagram, usually found on the access panel of appliances which are complex enough to require such information. Follow the steps outlined in the trouble-shooting charts until the failure is located.

Decide—again and finally—are you still going ahead with the job yourself? If you have gone this far to find out what the trouble is, you probably can. At the same time, some troubles way within the machine require special tools and equipment to repair.

Among items needing particular tools, equipment, and test apparatus are refrigerator compressor or evaporator, gear case assembly on a washer, bearings, an electric motor or coil needing rewinding, thermostats, timers, and and burner assemblies. This is the area where it is cheaper and safer to ask for professional help. G.M.

See also: INDIVIDUAL APPLIANCE LISTINGS.

Finishing an Attic Room on a Small Budget

Unused attic space in your home can be converted economically into an attractive living area

This is the kind of rough attic that the home handyman can convert to attractive living space, at a cost of about one third of what a contractor would charge to do the work.

MANY OWNERS of small single houses find they lack a spare room for unexpected guests or for the children when the size of their family increases.

The home handyman can build a finished room at comparatively small expense if there is a rough attic in the house with a stairway, which is used now only for storage. Such was the case with this bungalow-type house that has a large unfinished attic and only five rooms on the first floor; an extra guest room was badly needed.

While house designs vary considerably, in layout and construction, the procedure outlined here can be used as a general guide to the work by modifying the plans as required to fit the individual house.

The cost for materials to build this attractive room was about one-third of the cost of having a contractor do the work.

There was no dormer on this house which, of course, would be desirable to admit added light and ventilation to the new room, but it was felt that the expense would not be justified in having one built by a professional carpenter. Therefore, this was not considered.

A large window facing west will provide good afternoon sunlight. With a similar window in the unfinished section, it is possible to get cross ventilation with both windows open, if the doors separating the two sections are left open.

This project called for framing off with studding an area 14x15 feet, not counting the space taken by the stairway and the closet. A partition divides the finished from the rough part. The chimney is in the rough section, and the soil pipe that extends up through the roof is enclosed in the closet wall. A door leads from the finished room to the closet and another door goes from the back wall of the closet into the storage area.

Most attics have a single flooring overlay over the joists. If one doesn't, then it is necessary to lay some spruce boards for a flat, smooth sub-floor before putting up the studding. Later, hardboard is layed over the sub-floor and floor tiles are used for the finished floor.

First step is to lay out your room area, taking care to get the marked out space square. This can be done with the usual corner measurements, and snapping a chalk line guide on the floor.

audio master control: see intercoms
auger: see plumbing
automatic choke: see choke, automatic
automatic garage door operator: see garage door, overhead
automatic washer: see washer and dryer

A knee wall is required at two sides of the room which should be a minimum height of three feet. Short studs cut on an angle at one end should match the slope of the roof rafters. Minimum height of the ceiling should be about seven feet from the finished floor.

Collar beams are nailed to the rafters as the supports for the ceiling. Where the distance is only about four to five feet, 1x6-inch fir boards can be used for collar beams. Use 2x4 or 2x6-inch lumber for longer spans between nailing points on the rafters. These beams should be leveled, and their lower edges properly lined up to get a good level ceiling. Nail furring strips to the collar beams on 12-inch centers for the tiles used to finish off ceiling.

Use 2x3-inch studs in the dividing partition between the finished and unfinished areas since this partition carries no weight, or substitute 2x4s if preferred or required by a building code. The sole plate consists of furring strips which are nailed to the sub-flooring. Studding can be used for the sole plate at somewhat higher cost.

Put the studs up on two-foot centers so a standard sheet of four-foot wide wall board can be conveniently nailed in place. If more studs are desired locate them on 16-inch centers. Make sure all studs are installed level.

Short pieces of 2x3s are used for the knee wall. They are attached to the lower edges of the rafters to provide nailing points for the top ends of the partition studs where they come between rafters. These studs for the knee wall are cut at an angle and nailed to the existing rafters. There is a limited height for the door, due to the sloping rafters, but it is possible to use a 74-inch door.

Short pieces of furring, with end cleats, or 2x3s must be nailed between the knee wall studs where they are attached to the rafters for supports and to provide a nailing surface for the wallboard. Remember to use double-studding in the closet.

Install the heating outlets while the walls are still open. In this case the original contractor had carried a riser from the steam boiler up the side of the chimney to the attic floor line, where it was capped, thus providing for future expansion.

It was a simple job to remove the cap and extend the 1¼-inch pipe to the location for the new radiator. Measurements

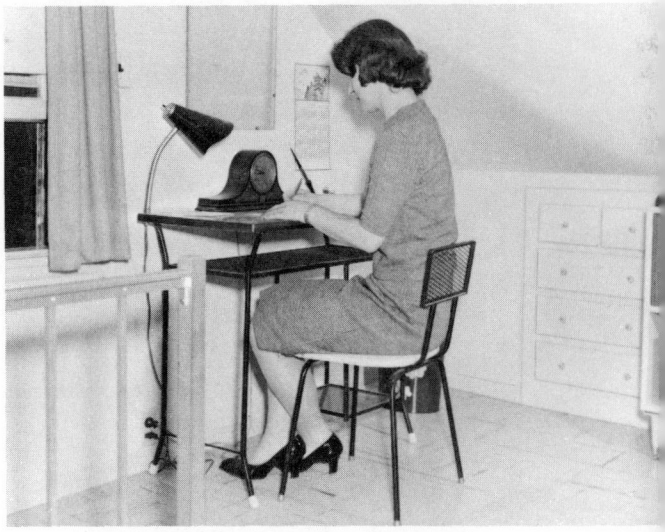

Completed conversion, shown in these two photos, includes built-in bookcase (at left of room) and built-in chest of drawers (at right). Railing in background next to the stairwell was purchased as a unit from a department store.

FLOOR PLAN

BUILT-IN BOOK SHELVES

42" CLOTHES POLE

48"

CLOSET

PASSAGEWAY

CLOSET DOOR

S S

DOOR TO UNFINISH STORAGE AREA

14'6"

6'

ALUMINUM RAILING 30" HIGH

DOWN

S3

EXISTING WINDOW 28 x 36" FRAME AND SASH ONLY INSTALLED ORIGINALLY

15'6"

RADIATOR

KNEE WALL 3-4' HIGH

BUILT-IN BOOK SHELVES

BUILT-IN CHEST OF DRAWERS

CEILING LIGHT

WALL LIGHT

RECEPTACLE OUTLET

S SINGLE POLE SWITCH

S-3 3-WAY SWITCH

RECEPTACLE OUTLETS SPACED NOT OVER 12' APART

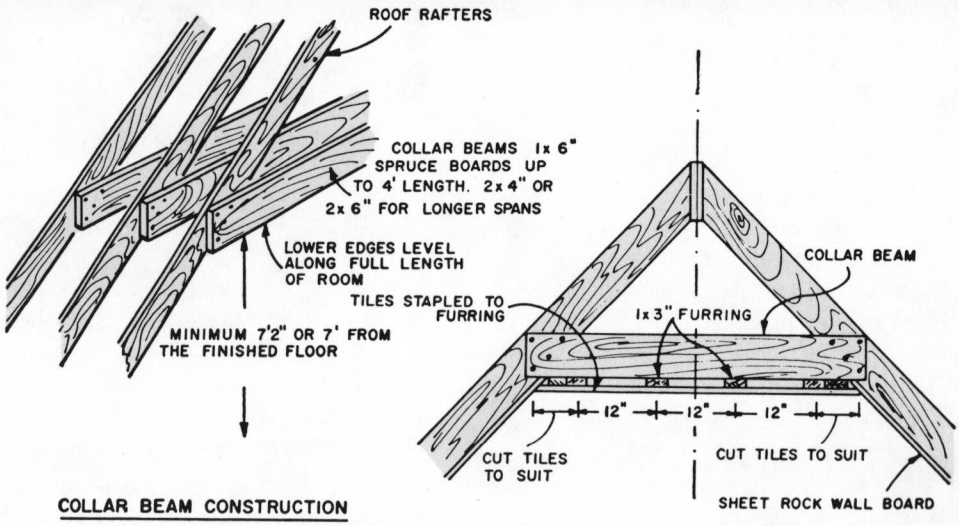

COLLAR BEAM CONSTRUCTION

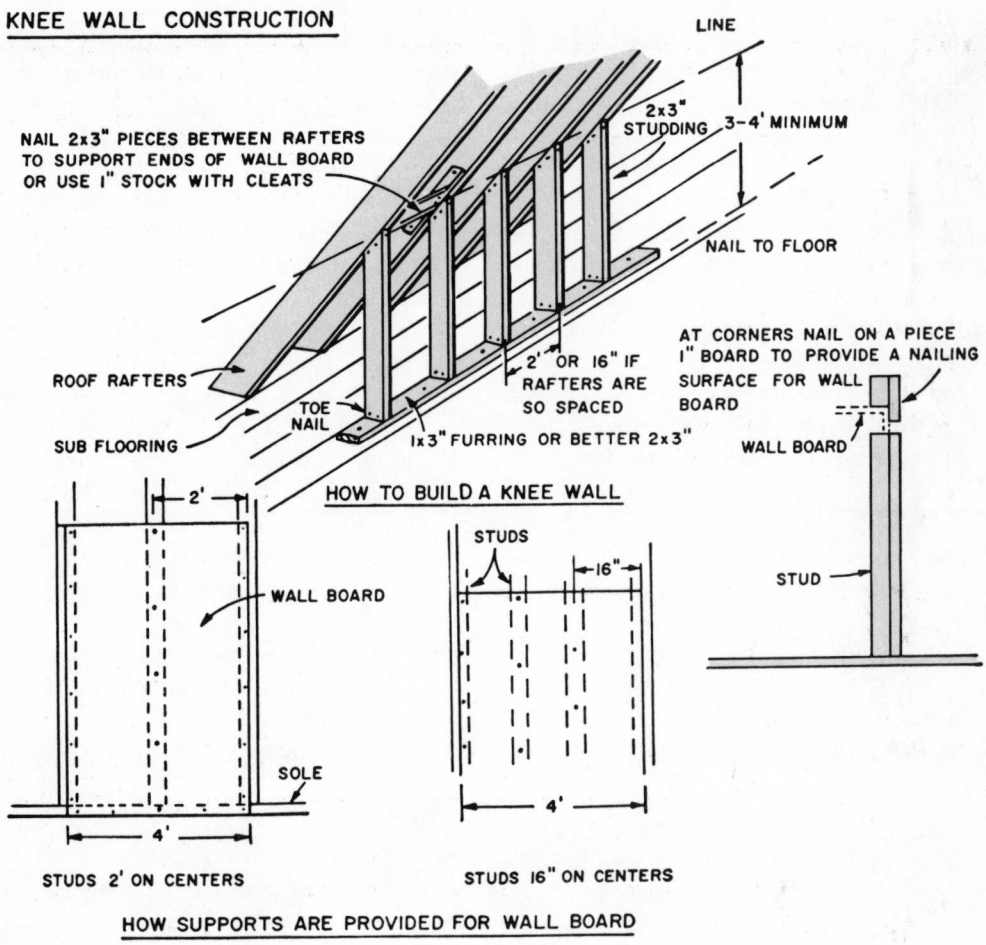

were taken and the pipe cut and threaded at a local plumbing supply dealer.

We bought the radiator from a dealer in used plumbing supplies for about half of what a new one would cost. Select a radiator that's as clean as possible and is large enough to provide adequate heat.

In cases where there is no extension from the boiler provided for future use, or where another type of heating system exists, it is necessary to call in a heating man to do this part of the work for you. In some cases the extra piping or duct work can be brought up from the basement by running it through a closet. Any exposed duct or pipe can be completely covered with asbestos sheathing.

In any case, use insulation over the heating pipe to conserve the heat. The pipe should have a slight downward slant which allows condensed water to flow back to the boiler.

Electrical wiring, like heating, should be installed while the walls are still open. One way to bring power to the room is to run a new cable to the attic from the main fuse box. You might be able to snake it up next to the chimney. Another method: hook the attic system to the junction or fixture boxes of the wiring for the rooms below, especially if these boxes are in the ceiling. If you do use existing wiring, make certain you do not overload any circuits.

Insulation necessary. For maximum effectiveness, try to cut insulation to exact length required so you won't end up "patching" one channel with a series of small pieces. The thick fiberglass in the material used here ensures maximum effect, and the reflective aluminum foil serves both as a vapor barrier and to reflect heat back in the room in winter.

Attach insulation to the sides of the roof rafters with ⅜ or ½-inch staples that are placed every 12 inches. Staple length is determined by the hardness and condition of the rafters. Fold the edges of the paper over the front corners so that when the finished wallboard material is on, a good seal is provided.

Edges of the insulation may have to be cut a bit at points where projections exist to fit the material tightly and smoothly in place. In this house 23-inch insulation was required for the roof because the rafters were on 24-inch centers. Some houses have rafters that are on 16-inch centers; 15-inch insulation should be used. With the 23-inch size, it took just about one roll to a bay in a continuous length.

One wall of the room was also insulated. The fiberglass was cut off at the top ends and stapled to the last roof rafter to make a tight and weatherproof barrier.

Variety of wall covering. After the insulation is securely fastened you can install the wallboard. Sheetrock makes a very suitable material if care is taken to make the joints as invisible as possible. It is also one of the lowest cost materials for the job.

Or you can use wood paneling with V grooves that is available in several attractive finishes and grains. However, it is necessary to add horizontal cross braces in your framing to support the panels properly. The cost of such paneling will be considerably higher.

In the interests of economy, sheetrock

➤ *Use level to check all studs for plumb. The doorways are framed with double studs. The doorway in the foreground is for the closet. The one beyond it is in the back of the closet and opens to the unfinished portion of the attic.*

Fiberglass and aluminum foil insulation is held in place by staples driven into studs and rafters every 12 inches.

was used. This material is available in ⅜-inch thickness. The side edges taper slightly so the joint can be sealed without causing a seam that can be easily noticed.

A special plaster compound is troweled into the joint, then a strip of perforated tape pressed down into the plaster. More plaster is then applied over the tape, finishing it off smooth with the surrounding surface. If carefully done, the joints will be practically invisible and will not crack open later.

Plan storage areas. A built-in chest of drawers was installed in the knee wall which is one of the attractive features of the new room. These units can be purchased in lumber yards complete, all ready to fit in the opening provided in the wall. Install by nailing through the finish trim at the sides and into the studs. The one used here is a 24-inch size, which fit between the knee wall studs.

Two built-in bookshelves were made up from one-inch pine stock and installed in the knee wall at opposite sides of the room. It was assembled with glue and finishing nails, with the shelves fitting in dadoes cut in the sides. The back is a piece of ⅛-inch *Masonite* hardboard. Finish nails were driven through the sides and into the studs. Pine trim was used to cover the raw edges of the cabinet.

Apply finish trim around the window, using materials commonly sold for this purpose by lumber yards. Originally, only the window frame and the two sash sections were in place in the rough attic.

Molding and ceiling tile. This finish trim consists of a stool and apron at the bottom of the window, and smooth stock for the sides and top. Install stop molding around

Pine bookcase with hardboard back was designed to fit into opening between studs of kneewall.

the sides and top so it lines up close to the lower sash to keep it in place.

Screws should be used for this molding so it can easily be removed to replace a broken window or broken sash cords. Fin-

CORNER DETAIL OF WINDOW

SHOWING RELATION OF FINISH MATERIAL WITH NAMES

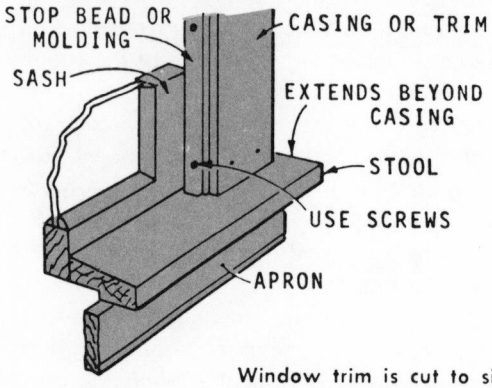

Window trim is cut to size and attached with 6D finishing nails. Use screws to hold the sash stop molding.

Finishing an Attic Room on a Small Budget

ish nails were used for the trim, but they should not be driven all the way in with a hammer. To avoid indenting on the wood, use a nail set to drive them in the last ⅛-inch and countersink the head just below the surface.

To complete the ceiling, block tiles are put up, which come in 12x12-inch squares and are made of ½-inch insulating material that is painted on one side. The furring strips were spaced so the ceiling tile could be attached with $\frac{9}{16}$-inch staples.

Next step is to apply the rest of the finish, which includes the door frame, the finish molding, and nailing the base molding in place.

Frame the door opening. The door frame was constructed from 1x3½-inch

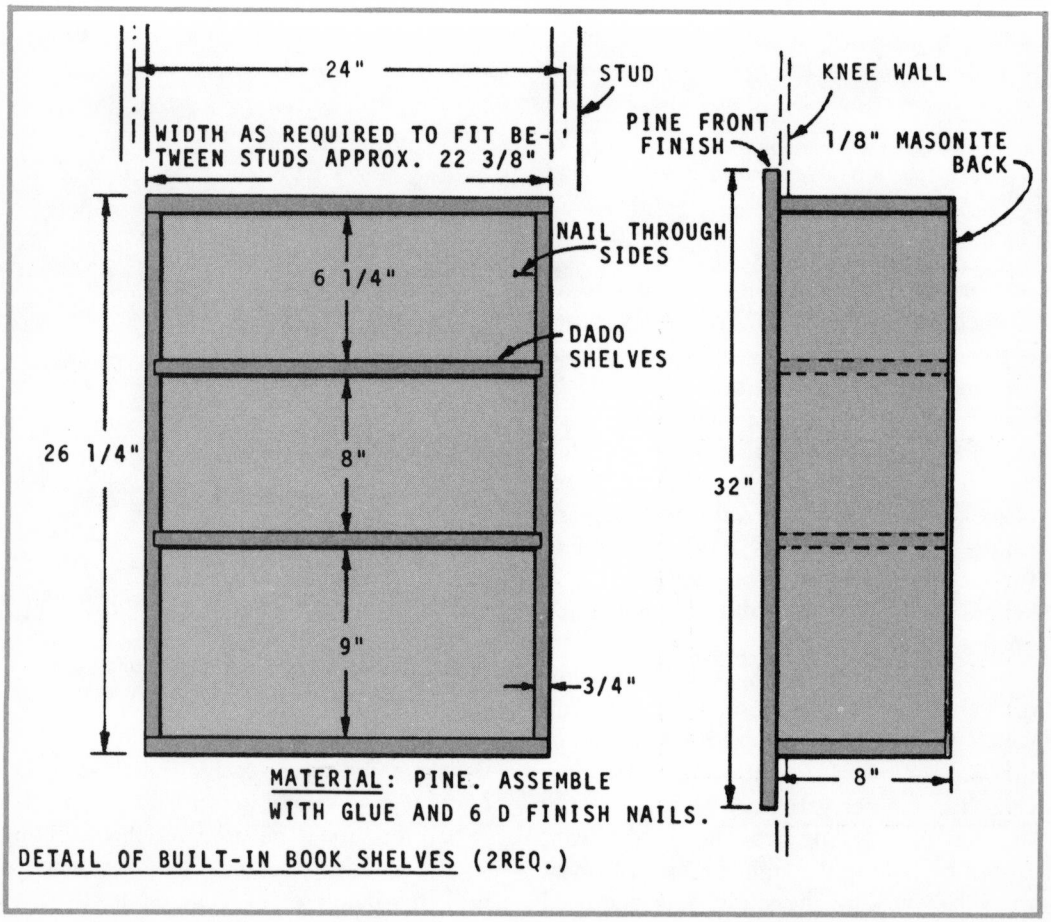

DETAIL OF BUILT-IN BOOK SHELVES (2REQ.)

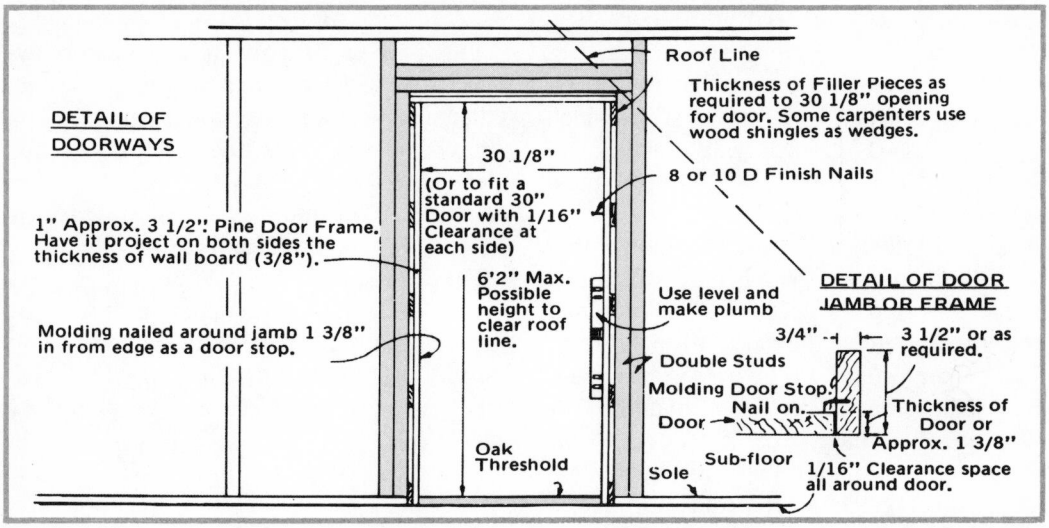

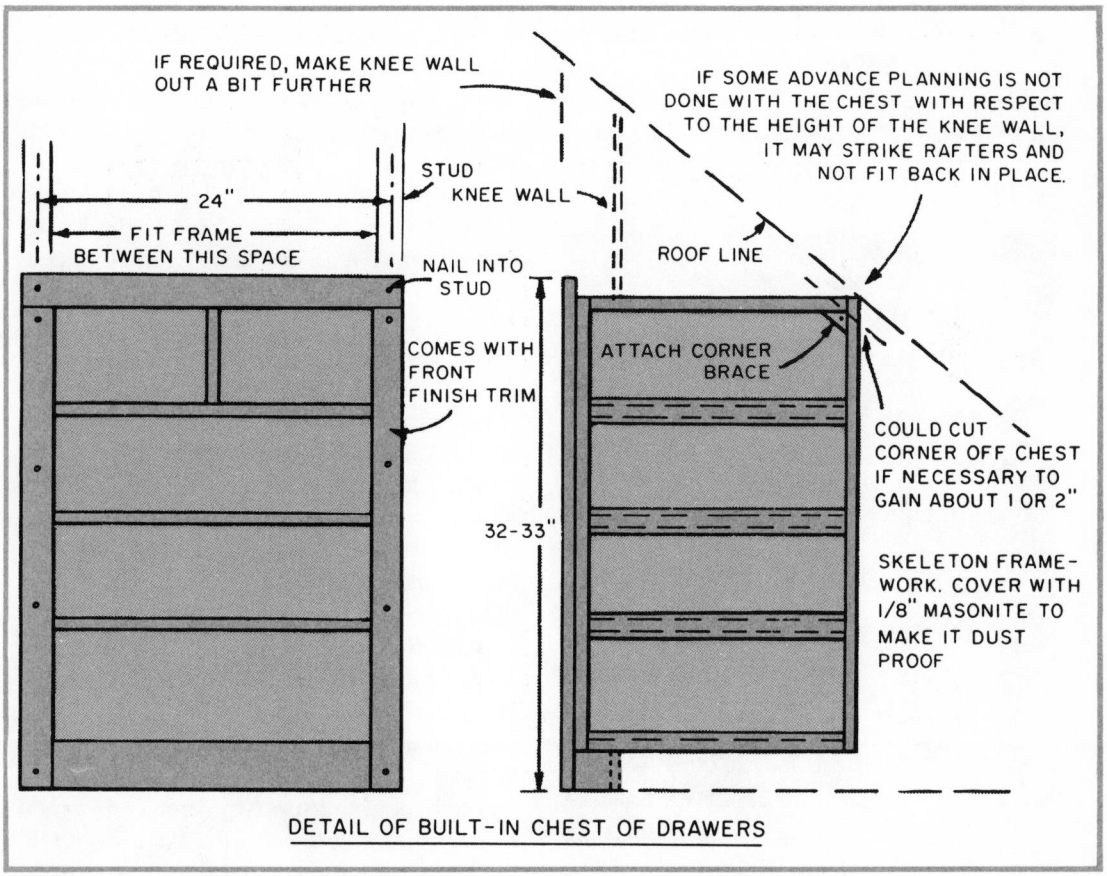

DETAIL OF BUILT-IN CHEST OF DRAWERS

clear pine, with an oak threshold. The frame, or jamb as it sometimes called, should be wide enough so it is flush with the wallboard at both sides. If 2x3-inch studs are used, 3½-inch wide molding will be about the right size. For 2x4-inch studs, it will have to be wider.

Cut the stock to fit the opening so that with the addition of small blocks between it and the studs, a space will be provided to properly fit a standard 30-inch door. Figure the height to take the maximum height door that can get in. A standard 78-inch door will have to be cut down to fit.

Provide a stop for the door by nailing some molding around the sides and at the top of the jamb. Position this molding so it will allow the door to come flush with the edge of the jamb. Oak threshold stock can be easily purchased, and it should be cut and fitted between the lower ends of the jamb and nailed to the floor. Lay out this work to allow about 1/16-inch clearance all around the door so that it will open and close without binding in the door framework.

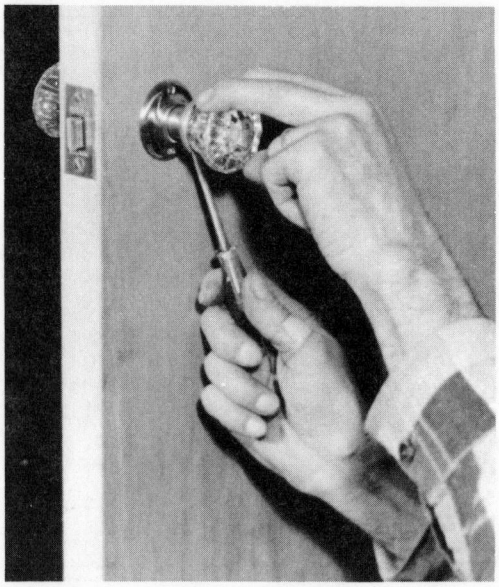

▲ *Tightening the doorknob setscrew is the final step in installing the door latch.*

Cut door to size. A flush door can be cut down to fit your needs. Clamp two pieces of 2x3-inch stock on the guide line, then use a sharp, fine-tooth hand saw to make the cut. Since these doors are hollow except at the sides and ends for a distance in of around 4 or 5 inches or so, cut across the hollow section and glue in a filler piece.

Make the filler piece from any soft wood stock of a thickness to fit in the hollow space, and about 2 or 3 inches wide. After the glue sets, the piece can be planed off flush.

Fit the door in the jamb by shaping it to get spacing all around for clearance, then hang it with two standard butt hinges that are set into a chiseled recess.

Position the hinges about 7 inches from each end of the door. Assemble the leaves with the pins, then place the door in the jamb. Insert a 1/16-inch piece of stock between the lower end of the door and the threshold for clearance, then mark the positions of the hinges on the jamb.

Chisel a recess for the top hinge leaves to bring them in flush and screw the leaves to the jamb. With the door again in place, insert the hinge pins and try it for a fit.

A little adjustment may be required, such as placing a piece of carboard in back of the hinges to shift the clearance to make it uniform, or perhaps a bit may have to be planed off the door if it strikes.

The door latch ordinarily used on a closet comes in a variety of types so you have many to choose from. They usually require that a large hole be bored in the door edge to pass the body of the latch, and another hole bored through the door at the point where the spindle is to pass through.

A latch plate must be fitted on the jamb. Let it in flush with a chisel at the correct marked spot, and use two screws to secure it. It's important to have the latch fit in the opening correctly to hold the door closed.

➤ *Mastic for vinyl-asbestos tile is spread with a notched-edge trowel obtained from the tile supplier.*

➤ *To cut edge pieces, warm vinyl-asbestos tile with a torch, then cut it with scissors.*

➤ *Apply two coats of flat wall paint after all plastering and filling work has been completed and all plastered surfaces have been sanded.*

Trim around the door can be applied now, using any type of molding finish desired. Carefully miter the corners, and keep edge back about ¼-inch from the side of the jamb. Set the nails in so the holes can be filled later.

Complete the finish by installing a base molding that goes all around the room. It can be about 2½ to 3 inches wide, as commonly used in many modern houses today. Countersink the finishing nails. They should be large enough so they hold the molding securely to the wallboard. Miter all corners.

Work in the closet consists of applying the wallboard to the studding in the same general manner as in the rest of the room. The door that leads out to the unfinished section is hung exactly the same way as the room door just completed. A base molding is also installed.

Paint suggestions. Use a brush or roller to apply two coats of flat paint to all the wallboard surfaces. The use of one of the water-base paints is suggested for easy application. This goes on well and dries to a uniform flat finish that is very attractive. It comes in a variety of colors, and in this case beige was selected.

The finish trim was painted with semi-gloss beige enamel. Before applying the enamel to the woodwork make sure all finish nails have been set and the filler used to cover the holes sanded down to provide a smooth and uniform surface.

Lay the flooring. One of the final major steps in the job is to lay the flooring. Sweep the floor and make sure there are no nails protruding or bits of material remaining. Hardboard, in ¼-inch thickness can be obtained from lumber yards in 4x4-foot sheets for easy handling, or cut to that size.

It should be nailed securely to hold the hardboard flat over the entire room. It may be necessary in a few spots to plane down some of the boards of the sub-floor or drive in some nails to level up the boards.

The tiles used were vinyl-asbestos which proved satisfactory, but one of the other available types may be used if desired.

Safety measures. One of the attractive features of the room is the aluminum stairway railing that was purchased from a department store in partially knockdown form. A few holes were required to be drilled in the posts during assembly, but otherwise it was quite complete. It was bolted down to the floor at the post flanges with lag screws. Railings come in six-foot lengths which was just right for our purpose, and the posts are 30 inches high.

A hand railing for the stairway was built from a length of one-inch electrician's aluminum conduit. Two hardwood plugs were used to cap the ends. Brackets commonly sold for use with wood hand rails were attached to the wall with wood screws that must turn into the studs.

Cost of new room. A breakdown in cost figures was approximately as follows:

Insulation	$100
Sheetrock	42
Ceiling tiles	6
2x3-inch studs, boards, and other lumber	45
Flush doors and all finish trim	25
Floor tiles	40
Wiring and fixtures	35
Used radiator and piping	30
Built-in drawer chest	18
Pine for bookshelves	6
Aluminum railing	16
Hand rail and brackets	4
Hardboard floor underlay	15
Paint, nails and miscellaneous	15
	$397

The cost of course will vary somewhat in different localities and your sources of supply. A little shopping for prices among various firms dealing in building materials will often effect a saving. H.P.S.

See also: WIRING, ELECTRICAL; INDIVIDUAL HOME ADDITIONS LISTINGS.

BLUEPRINT LANGUAGE

Here is a listing of abbreviations, terms and symbols most often used on blueprints and specifications noting materials, structure and conditions. You will find this list quite useful as reference after choosing a new home plan and ordering the working drawings

A.W.	Automatic Washer
A.D.	Ash Dump
Cab.	Cabinet
Ceil.	Ceiling
℄	Center Line
C.I.	Cast Iron
CL.	Closet
Cl.W.P.	Clear White Pine
Conc.	Concrete
Contr.	Contractor
C.o.	Clean Out
C.O.	Cased Opening
Cols.	Columns
Corr.	Corrugated
Csmt.	Casement
Cu. ft.	Cubic feet
D.A.	Double Acting Door
D.H.	Double Hung
Diag.	Diagonal
D & M	Dressed and Matched
Dn.	Down
D.W.	Dish Washer
Exp.	Exposure
Ext.	Exterior
F.A.I.	Fresh Air Intake
F.	Fill
Fin.	Finished
Ftgs.	Footings
Fxd. (or F)	Fixed
Ga.	Gauge
Galv.	Galvanized
Gl. (Glazed)	Glass
Hd. Rm.	Head Room
Hor. (Horiz.)	Horizontal
H.T.	House Trap
Htr.	Heater
L.	Angle Iron
L. (Lin.)	Linen
Lav.	Lavatory
Lino.	Linoleum
L.T.	Laundry Tub (Or Trap)
Lts.	Lights (Glass Areas)
M.C.	Medicine Cabinet
Min.	Minimum
O.C.	On Centers
O.H.	Overhead Door
Part.	Partition
P.C.	Pull Cord
Pl.	Plate
Plwd.	Plywood
Prefab.	Prefabricated
R.C.	Reinforced Concrete
12 R	Twelve Risers (Vertical part of steps)
S.	Sink
Sect.	Section
Shr.	Shower
Sl.	Sliding
T. C.	Terra Cotta
Temp.	Tempered
T.H.	Top Hinged
T.O.	Trimmed Opening
T & G	Tongued and Grooved
Unex.	Unexcavated
V (or Vd)	V Groove
Vert.	Vertical
T.W.	To Weather
W.C.	Water Closet
W.I.	Wrought Iron
W.P.	Waterproof
ϕ	Round
Φ	Square foot

ELECTRICAL SYMBOLS

Light—Wall or Ceiling

Ceiling Light with Pull Cord

Wall Receptacle

Waterproof Base Receptacle

Combination Wall Receptacle and Light Outlet

Heavy Duty Outlet

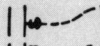
Wall Switch

3-Way Switch

Telephone Outlet

Make an Automobile Headlight Switch

This device will keep your car lights on while you walk to your door, then turn them off automatically

THE NIGHT may be dark and dismal when you pull in your driveway, but thanks to your automatic headlighter you'll have no trouble seeing the way to your doorstep. This automatic headlight timer is a two-transistor circuit that keeps your headlights illuminated for 60 seconds after you leave your car. A simple ten-dollar project (all new parts), it's connected in parallel with your existing auto headlight switch and is operated by a single pushbutton. The timer has been field-tested and has been proven extremely reliable. It is for installation in a 12-Volt negative ground electrical system, but installing the unit in positive ground systems is a snap for hobbyists.

The how of it. When the driver depresses pushbutton switch S1, timing capacitor C1 charges to 12 volts and turns on transistor Q1, which drives power transistor Q2 into conduction. This, in turn, energizes the relay which has its contacts connected in parallel with the headlight switch. The relay will stay energized until C1 discharges to the Q1 turn-off level. The lights-on period is determined by the value of C1, R1, and the characteristics of transistor Q1. With values shown on the schematic drawing, about 60 lights-on seconds are provided.

What to do. Construct the timer in a small 3¼x2⅛x1⅝-inch mini-box where all components except the relay and pushbutton switch S1 are mounted on a 1⅞x1⅜-inch printed circuit card. The circuit card may be made by any of the conventional methods.

Special attention must be given in mounting some of the components on the printed circuit card. Capacitor C1 must be mounted with its + terminal connected to R1. Also, special attention must be given to spacing the transistors at least ⅛-inch

automobile alternator: see alternator, auto
automobile battery: see batteries
automobile electrical system: see electrical, auto
automobile electronic equipment: see electronics

away from the circuit card to avoid overheating during soldering. Two insulated washers are used to mount power transistor Q2 to the printed circuit board.

Interconnecting wires from the circuit board should each be at least 4 inches long. They can be cut to proper length just before wiring in the mini-box. Mount RY1 and S1 in the mini-box, with heavy gauge (#14) wires soldered to the relay terminals as shown on the schematic. Make these wires about 24 inches long and mark "+" and "Lights" for easy identification during installation. The last step is to mount and connect the printed circuit card in the mini-box.

Under the dash. The protruding mounting screw of RY1 may be used to mount the timer under your dash, or make a bracket of your own design for your particular automobile and installation. Just make sure the timer chassis is well grounded to the dashboard frame before proceeding.

At the headlight switch, find the wire coming from the headlamps and select a convenient point (probably a wire right on the switch) to tap into the 12-Volt battery power. You can locate these two wires by checking for voltages with a VOM at the headlight switch. A +12-Volt battery wire will be the only wire that will read +12 volts with the headlight switch in the *off* position. The wire that reads +12-Volts only when the headlights are *on* is the other correct one; it normally runs directly to the foot dimmer switch. After locating these wires and marking them "+" and "Lights," disconnect the battery cable at the battery so there will be no accidental shorts. Remove ½-inch of insulation from the two underdash headlamps and battery wires you have located. Now connect each

PARTS LIST	
C1	500-uF electrolytic capacitor, 15 VDC or better
Q1	NPN transistor, 2N1302, HEP-641
Q2	PNP transistor, RCA 40254, HEP-628
R1	3,300-ohm, ½-watt resistor
R2,R3	560-ohm, ½-watt resistor
RY1	Relay, DPDT, 10-amp contacts, 12 VDC coil resistance at least 100-ohms, Potter and Brumfield type MR11D or equivalent. (BA stock no. 19A387, Lafayette stock no. 30-20047 or Allied type KN105-2C-12D)
S1	SPST pushbutton switch, normally open (time-start switch)
Misc.	3¼x2⅛x1⅝-inch case, 1-amp SB fuse with pigtail leads, #14 wire, hook-up wire, printed circuit material, hardware, solder. etc.

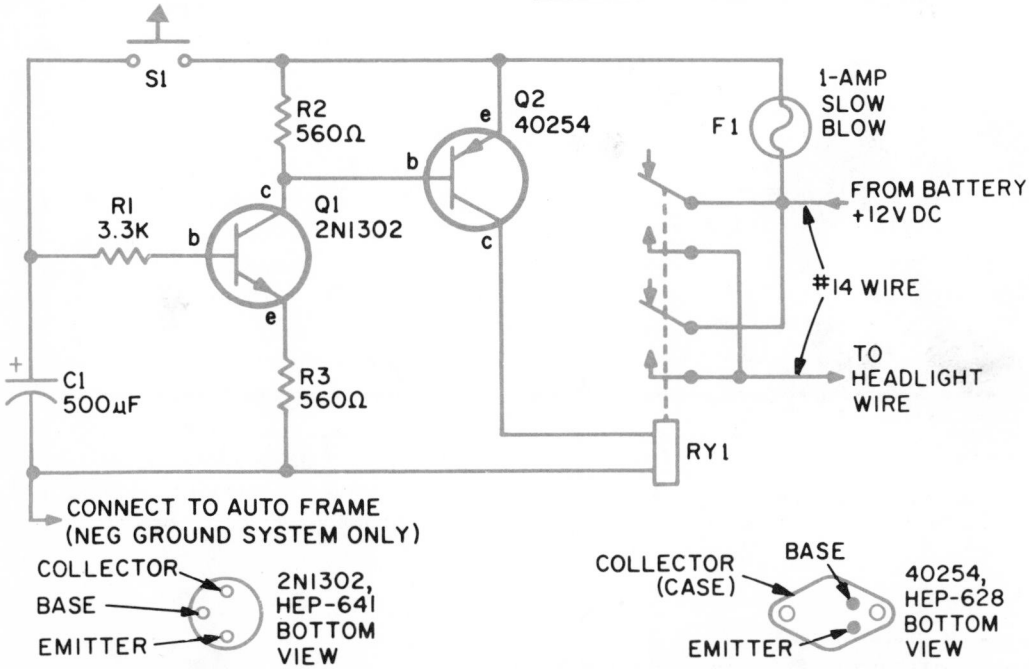

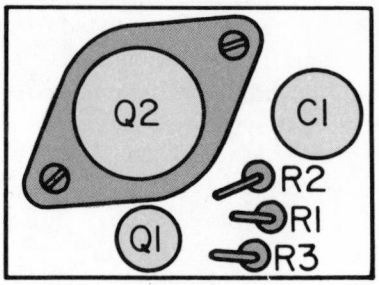

Actual size copper (bottom) side of your board on left and component (top) side on right.

timer wire to the corresponding automobile headlamp and battery wire. Wrap electrical tape over the exposed wires and arrange them in an out-of-the-way spot under the dash. Reconnect the + battery cable and the timer is ready for use.

Modifications anyone? If more than 60 seconds delay is desired, a larger capacitor can be installed in place of C1. For example, a 1,000 μF capacitor will give two minutes or more of time delay. If you wish, a 10K trimmer resistor in series with R1 will allow exact adjustment of the time interval.

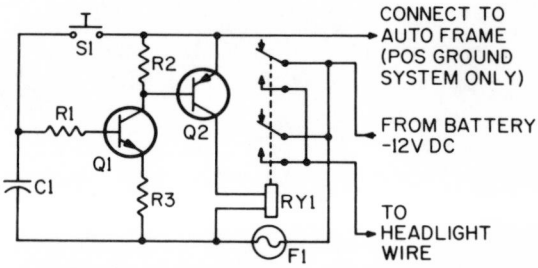

Use this schematic in positive ground cars only. There are no connections made to the normally open contacts of the relay. Use the same printed circuit board. All of the necessary changes are made around a board.

Several fixed timing periods such as 60, 30 and 15 seconds can be chosen with a switch wired to select different discharge resistors connected in parallel across capacitor C1. All of these modifications combined would give a longer delay period and a variable delay with your choice of lights-on times.

Positive ground? To modify the basic timer for a 12-Volt positive ground system, do not ground the printed circuit board to the chassis. Instead, use insulated standoffs when mounting the circuit board in the mini-box. Ground the "+" point on the *circuit card* to the chassis using a solder lug mounted under one standoff. Run a wire from the circuit card negative points to the relay. Operation will be identical to negative ground systems.

W.R.D.,JR.

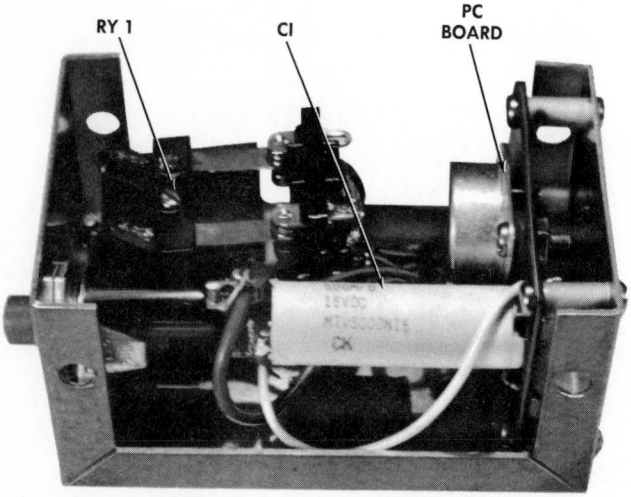

With the relay mounted on left, PC board at right, all parts fit into the minibox case.

See also: ELECTRONICS; ELECTRICAL, AUTO.

How the Wankel Rotary Engine Works

Few moving parts and relatively small size keynote the revolutionary Wankel

THE REVOLUTIONARY Wankel engine, invented in Germany by Dr. Felix Wankel but pioneered for wide automotive use by engineers of the Japanese Toyo Kogyo Machine and Auto Manufacturing Company, is finding wide use in an automobile.

The engine has proved to be economical, smooth-running, capable of exceptional acceleration, and smaller in size and weight than piston engines delivering the same amount of mechanical power. Detroit car makers for long shied from the Wankel engine, ostensibly because it was considered to be inherently too "dirty" in terms of air-polluting exhaust emissions. But practical experience with the engine, as used in the Japanese Mazda car, has demonstrated that the Wankel rotary engine's thermal reactor is a more reliable pollution control device than any catalytic reactor yet developed for use with piston engines.

The Wankel is unlike any other engine that ever pushed or pulled a car along the road. Instead of the usual piston system, the guts of the Wankel consist of a relatively simple rotor inside a roughly oval chamber. Instead of moving up and down with full stops in between, as do the pistons in a reciprocating engine, the rotor

automobile repairs: see repairs, auto
awls: see hand tools
axes: see knives and axes
baby photographs: see photography
back pack: see hiking

Wankel rotary engine for the Mazda with the cover of the forward combustion chamber removed. Combustion of fuel and air drives the rotor—which looks like an overstuffed triangle—around in the chamber. The ring gear on the inside of the rotor transmits power to gear on the drive shaft in the middle.

just keeps going round and round in the same direction. The result: elimination of virtually all vibration.

The rotor looks like a sort of "bulged out" triangle. It revolves around an *eccentric* shaft having a gear that engages an inner-toothed gear that is part of the rotor. The chamber in which the rotor is housed looks like an oval that has been pinched in at the sides. (This shape is technically known as an *epitrochoid.* This term is applied to the path drawn by a point within a circle when that circle rolls around a second circle while maintaining constant tangential contact. The Wankel engine rotor housing is a *two lobe* epitrochoid, which is what you get when the radius of the inner circle is double the radius of the rolling circle.) As the rotor turns, its three tips make constant contact with the chamber walls to create three constantly moving compartments between the rotor sides and the epitrochoid chamber wall. The tips of the triangular rotors maintain this contact with the chamber wall because the rotor "wobbles" around on its eccentric shaft. The action has been compared to the twirling of a hula-hoop on the hips of a child.

As each of the rotor's three sides makes a complete sweep of the chamber, it performs the same four functions that the "strokes" of a piston do in a conventional reciprocating engine—intake, compression, power and exhaust.

When any one of the three rotor tips (call it the advance tip) passes a fuel inlet port in the chamber wall, the fuel mixed with air enters the moving compartment following the advance tip. No valves or valve-operating mechanisms are required to accomplish this job; in this respect, too, the Wankel has it all over the piston engine. The compartment continues to increase in size and, in doing so, sucks the gas-air mixture into the combustion chamber. This fuel intake action ceases only when the next rotor tip passes the intake port. The entrapped fuel mixture is now ready for compression. (Note that the second rotor tip, which acts to seal up the first fuel compartment by passing past the fuel intake port, simultaneously becomes the advance tip for the second of the three compartments.)

Now let's go back to the compartment

that has just been filled with gas-air mixture. As the rotor continues to turn, the space between the rotor and the chamber wall must become smaller and smaller because the rotor is *not* following a circular path but is instead wobbling closer to the chamber wall at this point. Thus the gas-air mixture is compressed to approximately one-ninth of its original volume.

When the gas-air mixture is fully compressed, the rotor side has reached a position opposite the two spark plugs. The first of the two spark plugs fires to initiate combustion of the fuel; a split second later the second spark plug fires to make sure that combustion is completed. Note that here we are talking about two spark plugs acting jointly in the *same* chamber. In a typical rotary car engine there are two chambers, each with its own rotor and pair of spark plugs. Two distributors are used to fire the four plugs. One distributor fires the first plug in each of the two rotor chambers, and the second distributor fires both delayed action plugs. This one-two punch provided by the paired spark plugs does much to make the Wankel run smoothly and reliably.

As the gaseous combustion products expand, they exert pressure on the rotor and drive it along its eccentric path. By the time these gases have expanded about as much as they can, the advance rotor tip passes the exhaust port and the combustion products escape through the port as the advancing rotor side exerts exhausting pressure.

Bear in mind that we have considered

Cutaway view of a rotary engine shows two rotor chambers mounted in line. These perform the same functions as the cylinders and pistons of a reciprocating engine. Other parts, such as the carburetor, starter, radiator (not shown) and transmission, are similar to those used with piston engines. Dual distributors and spark plugs are also used.

HOW THE ROTARY ENGINE WORKS.

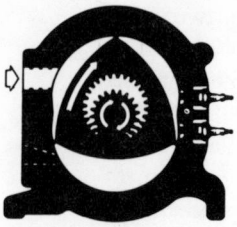

1. Intake.
Fuel/air mixture is drawn into combustion chamber by revolving rotor through intake port. No valves or valve-operating mechanism needed.

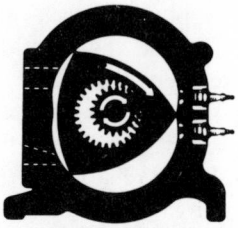

2. Compression.
As rotor continues revolving, it reduces space in chamber containing fuel and air. This compresses mixture.

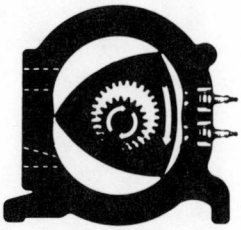

3. Ignition.
Fuel/air mixture now fully compressed. Leading sparkplug fires. A split-second later, following plug fires to assure complete combustion.

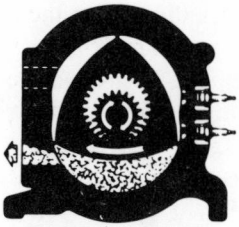

4. Exhaust.
Exploding mixture drives rotor, providing power. Rotor then expels gases through exhaust port.

HOW YOUR PISTON ENGINE WORKS.

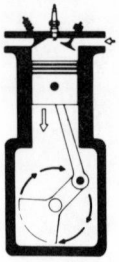

1. Intake.

2. Compression.

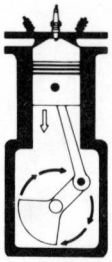

3. Ignition.

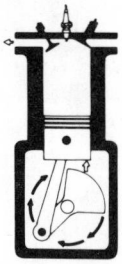

4. Exhaust.

only one third of the total action that goes on inside the operating engine. The two other compartments are in various other stages of the same four-step cycle. Thus, when the first compartment is being exhausted, gases in the next following compartment are being compressed while fuel is being sucked into the third compartment.

Each rotor has the same number of power pulses per shaft rotation as a two-cylinder, four-stroke piston engine, hence each rotor can be considered to be the equivalent of two conventional cylinders in a reciprocating engine. And, since the rotary engine used in Mazda cars has *two* ganged, in-line rotors spinning in their separate combustion chambers, the engine is comparable to a conventional four-cylinder piston job—only much smoother operating. The rotors in a Wankel apply power directly to the shaft for 270 degrees of each complete 360-degree shaft revolution. On the other hand, a piston engine produces power through only 180 degrees of each shaft revolution. That is another reason why the Wankel operates smoothly.

Various estimates of the relative efficiencies of the Wankel and conventional piston engines are quoted. Sometimes the claim is that a rotary engine that is only two-thirds the size of a piston engine delivers the same horsepower; or that a rotary engine produces about twice the horsepower of a reciprocating engine of equal size and weight. Actually, it is virtually impossible to make any absolute comparisons. But some studies indicate that the weight and size versus performance benefits of the rotary engine becomes more apparent at higher horsepowers. Up to about 75 BHP ("brake horsepower") it's no contest between the two types of engines in relation to size and weight. When you get into engines rated 150 BHP or higher, the Wankel becomes significantly lighter and smaller than its piston counterpart. You can assume that between these two ranges a Wankel engine will match the weight or size of the smallest or lightest reciprocating engine having the same power output. As a rule of thumb, figure that, in terms of production engines, a Wankel is likely to be 30% smaller and perhaps 10-12% lighter than a piston engine of comparable power.

The rotary engine has certain advantages even if it doesn't weigh significantly less and if it isn't appreciably smaller than a comparable reciprocating engine. The main advantage is the incredibly small number of moving parts that can wear or malfunction for some other reason. Only three moving parts (two rotors and the eccentric shaft) put of a total of 70 basic parts in the Wankel engine take the place of 166 moving parts (from a total of 230 basic parts) in a comparable six-cylinder piston engine. These three parts replace pistons, rods, valves, cams, lifters and a host of other conventional parts that can and do wear and cause engine failure.

Those three moving parts provide far smoother, nearly vibration-free performance. Why? Because there is none of the inevitable vibration and jerkiness associated with pistons that must go rapidly through a series of go-stop-go-actions. It's not so much what the tiger in gas tanks can do, as how the two power tigers in a piston cylinder and in a rotary chamber are able to perform. The piston in a reciprocating engine moves much like a tiger in a cage; it can only go a short distance before it must stop, change directions, pick up speed, then stop once again and repeat the process—endlessly. Think about that the next time you visit the zoo. On the other hand, the rotor in a Wankel engine just keeps on going in one direction, albeit in a wobbly sort of oval, so the Wankel tiger purrs as it speeds along without ever having to stop and abruptly change directions. You can tell the difference between these caged and free-running tigers just by listening to the sounds of comparable rotary and reciprocating engines.

Other performance characteristics that are winning new friends for the Wankel engine include superior high speed performance, better throttle response (resulting in eye-opening acceleration performance), operation on unleaded, low-octane gasolines, and ease of maintenance.

Emission control simplified. The Wankel engine used in the Mazda meets the stringent 1975 Clean Air Act standards. Fresh air injection mixes oxygen with the raw *exhaust* gas, and this oxygenated exhaust goes into a *thermal reactor* (a special kind of exhaust manifold) where toxic hydrocarbons and carbon monoxide pol-

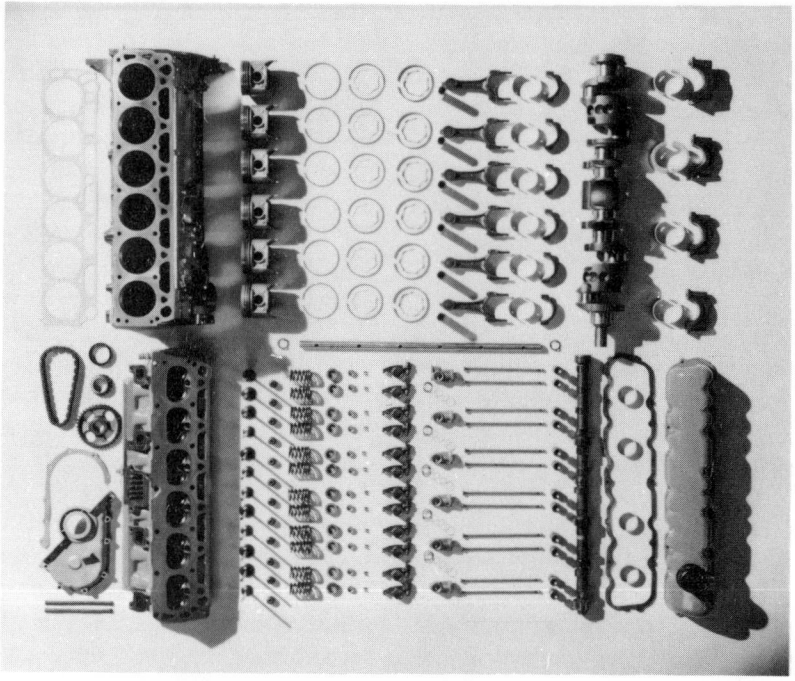

Array of parts illustrate the mechanical simplicity of the Wankel design. Standard six-cylinder engine (top) has 230 basic parts, of which 166 are moving parts. Only three of the Wankel's 70 parts (bottom) are moving parts.

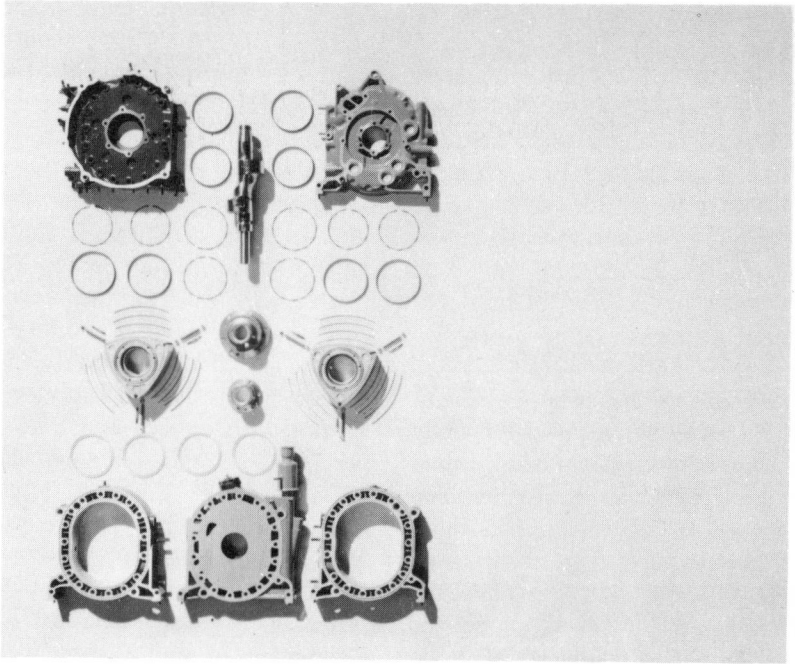

How the Mazda clean-air system works

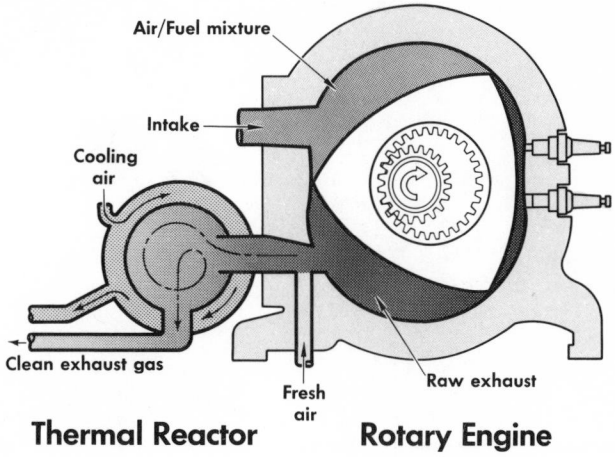

Incompletely burned exhaust gases from a Wankel engine are oxidized in Mazda's thermal reactor to form water vapor and carbon dioxide. Exhaust of the Wankel is hot enough for the reactions to occur without a catalyst. This system exceeds the requirements of the strict U.S. anti-pollution regulations scheduled to take effect in 1975.

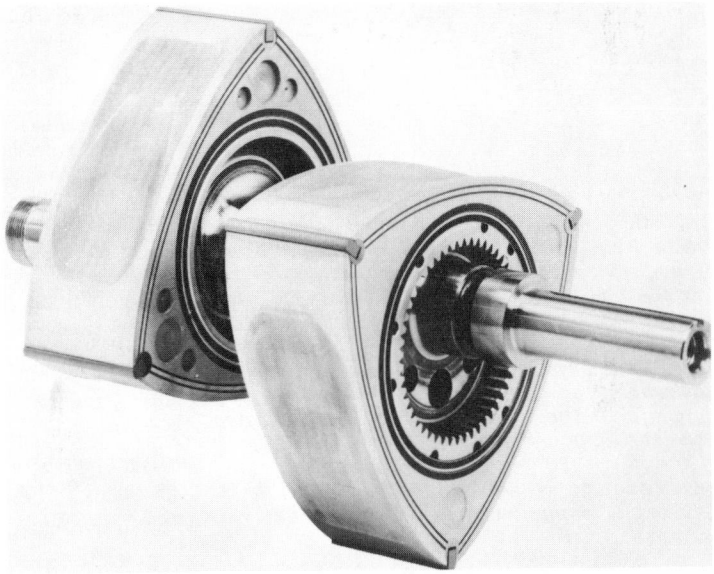

The three moving parts of a two-chamber Wankel are the two rotors and the eccentric drive shaft.

lutants are further oxidized to form water vapor and harmless carbon dioxide. Actually, the thermal reactor is little more than an air-cooled chamber in which the hot exhaust gases can mix with more oxygen and complete the combustion process that started inside the engine.

According to Environmental Protection Agency test data, Mazda vehicles equipped with this "clean-air" system are able to come well under the tough 1975 air pollution standards, with no loss of fuel economy, driveability or performance as compared with earlier model cars. This is in sharp contrast with the noticeable reduction in performance of cars powered with piston engines that use different methods of pollution control. After 50,000 miles on the road, a Mazda RX-3 car tested by EPA averaged emissions that

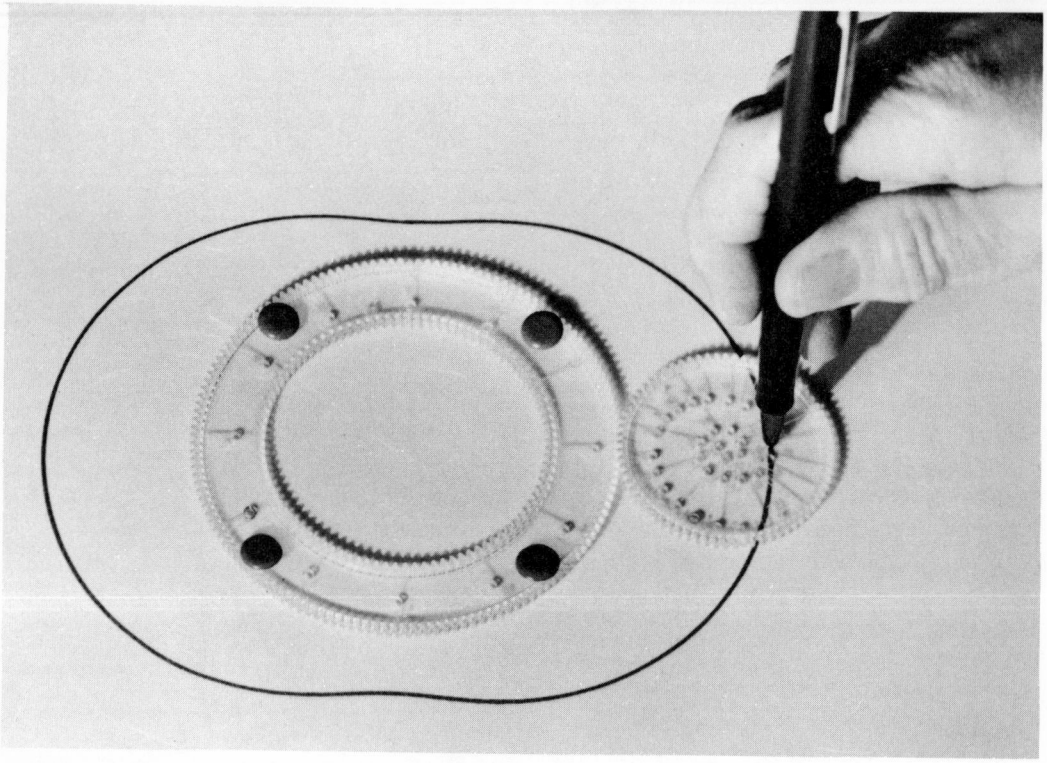

You can draw the epitrochoid shape of a Wankel combustion chamber by using two gears from a pattern drawing kit, such as a Spirograph. For the stationary center gear, choose one of the largest, with 144 teeth. The second gear must have half the radius, hence half the number of teeth (72). Pick a pencil hole about half way between the center and rim of the smaller gear and run the gear around the larger one. The shape that is generated is a two-lobe epitrochoid. If you have no Spirograph, you can cut out two circles of cardboard, one twice as large as the other with the pencil hole in the smaller circle about half way between the center and rim.

were substantially lower than the maximum permissible levels set by EPA. Hydrocarbon and carbon monoxide levels were about 50% of maximum; the oxides of nitrogen level was about 33%.

Why is it possible to use such a simple thermal reactor on the Wankel engine and not on a piston engine although both use gasoline as fuel? Primarily because the gases exhausted from a Wankel engine are much hotter than those exhausted by a piston engine, and these hot gases can be made to burn by the addition of some extra oxygen. The big advantage in this process is that there is no expensive combustion catalyst to be "poisoned" and thus be made ineffectual by inadvertent use of leaded gasoline, as could happen if a catalytic emission control system is used. Although the rotary engine runs perfectly on unleaded, low-octane gasoline, the use of ordinary leaded fuel would not harm the thermal reactor. Moreover, no power-robbing exhaust gas recirculation (EGR) system, of the kind essential to control emission in piston engines, is needed.

At this point it might seem that the Wankel is the end-all in the development of automotive power plants. However, the engine still has some drawbacks. First, the Wankel-thermal reactor system uses 30% more gasoline than a comparable piston engine. This is no small disadvantage. In city driving, you can get 20 to 25 miles per gallon driving a small foreign-made car powered with a piston engine; you can expect only around 13 miles per gallon when driving a Wankel-powered Mazda under the same conditions, according to trade reports.

Standards for servicing the Mazda engine are very conservative. Owners are urged to bring the cars in for check-ups and oil changes every 4,000 miles. The operating instructions also call for gentle breaking in of the engine during the first 1,000 miles of driving; this period engine revolutions should not exceed the 4,000 to 5,000 rmp range.

At one time there was concern that the seals on the three points of the triangular rotor would be subject to damaging friction as they rub against the wall of the containing chamber. These seals, made of carbon impregnated with aluminum alloy, are rather soft and brittle although they look much like metal. These seals make rubbing contact with the chromium surface of the rotor housing. But as it turns out, wear of the seals is not a problem provided the engine is kept properly lubricated. After a test car powered by a rotary engine had been run for more than 50,000 miles, the engine was opened for inspection. The apex seals on the rotors were judged to be good for still another 100,000 miles. Thus it can be assumed that under ordinary use conditions, the apex seals on rotary car engines are good for at least

SPECIFICATIONS: MAZDA, RX-4, 1974 MODEL	
Number of Rotors	2 rotors in line
Type of Rotors	3-lobe
Cooling System	Water
Displacement	40 cu. in. x 2 (654 c.c. x 2)
Carburetion	Downdraft, 2 stage 4 barrel
Maximum Horsepower (SAE net)	110 HP @ 6000 rpm
Maximum Torque (SAE net)	117 ft. lbs. @ 3500 rpm
Fuel	Regular gasoline
Battery	12v 70 amp/H
Alternator	63 amp
Clutch	Dry disc, hydraulic linkage

Wankel-powered automobiles move down Japanese assembly line.

150,000 miles, although these seals, the counterparts of rings on ordinary pistons, will eventually need replacement. And, a rotary engine has no additional valves that might leak or burn. Side seals, made of special cast iron, have never posed serious problems and no wear limit is specified for them.

The rotary engine used in Mazda cars utilize two oil pumps: one to pump oil to the gears and bearings of the rotor to lubricate these parts and to help cool the interior of the engine; the other pump meters small amounts of oil to the carburetor, for mixing with the air-fuel mixture, to lubricate the rotor tip seals and the rotor chamber.

Although some potential buyers of cars powered with Wankel type engines worry that they may not always find competent mechanics to service these revolutionary engines until more dealer-repair shops are established throughout the country, do-it-yourself week-end mechanics have cause for considerable optimism. Those who have already played around with the rotary engine report that the Wankel is very easy to service and trouble-shoot for at least three good reasons: (1) you can easily get at all the components because of the relatively small size of the engine, as compared with piston engines, (2) there are relatively few moving parts that can get out of whack, and (3) you don't need a garage full of special tools—what you find in a typical handyman tool box will probably handle most ordinary maintenance and repair jobs.

Rotary engines are also being used to power some snowmobiles, and they find favor with some snowmobile enthusiasts because of reduced vibration and because the noise—even if not actually much lower than that generated by the best piston engines—is considered more tolerable because there is less high-frequency sound which is most bothersome. In time, you will probably be using lawn mowers and chain saws powered with small Wankel type engines. In these applications the same benefits—reduced vibration and more tolerable noise levels—may do much to help popularize the Wankel. And for the do-it-yourselfer who likes to service his own machinery, the prospect of maintaining simpler engines in the future is a very pleasant prospect indeed. J.H.

See also: ENGINE; TUNE-UP, ENGINE.